MW00761645

ABOUT THE AUTHOR

Dennis Foster is the author of more than 20 published books. His expertise is in computer applications for business, entrepreneurship, and various areas of the travel and hospitality industries.

As a consultant to major airlines and corporations during the last 10 years, Foster developed a curriculum for training travel professionals. The Mundus Companies, of which Foster is chairman of the board, have marketed this travel and tourism curriculum to private and public postsecondary schools with great success. The Mundus program, from which Glencoe/McGraw-Hill's *Travel Professional Series* is derived, has helped many schools achieve better than 90 percent placement rates.

The Travel Professional Series

First Class: An Introduction to Travel and Tourism
Reservations and Ticketing with SABRE®; Reservations and Ticketing with Apollo®
Destinations: North American and International Geography
Sales and Marketing for the Travel Professional
The Business of Travel: Agency Operations and Administration

Reservations and Ticketing with

APOLLO®

Dennis L. Foster

Glencoe/McGraw-Hill

A Macmillan/McGraw-Hill Company
Mission Hills, California   New York, New York

Photo and Illustration Credits   D. L. Foster, pages i, 122; Special thanks to M. Gruber, Covia, Inc., pages ii, xvi, 48, 106, 136; Photo from FPG, page 64; Hugh Rogers from Monkmeyer Press Photo Service, page 76, 158; M. Forsyth from Monkmeyer Press Photo Service, pages 92, 142, 206; Arlene Collins from Monkmeyer Press Photo Service, page 168; Photo Researchers, Inc., page 186; *Chapter 1* UPI/Bettmann, page 3; Fritz from Monkmeyer Press Photo Service, page 4; Ken Urban, illustrator, pages 6, 7, 9; Beryl Goldberg, photographer, pages 11.

Sponsoring Editor: Carole O'Keefe
Editing Supervisor: Katharine Glynn
Production Supervisor: Walter Healey

Production Services: Visual Education Corporation
Cover Design: Viviani Productions, Inc., New York City
Cover Photo: Courtesy IBM Public Relations Department, White Plains, NY

Library of Congress Cataloging-in-Publication Data
Foster, Dennis L.
    Reservations and Ticketing with Apollo/Dennis L. Foster.
        p. cm.
    ISBN 0-02-680863-3
    I. Airlines—United States—Reservation systems—
Handbooks, manuals, etc. I. Title
HE9787.5.U5F68   1990   90-32708
387.7'42—dc20   CIP

Reservations and Ticketing with Apollo®

Copyright © 1990 by Glencoe/McGraw-Hill Educational Division. A Macmillan/McGraw-Hill Company. All rights reserved. Printed in the United States of America. Except as permitted under the United States Copyright Act of 1976, no part of this publication may be reproduced or distributed in any form or by any means, or stored in a database or retrieval system, without the prior written permission of the publisher.

Send all inquiries to:
Glencoe/McGraw-Hill
29th floor
1221 Avenue of the Americas
New York, NY 10020

ISBN 0-02-680863-3

1234567890   WEBWEB   9876543210

Contents

APPENDIXES

Preface

Travel, if viewed as a commodity, is among the world's leading commercial products, accounting for $600 billion in economic trade. If viewed as an employment field—commercial travel, tourism, hospitality, and food and beverage service—produce 6 million jobs in the United States alone. Tourism is the first, second, or third largest industry in forty-one U.S. states and in 130 other nations. Yet, when most people think of travel, they envision leisure. Few think of the highly specialized knowledge and finely cultivated technical skills needed for a successful career in the industry.

In the past, a travel career was viewed as one in which travel experience weighed more heavily than technical skills. During the last decade, increasing global awareness and the widespread adoption of various technologies have altered both the image and the livelihood of the full-time travel professional. The emphasis has moved away from the accumulation of "war stories" about travel and tourism toward a structured discipline blending communication and human relations skills with technical proficiency.

Despite this dramatic shift, until now there have been few educational materials that have as their primary objective the creation of travel professionals with specialized knowledge and technological skill.

ABOUT THIS SERIES

The Travel Professional Series has been designed to meet the needs of students who seek to enter an exciting, growing field as productive and promotable employees whose skills are marketable in many segments of the industry.

Comprising five textbooks and software simulating the major computerized reservations systems, this Series provides:

- Thorough, current knowledge of the principles, practices, and scope of the industry.

- An understanding of the opportunities and responsibilities of a career in travel and tourism

- The skills to perform manual and computerized tasks with accuracy, skill, and efficiency.

- Effective communication and interpersonal skills.

- A context for and definition of *professionalism* that includes all aspects of demeanor and courteous, competent service to clients.

The textbooks in the Series include:

First Class: An Introduction to Travel and Tourism

Covers the history, scope, and functions of the industry, and provides an understanding of and skills in constructing itineraries; using the *Official Airlines Guide*; calculating air tariffs and fares; domestic and international ticketing; handling hotel, motel, resort reservations; arranging cruises; booking tours and car rentals; and using references and resources. An overview is given of job opportunities and responsibilities as well as of professionalism and ethics.

*Reservations and Ticketing with SABRE® or
Reservations and Ticketing with Apollo®**

Provides an understanding of industry automation with emphasis on computer skills, and covers the concepts and skills required to interpret and modify availability; sell air space; create and change Passenger Name Records (PNRs), client profiles, and seat assignments; access fares; modify and price itineraries; issue tickets and boarding passes; and handle hotel reservations, car rentals, and tours. Software simulating the functions of the system for an intensive computer lab accompanies both textbooks.

Destinations: North American and International Geography

Describes the world according to the International Air Transport Association—times, codes, and traffic conference areas—and explores international travel requirements and air and surface travel abroad. Students learn essential information to recommend and book travel arrangements in North, Central, and South America; the Atlantic and Caribbean; Europe; the Pacific and Asia; and Africa and the Middle East.

Marketing and Sales for the Travel Professional

Describes travel markets, customers, and product lines, and discusses techniques for targeting markets, market planning and positioning, and advertising and promotion. Explores personal selling, sales preparation, and telephone techniques. Students learn how to handle job stress, ethical questions, and client crises.

The Business of Travel: Agency Operations and Administration

Provides a thorough understanding of the agency business, including conference requirements, location and staffing, reservations and bookings, sales reports, and agency accounting, and commissions tracking. Students learn how to use an agency automation system and interpret computer-generated reports.

ABOUT THIS BOOK

Reservations and Ticketing with Apollo is designed both as an introduction to the field and as one component in a program for thorough career preparation. This book, like the other textbooks in the Series, is an outgrowth of an exhaustively researched curriculum that has been in use since 1977 in 200 postsecondary institutions. It is estimated that more than 100,000 skilled travel professionals have graduated from this program with a number of schools reporting placement rates as high as 99 percent. These graduates, far from being regarded as neophytes, are often considered technical authorities by their employers and co-workers.

This textbook uniquely combines student reading material with interactive role-play and hands-on computer experience. The instructional emphasis is on behavioral reinforcement of key concepts and the mastery of practical, job-related skills; throughout, the principle of "learning by doing" is followed. Each chapter is designed with a focus on job-related tasks and on the corresponding learning objectives required to achieve competency.

Students need little or no prior experience with either computerized reservations systems or the microcomputer. An easy-to-use, interactive Apollo simulation with role-play exercises accompanies the textbook. Students have the opportunity to practice basic Apollo functions as though they were using the live system. The textbook, of course, will also help train students using the live system.

---

* SABRE® and Apollo® are registered trademarks. The sign is used here only at the first mention of each system.

The text is divided into 15 chapters, each dealing with particular skills and Apollo functions. Four appendixes are included as quick-reference guides for students.

Although some chapters are self-contained and may be covered in the order that best suits the needs of students, it is recommended that the sequence of the text be followed.

Content

The following descriptions of the contents of each chapter and the appendixes may also serve as helpful summaries.

1. Introduction to Computer Reservation Systems

This chapter provides an introduction to data processing and microcomputer technology as well as an overview of computer use in the travel agency. Students master computer terminology and such concepts as input, output, and processing, and learn about auxiliary storage units, modems, the keyboard, monitors, printers, and the agent's set.

2. Availability

Basic sign on/sign off and city pair availability are introduced. Students also learn how to obtain return and additional availability, modify the current display, and use optional entries to access availability by connecting city, arrival time, class of service, or carrier.

3. Selling Air Space

This chapter introduces entries for selling from the availability display or by specified flight. Students learn how to read itinerary segments, interpret status/action codes, sell connections, waitlist seat requests, and book surface (arnk) and open segments.

4. Passenger Name Records

In this chapter students learn how to enter passenger names, received information, contact phone numbers, and ticketing advice, culminating in the creation of complete PNRs.

5. Supplementary Data

This chapter introduces the Remarks, Address, OSI, and SSR fields of the PNR. Students learn how to enter client and agency addresses and use OSI and SSR entries to send messages and request services from United Airlines and off-line carriers.

6. Modifying the Itinerary

Here, students learn several methods for retrieving PNRs and displaying all or part of a record. The chapter explores procedures for canceling a segment, rebooking the same flight and class, canceling and rebooking from availability, and canceling multiple segments. Students also learn how to insert new segments and change segment status.

7. Modifying the PNR

In this chapter students learn how to change or delete data stored in Name, Phone, Ticketing, and other data fields. The chapter also presents techniques for reducing the party and dividing a PNR.

8. Apollo Fares

This chapter explores the computer's comprehensive database of airline fares. Students learn how to access and interpret fares, using both Fare Shopper's and fare quote entries; modify a fare quotation; display domestic joint fares; and access fare rules. The chapter also examines methods of displaying city pair availability and fares simultaneously.

9. **Itinerary Pricing**

Students learn how to autoprice itineraries, using eight optional methods: passenger type, segment, passenger name, forced connection, future ticketing date, overriding fare basis, overriding class, and lowest available fare. The chapter also introduces the future ticketing entry.

10. **Demand Ticketing**

This chapter deals with initializing a ticket printer and issuing tickets on demand. Students learn how to override a validating carrier and agency commission, enter accounting lines, and issue invoices and boarding passes.

11. **Miscellaneous Entries: Seat Assignments and Queues**

Divided into two sections, this chapter deals with assignments and queues. The seat assignment section instructs students how to request automatic seat assignment, display seat maps, and assign specific seats. The queues section instructs students how to obtain a queue count, access a queue, and route PNRs. Students also learn how to initiate, halt, and interrupt continuous queue ticketing.

12. **Client Profiles**

Students learn how to display Master Account Records (MARs), Business Account Records (BARs), and Passenger Account Records (PARs), move mandatory data, and select optional data. The chapter also teaches students how to create and update client profiles.

13. **Apollo Hotels**

Students learn how to display a hotel index, determine room types and rates, obtain hotel availability, display reference points and descriptions, sell hotel space, enter guarantee information, and enter room options. The chapter also explores direct bookings, cancellations, and hotel codes.

14. **Apollo Car Rentals**

This chapter introduces the Apollo car rental system and teaches students how to display car availability, sell and modify car segments, and obtain rate quotations and vendor policies.

15. **Direct Link and General Information**

This chapter explores the Direct Link program and the General Reference programs. In addition, students learn how to access on-line carriers, access Amtrak, obtain weather forecasts and currency conversion rates, display a Universal Profile, and use Apollo's Help program.

Appendixes

Four appendixes contain an overview of fill-in formats and quick-reference guides to carrier codes, city/airport codes, and Apollo command formats.

Ease of Learning

The following aids to learning, and to teaching, are included in this book:

- *Learning Objectives*, clearly state expected knowledge and skill outcomes.
- *Format Guide*, provides a convenient permanent reference to Apollo command formats for use both in study and after obtaining employment.

- *Check-In: A Study Aid*, a series of review questions that are included throughout the chapter to reinforce learning, memory, and understanding.
- *Computer Laboratory*, directs the student to apply knowledge with hands-on computer practice, including interactive role-play exercises.

Motivation

The practical experience with Apollo functions at the microcomputer is the chief motivational feature of these materials. Without hands-on experience, students do not have clearly defined marketable skills. In addition to students' interest in actually practicing job tasks, they find a microcomputer to be a patient and nonjudgmental tutor, creating a vital learning experience. The accompanying software transforms the microcomputer into an Apollo workstation and provides the "look and feel" of a "live" system.

Instructor Support

An Instructor's Guide accompanies each textbook in The Travel Professional Series. The Guide contains plans and teaching suggestions, references and materials needed to teach each chapter, transparency masters, testing materials, and keys to all testing material. For *Reservations and Ticketing with Apollo*, two alternative sets of computer laboratory exercises are included: for teaching with a "live" system or with a simulated system.

SUMMARY

The travel and tourism field is fast-paced and is rapidly growing. It is becoming increasingly more difficult for employers to undertake the training of new workers in the field. The parallel growth in the use of sophisticated, rapidly changing technologies has complicated this situation. At the same time, travelers throughout the world have become more sophisticated, more knowledgeable, and more demanding.

In the 1990s, the primary need of the field is for *professionalism*—the combination of demeanor, knowledge, and skill necessary for industry growth and career success.

It is this need voiced by employers and reflected in the educational efforts of instructors that has inspired the writing and publication of The Travel Professional Series.

Dennis L. Foster

ACKNOWLEDGMENTS

We are grateful to all of the educators who gave of their valuable time and creative energy. Our Advisory Board and reviewers have been critical, caring, and articulate. This Series owes much to their contributions.

Glencoe/McGraw-Hill Advisory Board for The Travel Professional Series

Lisa Courtney
Department Chair and Program Director
Murieta Travel School
Rancho Murieta, California

Paul Lacroix
Director of Travel and Tourism
Johnson & Wales University
Providence, Rhode Island

Richard Harvey
Director of Travel and Tourism
Patricia Stevens Career College
St. Louis, Missouri

Sandra Lockwood
President
Advanced Career Training
Atlanta, Georgia

Reviewers

Pat Schultz
Northwestern Business College
Chicago, Illinois

Bruno Ociepka
Northwestern Business College
Chicago, Illinois

George Morgan
Edmundson Junior College of Business
Chattanooga, Tennessee

Steve Ward
Valencia Community College
Mid Florida Tech
Orlando, Florida

Marilyn Ward
Consultant
Ward & Company
Clermont, Florida

Donna Licas
Lakeland Community College
Mentor, Ohio

Becky Emerson
Parks Junior College
Denver, Colorado

Joann Yurchifon
American Business and
   Fashion Institute
Charlotte, North Carolina

Karen Rogers
Executive Vice President
Advanced Career Training
Atlanta, Georgia

JoAnn Daniels
Corporate Director of Education
Advanced Career Training
Atlanta, Georgia

Roberta Sebo, CTC
Assistant Professor and Travel Internship
   Program Coordinator
Johnson & Wales University
Providence, Rhode Island

AUTHOR'S ACKNOWLEDGMENTS

The author gratefully acknowledge the numerous individuals, companies, associations, agencies, and educational institutions that have contributed, in one way or another, to the development of the Travel Professional Series textbooks and software. To name every individual would require an entire book itself.

However, special acknowledgment is due the staffs of the following organizations, whose various contributions helped make this series possible: American Airlines, United Airlines, TransWorld Airlines, Eastern Airlines, Delta Airlines, AMR, Inc., Covia, Inc., Hertz, Inc., Budget Rent A Car, Firstworld Travel, Ask Mr. Foster Travel, Uniglobe Travel, Time Travel, Hilton Corporation, Marriott Corporation, and Mundus Institute of Travel; Airline Reporting Corporation, International Airlines Travel Agent Network, American Society of Travel Agents, Association of Retail Travel Agents, and Society of Travel and Tourism Educators; the U.S. Department of Transportation, Travel Data Center, Travel and Tourism Administration, Industry and Trade Administration, Federal Aviation Administration, International Trade Conference, and the Central Intelligence Agency; the Africa Travel Association, Caribbean Hotel Association, European Travel Commission, Fiji Visitors Bureau, Tahiti Tourism Board, Intourist, and other bureaus too numerous to name here.

Special appreciation is also extended to Marty Rosholt, Cathy Cedarblade, Ralph Miles, Jennifer Dietz, Portia Flynn, Nanette Kelly, Roz Horwich, Katherine Oberlin, Cathy Doody, Greg Wynn, Russel Stamm, and innumerable others who helped in various ways over the years.

Thanks also to my unending inspiration, Dawn.

CHAPTER 1

INTRODUCTION TO COMPUTER RESERVATION SYSTEMS

CHAPTER OBJECTIVES

At the end of the chapter, you should be able to perform the following tasks:

- Define *computer reservation system.*

- Define *input, output, processing, storage operation, modem,* and *data processing system.*

- Define *agent's set.*

- Define the meanings of the abbreviations CRT, VDT, and PC.

- Identify the distinguishing features of United Airlines' Apollo® system.

- Identify the primary keyset groups on the keyboard of the agent's set.

- Identify the primary differences between the keyboards of VDTs and PCs.

Copyright © 1990 by Glencoe/McGraw-Hill Educational Division. All rights reserved.

There is a romance novelist in Connecticut who rises early each morning, throws on a robe, heats the teapot, and switches on the computer perched atop her kitchen counter. Not long ago, she could not have told you the difference between a fast modem and a slow burn. But today, when she finishes her latest manuscript, she will use a modem to send the entire novel over the telephone line to her publisher's typesetting machine.

There is a famous chef in New Orleans who searches for exotic dessert recipes by sliding a disk into a computer and lighting up the screen. Six months ago, he could not have explained the difference between a floppy disk and a flaming platter. But tonight he will display on his computer screen twenty different ways to make *crépes Heléne flambée*, all neatly stored and categorized on a floppy disk.

There is a travel agent in San Francisco who specializes in ocean adventures; when she wants to know the lowest fare to St. Croix, she types in a code on her personal computer. In the not too distant past, she could not have distinguished between a database field and a baseball diamond. Yet, today she will pore through hundreds of database fields to find the best fare for her client.

All these professionals—and 50 million others—have at least one thing in common: All rely on the power of computers to perform their jobs. Nowhere is this impact more profound than in the travel and tourism industry. Over the last decade, the computer has become an essential tool of virtually every travel professional. It is said that 90 percent of a travel agent's job entails booking airline reservations. Indeed, the overwhelming majority of all airline reservations today are made by computer. Besides travel agents, airline reservationists, tour operators, and corporate travel managers, others must also know how to use computer reservation systems, or as they are commonly called in the industry, "res systems."

The term **computer reservation system** (CRS) refers to a specialized computer system designed to store information about travel reservations—primarily airline, hotel, and car rental arrangements. A typical computer reservation system has an enormous database of scheduled flights, plus fare information, lodgings, automobile rental rates, and other essential travel data. When a reservation is booked by a travel agency, the information is stored in the computer.

Besides airline commissions, the major automation vendors—including SABRE®, United Airlines' Apollo®, Eastern Airlines' System One, and Worldspan, used by TWA, Northwest, and Delta—offer cash rebates to travel agents who book hotel and car rental reservations through their respective systems.

The first major computer reservation system was developed by IBM Corporation for TWA Airlines. This system was used to store flight schedules and book passenger reservations for TWA flights and other participating carriers.

Not long afterward, American Airlines introduced its own reservation system (SABRE), which is now widely used by many independent travel agents. United Airlines created the Apollo system, similar in its functions and storage capabilities

Copyright © 1990 by Glencoe/McGraw-Hill Educational Division. All rights reserved.

to both SABRE and PARS. Together, SABRE and Apollo are presently used by approximately 70 percent of all travel agencies.

What made all these systems possible was the development of powerful computer systems adapted first for use by the airlines and finally by travel agencies with appointments to sell airline tickets.

THE IMPACT OF TECHNOLOGY

Clearly, the computer is one of the most influential inventions of this century. Almost every human endeavor has benefited from the advent of affordable computers. Yet it was not so long ago that computers were rare and their role in the affairs of humanity was minor. Only fifty years ago there were virtually no computers anywhere in the world; in 1950 there were about 250 computers in the United States. Today, there are more than 100 million computers in use worldwide.

The first computers were enormous and required massive amounts of electricity. ENIAC I, developed in 1939, was as large as a warehouse; when the computer was turned on for the first time, the power drain caused all the lights in Philadelphia to dim. For nearly three decades, the size and cost of computer technology were prohibitive to all but the wealthiest corporations and government departments.

In the late 1960s, Large Scale Integration (LSI) was introduced. This technology made it possible for computer engineers to place thousands of electrical circuits on a small slice of silicon, called a microchip. By the late 1970s, all of the parts of a computer "brain" could be produced on a single microchip, or microprocessor. In 1982, IBM introduced the personal computer, abbreviated PC. Today, **PC** is used to refer to any computer that uses a microprocessor.

Figure 1–1 A view of the first general purpose "electronic calculator." It was named the "Electronic Numerical Integrator and Computer," and was called after its initials, the ENIAC. ENIAC was composed of more than 15,000 vacuum tubes, and its power source occupied about half as much space as the computer itself.

Copyright © 1990 by Glencoe/McGraw-Hill Educational Division. All rights reserved.

In recent years the cost of computer technology has fallen within the reach of virtually every business and self-employed individual. As a result, it is difficult today to find even a small travel agency that does not rely on a data processing system to perform reservations and ticketing.

Figure 1–2 A computer operator prepares to load a magnetic tape onto the tape drives of a mainframe computer.

Copyright © 1990 by Glencoe/McGraw-Hill Educational Division. All rights reserved.

DATA PROCESSING CONCEPTS

A data processing system is essentially an input/output system, or I/O system. What goes into the system is called "input"; what comes out is "output." What happens in between is "processing."

A data processing system can be compared with the brain of a human being watching an opera. Information in the form of sights and sounds flows into the brain via the eyes and ears. The brain processes the information and produces output, in the form of actions and speech. For example, when a particular shrill note is sung, the brain might signal the hands to clasp the ears tightly. The shrill note constitutes "input," and clasping the ears is a type of "output." By reacting to the note and signaling the hands, the brain is "processing" information.

A data processing system also processes information. Information goes into the system, is processed by the computer, and comes out in a different form. When the computer receives information to process, it performs an "input operation." An example of an input operation is typing an airline reservation at the keyboard to be sent to the computer. When information comes out of the computer, the computer performs an "output operation." An example of an output operation is sending information from the computer to the ticket printer, to produce an airline ticket.

The brain remembers by storing information that can be recalled later. Similarly, a computer stores information for future recall and use. This process is called a "storage operation." An example is saving information on a computer disk or tape.

Data Processing

Thinking is an important function of a human's brain. In its own way, the computer also "thinks." Computer thinking is referred to as "data processing." The term **data** refers to any information that can be processed by a computer. For example, the letters of the alphabet are data, as are numbers. Things made up of letters and numbers, such as flight numbers, passenger names, telephone numbers, fares, and so forth, are other examples of data.

Components of a Data Processing System

To summarize, a data processing system can do four types of operations: (1) input, (2) output, (3) storage, and (4) data processing. To perform these operations, the system must have four different components:

1. Input device
2. Output device
3. Storage device
4. Processor

A device used to enter data into the computer is called an input device. The most common type of input device is a keyboard used to type words for computer processing. Any device used by a computer to generate output is known as an output device. An example of such a device is the printer that produces an airline ticket.

A device used by the computer to store data for future use is generally referred to as a storage device. An example of an auxiliary storage device is a disk used to save data. Computer programs are generally referred to as **software.** The physical devices that make up the parts of a computer are generally referred to as **hardware.** For example, word processing programs that type, revise, and print text are software; printers or disk drives are hardware.

Copyright © 1990 by Glencoe/McGraw-Hill Educational Division. All rights reserved.

Microcomputers and Mainframes

A microcomputer is the smallest type of data processing system currently in use. The main feature of a microcomputer is the use of the microprocessor; and most microcomputers are used by one person at a time.

A mainframe is the largest and most complex type. A typical mainframe system can be used by many different people at the same time, working at separate terminals. A minicomputer is a small computer that is larger than a microcomputer and can be used by several individuals simultaneously.

How much larger and more powerful is a mainframe than a microcomputer? As an example, a typical personal computer can execute 100,000 instructions per second, whereas a powerful mainframe can execute more than 10 million instructions per second. A typical mainframe has a main memory about 20 times greater than the average microcomputer.

COMPUTER RESERVATION SYSTEMS

A computer reservation system consists of a large and complex mainframe in a central location which serves many different sites, including travel agencies and airport ticket counters. The part of the mainframe that processes data is called the **central processing unit,** abbreviated **CPU.** Flight information, air fares, and reservation data are stored in the mainframe's storage unit. At each site linked to the mainframe one or more terminals may be present. A terminal is a device

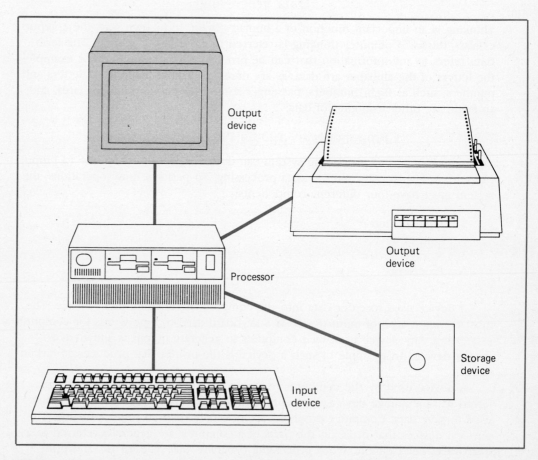

Figure 1–3 Components of a data processing system.

Copyright © 1990 by Glencoe/McGraw-Hill Educational Division. All rights reserved.

with a keyboard to input data to the computer and a video display screen, or monitor, to receive output.

A terminal is often referred to as a **CRT,** an abbreviation for *cathode ray tube*—the type of television tube that is used for the display of information. A more contemporary term for a computer terminal with a keyboard and display screen is a **VDT**—or *video display terminal*. The terminal used in a travel agency to communicate with a computer reservation system is called an **agent's set.** Two types of agents' sets are common in travel agencies today: **VDTs** and **PCs.**

A VDT has a keyboard and a video display screen, which are used to communicate with the computer reservation system. Prior to 1985, the most common VDTs used with computer reservation systems were special-purpose terminals designed specifically for airline reservations and ticketing. These "dedicated" terminals featured unique function keys and produced only uppercase characters.

Since 1985, the PC has been used increasingly by travel agents to communicate with computer reservation systems. Like a VDT, a PC has a keyboard and display screen, but also has its own internal microprocessor and a storage device, usually a disk drive. In this context, the term PC refers to any make or model of microcomputer, not just the IBM personal computer. Common types of PCs found in travel agencies include the IBM PC-XT, IBM PC-AT, IBM PS/2, and equivalent microcomputers manufactured by other computer companies.

Modems

To send and receive data, the agent's set must be connected to a **modem,** a device which allows two or more hardware devices to communicate over a tele-

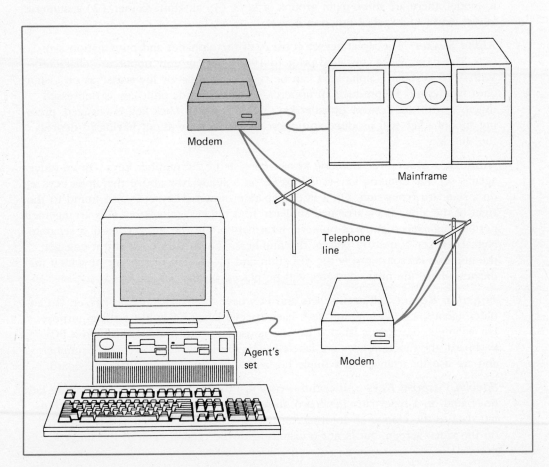

Figure 1–4 Components of a computer reservations system (CRS).

Copyright © 1990 by Glencoe/McGraw-Hill Educational Division. All rights reserved.

phone line. The term "modem" is short for *modulator-demodulator.* Information from the sending device is coded or *modulated* prior to transmission. It is then decoded or *demodulated* at the receiving end of the line. Each agent's set is connected to a modem that sends and receives data, permitting the user to communicate with the mainframe.

Auxiliary Storage Units

When a PC is used as the agent's set, one or more disk drives may be present for storing data. Disk drives fall into two categories: flexible disks and hard disks.

Flexible disks, often called floppy disks, are inserted and removed from the disk drive as desired. Two sizes are commonly used: a 3.5-inch disk, which is manufactured inside rigid plastic sleeves; and the 5.25-inch diskettes, which are housed in flexible vinyl skins. (The IBM PS/2 accepts only the 3.5-inch disk, whereas the IBM PC and its equivalents use the 5.25-inch format.)

A fixed disk may be mounted internally in the computer system unit or may be connected externally. The fixed disk is made of heavy steel and is never removed; it is capable of storing 50 to 60 times more data than a floppy diskette.

Flexible disks are generally referred to as "diskettes." Both floppy diskettes and fixed disks must be magnetically "formatted" before the computer can use them to store data and programs.

The Keyboard

The keyboard of an agent's set is similar to that of an electric typewriter. However, several keys have special functions or additional uses. Depending on the specific model, there are three main groups of keys: (1) an alpha keyset, (2) a numeric keyset, and (3) a special function keyset.

Alpha Keyset The alpha keyset consists of the alphabet and punctuation symbols. The older VDTs (installed prior to 1985) display only uppercase characters. With a PC keyboard, alpha keys can be typed in upper- or lowercase as on a standard typewriter. To produce an uppercase character, the Shift key is depressed together with the desired alphabet key. When the Cap Lock key is engaged, pressing an alpha key will produce an uppercase character without having to depress the Shift key.

Numeric Keyset The numeric keyset consists of the number keys. On an older agent's set, the numeric keyset is located on a single row above the alpha keys as on a standard typewriter. On a PC, a separate numeric keyset is also found to the right of the alpha keys, arranged similarly to a ten-key calculator. This arrangement permits high-speed entry of numeric information. On the PC keyboard, a separate Num Lock key is used to engage the numbers. When Num Lock is not engaged, the numeric keyset controls the direction and movement of the cursor which indicates where the next character will be placed on the screen.

Function Keyset All agents' sets and PCs have a special function keyset. On an older agent's set, the function keys have special labels to indicate their purpose. For example, one key is labeled ET and is used to "end transaction." On a PC keyboard, the function keys are labeled with the letter F followed by a number and are usually arranged in a single horizontal row at the top of the keyboard.

Special Purpose Keys All agents' sets and PCs have certain special purpose keys not found on a typewriter keyboard, including an Enter key that is used to transmit data to the computer. Information that is typed at the keyboard is displayed on the video screen, but is not transmitted to the computer until the Enter key is pressed.

Copyright © 1990 by Glencoe/McGraw-Hill Educational Division. All rights reserved.

Many terminals used with computer reservation systems have two special keys not found on an ordinary computer keyboard: One is called a "lozenge" or "pillow" and produces the character □. The other is called a cross of Lorraine and produces the character ‡. As you will discover in a later chapter, these keys have special uses, depending on the computer reservation system that the terminal is using.

The PC keyboard has two important keys not found on a standard typewriter. One is labeled Ctrl and is called the Control key. The other is labeled Alt and is called the Alternate key. These keys are used in conjunction with other keys to transmit special signals to the computer. For example, a special signal is sent when the Ctrl key and the C key are pressed at the same time, and a different signal is sent when Alt and N are pressed in conjunction.

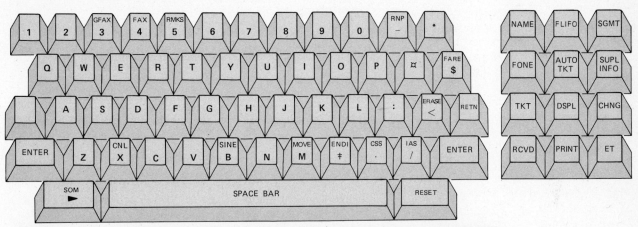

Key	Screen Display	
NAME	N:	Data field key used to record the passenger name(s) in a PNR.
FLIFO	F:	Used to display current flight information (United only).
SEGMENT	Ø	Data field key used to record (sell) air and non-airline segments in a PNR.
FONE	P:	Data field key used to record agency and passenger phone numbers in a PNR.
SUPPLEMENTARY INFORMATION	□:	Data field key used to enter remarks and other special information.
TICKET	T:	Data field key used to record ticketing information.
DISPLAY	*	Used to display PNRs or parts of PNRs.
CHANGE	C:	Identifier key which allows user to change or delete items contained in a PNR.
RECEIVED	R:	Field key used to store name of person who requested the reservation or change to reservation.
ET	E	End Transaction key causes the complete message to be transmitted to the central processor.

Figure 1–5 The keyboard panel of an agent's set.

Copyright © 1990 by Glencoe/McGraw-Hill Educational Division. All rights reserved.

The keyboard acts primarily as a typewriter. However, several keys serve dual functions and are both alphanumeric as well as function keys.

Function Keys (located on the keyboard)

GFAX (3)   General Facts—Data field used to record supplementary information such as "SSR" and "OSI" items for notification to airlines.

RMKS (5)   Remarks—Data field used to store information in a PNR for agency use that will not be transmitted to the airlines.

☐   Used as a separator of items and with GFAX and Remarks entries.

FARE ($)   Used in fare quotations and pricing functions.

ERASE (<)   Used to backspace and erase characters printed on the screen.

RETN   Return—Used to return the cursor to the beginning of the next line.

ENTER   Initiates the transmission of the message just printed on the screen.

ENDI ‡   End Item—Normally used to segment the input and simulate carriage return. It does not release the message.

CSS (.)   Change Segment Status—Used to change action/advice codes as well as times.

IAS (/)   Insert After Segment—Used to insert a new segment between existing segments.

RNP (-)   Reduce number in party—Used for the specific action of reducing the number of passengers in a party.

The Display Screen

Usually placed atop the terminal or on a swivel base, the display screen, or monitor, is the agent's "window" to the computer reservation system. Because the screen uses the cathode ray tube, the monitor is often referred to as the *CRT*. An older agent's set typically produces a display of 30 lines with 64 characters per line, whereas a PC monitor has a display of 25 lines with 80 characters per line.

Computer Printers

A printing terminal or printer produces hard copy output—data typed on paper. Computer printers use different mechanisms to form characters. A dot matrix printer creates characters by printing a series of dots in a rectangular box. Hammers strike the paper through a ribbon, creating characters one after the other to produce a line of text. This technique permits the printer to work at a relatively high speed—usually 120 characters per second (cps) or greater. The denser the dot formation, the more legible the character.

In contrast, a daisy wheel printer produces typewriter-quality output, but only by sacrificing output speed. The daisy wheel is a circular print mechanism with spokes radiating from its center. At the end of each spoke is an embossed character which strikes against a ribbon as the wheel moves across the paper. Daisy wheel printers function at speeds of 10 to 65 cps.

Most ticket printers used by travel agencies and airlines are dot matrix printers, although either can be used in training.

Copyright © 1990 by Glencoe/McGraw-Hill Educational Division. All rights reserved.

The Agent's Set

Since 1985, PCs with standard computer-style keyboards have begun to replace the older agents' sets which produce only uppercase characters. The agent's set or PC connected to a modem communicates with the mainframe over telephone lines. When reservations are booked at the agent's set, the data are stored temporarily at the travel agency, then eventually transmitted to the mainframe. Besides reservation data, the mainframe also stores flight schedules and other information that is retrievable by the travel agent.

One obvious difference between the PC keyboard and the keyboard on an older agent's set is the location of the special function characters. There are also some minor differences in the way each character is typed. For example, on older Apollo keyboards, a key called the *Fares* key is used to produce the character $. On a PC keyboard, the agent can produce the same character by pressing Shift and 4, just as on a standard typewriter. On older keyboards, a key called the "lozenge" or "pillow" produces the character ▢. On the PC keyboard, the [key is used in place of the lozenge and produces the character ▢.

Figure 1—6 An IBM PS/2 being used as an Apollo agent's set.

Figure 1—7 Apollo agent's set.

Copyright © 1990 by Glencoe/McGraw-Hill Educational Division. All rights reserved.

Despite the use of different keys for special functions, all major computer reservation systems have several characteristics in common. All store flight information, seat availability, and air fares for numerous domestic and international city pairs (a city pair is a "from" city paired with a "to" city). Various hotel chains and car rental companies also participate in the systems. The travel agent receives the normal commission for selling airline tickets, and many vendors also provide rebates—cash bonuses—when hotel and car bookings are made through a computer reservation system.

United Airlines' Apollo

The Apollo system, administered by Covia, Inc., a contractor designated by United Airlines, is utilized by approximately 25 percent of the retail travel agencies in the United States, second only to American Airlines' SABRE. In the Apollo data base are stored flight availability for 125,000 city pairs, 7.5 million fares, and room rates for 12,000 hotels, including 4,000 overseas properties. The participating vendors include 60 hotel chains, 16 car rental companies, and 20 cruise ship lines. Twenty different tour packagers are also in the Apollo system. Apollo can automatically price 97 percent of all domestic itineraries.

Although United Airlines is the "host" carrier, Apollo also provides direct access to seat availability for Eastern, TWA, Delta, KLM, and British Airways, among others. Apollo can issue boarding passes for United, American, Delta, TWA, Eastern, USAir, SAS, and other carriers. Travel insurance and bookings for Las Vegas and Broadway shows, sporting events, restaurants, and nightclubs are also booked on the Apollo system.

The Future of the CRS

Computer technology has had a major impact on the travel industry in the form of increasingly more sophisticated computer reservation systems. Older video display terminals with limited keyboard capabilities are being replaced by "intelligent" microcomputers which perform a range of functions. Originally designed just for airline reservations, today's computer reservation systems have enormous databases of airlines, hotels, car rentals, cruises, tours, and other vital travel data.

What does the future hold for computer reservation systems and the professionals who use them? One development is the spread of corporate "in-house" agencies. Corporations that have a high frequency of airline travel are eligible to participate in special corporate programs administered by CRS vendors. Under these programs, a company serves as its own travel agency, complete with on-site agents' sets operated by company employees. By agreement, the "in-house" agency's only clients are employees of the company.

At various times airlines and other vendors such as Official Airline Guides Publications, Inc., have experimented with making computer reservation systems available to the general public. For example, an airline information and reservation system called the *Electronic OAG* may be accessed by anyone who has a microcomputer and a modem. Those who access the Electronic OAG find flight schedules, fares, and restrictions, and can book reservations using their personal computers as agents' sets. The tickets are actually issued by a travel agency under a contract with Official Airline Guides Publications, Inc. It is important to note that a relatively small portion of airline reservations are made via programs such as the Electronic OAG. Recent studies show that many people prefer flight arrangements made by a trained professional—an airline reservationist or a travel agent.

Copyright © 1990 by Glencoe/McGraw-Hill Educational Division. All rights reserved.

GLOSSARY OF NEW TERMS

Agent's set   A computer terminal utilized by a travel agent to communicate with a computer reservation system.

Apollo   The computer reservation system hosted by United Airlines and administered by Covia, Inc.; utilized by approximately 30 percent of all travel agents to book airline reservations.

Computer reservation system (CRS)   A special purpose data processing system designed to store information about airline and other travel reservations, hosted by a major carrier.

CRT   Abbreviation for cathode ray tube, used generally to refer to any computer terminal with a video screen.

Disk   A medium used to store computer data electronically. A *floppy disk* may be inserted and removed from the computer as needed.

Input   Refers generally to any information that can be entered into a computer for processing; examples are numbers or letters typed on a computer keyboard.

Large scale integrations   The technique of creating 1,000 or more electrical components on the surface of a micro chip.

Mainframe   The largest and most complex type of data processing system, capable of being operated by several individuals at the same time.

Microcomputer   The smallest data processing system usually operated by only one individual.

Output   Refers generally to any information that is produced by a computer; examples are data displayed on a computer screen and documents, such as airline tickets, generated by a computer printer.

PC   Abbreviation for *personal computer,* generally used to refer to any microcomputer.

Processor   The part of a computer that performs arithmetic and logical operations; the "brains" of a data processing system.

Copyright © 1990 by Glencoe/McGraw-Hill Educational Division. All rights reserved.

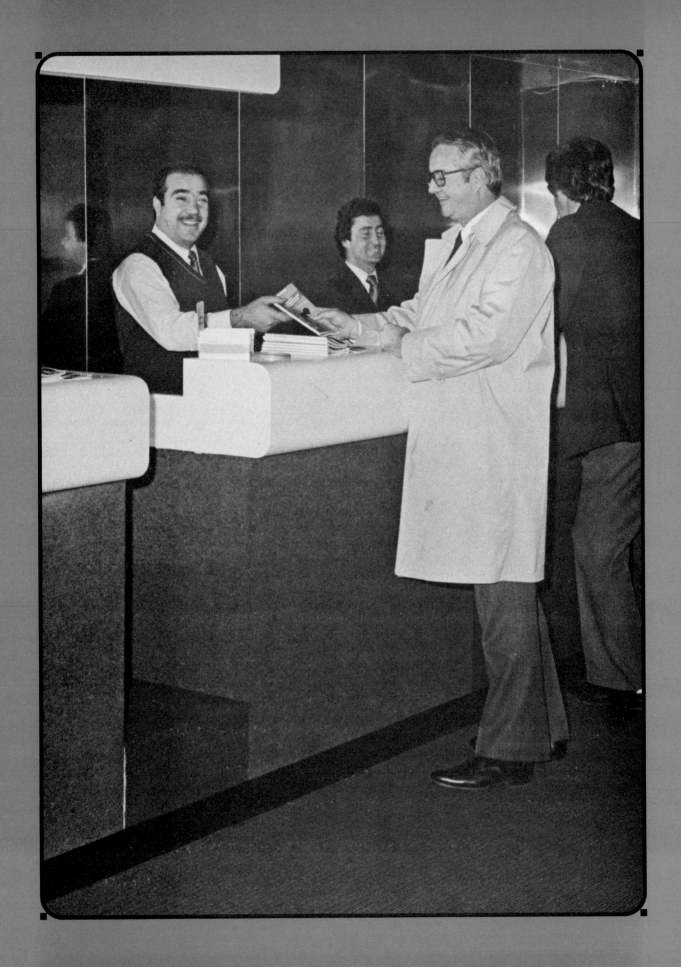

CHAPTER 2

AVAILABILITY

CHAPTER OBJECTIVES

At the end of the chapter, you should be able to perform the following tasks:

- Display city pair availability for any travel date and departure time.
- Locate the carrier, flight number, and available seats in each class of service on a given flight.
- Determine the origin and destination airports, departure time, arrival time, aircraft, meal service, and number of stopping points.
- Display availability for the return.
- Display additional availability and modify the display.
- Display availability via a specified connecting city.
- Display availability by arrival time.
- Display availability by class of service.
- Display availability by carrier.

Copyright © 1990 by Glencoe/McGraw-Hill Educational Division. All rights reserved.

Problem

An account executive in San Francisco must visit a customer in Chicago on the 17th of March. The following morning, he must travel to New York in time to make a lunch appointment. He then must be in Atlanta to make a 9:00 A.M. meeting on the 19th. Returning to San Francisco, he wishes to stop at the Los Angeles airport for a one-hour meeting.

Apollo Solution

Use city pair availability (CPA) to display regularly scheduled airline flights between each set of cities. In this chapter, you will learn various methods of checking availability for outbound and return segments, connections, and specific flights.

SIGN ON/SIGN OFF

Before Apollo can be used to access air fares or book passenger reservations, the travel agent must first "sign on" at the CRT. The sign-on procedure identifies the agent who will be using the computer and the work area in which the task is performed.

The **work area** is an electronic holding area assigned to each agent's set. In the work area, the agent assembles information such as the traveler's name, contact telephone number, and desired ticketing date. This information may be entered in any order. Together, this collection of data is referred to as a **passenger name record** or **PNR.** When all the data has been assembled, the agent "ends the transaction," and the record is sent from the agent's work area to permanent computer storage. The work area is then erased so that another passenger record can be assembled.

Whenever the terminal is not used for an extended period, the agent should "sign off." The entry to sign on or off consists of a combination of letters and numbers. Each travel agent who uses the Apollo system is identified by a unique agent ID code.

Basic Sign-On

The basic sign-on entry is used to identify the agent and gain access to the computer.

Copyright © 1990 by Glencoe/McGraw-Hill Educational Division. All rights reserved.

Format:

SON/<Agent ID Code>

Example:

SON/12T

Sign on: SON
Slash: /
Agent ID::   12T

The agent ID may consist of from one to three alphanumeric characters (letters or numerals).

Sign Off

Before leaving the agent's set for an extended period of time, or at the end of the work day, the agent is instructed to sign off the system.

The sign-off entry has the following format:

Format:

SOF

The letters *SOF* stand for "sign off." Any agent set that has been left on and not used for three hours is automatically signed off.

ENTERING APOLLO COMMANDS

A **command** is an entry that is typed at the terminal to instruct Apollo to perform a certain task. Apollo commands are used to enter passenger information, display flight schedules, book reservations, and make changes to the passenger record, among other functions.

An Apollo command begins with a **field identifier** or command code. Each command has a specified **format** that determines what information is typed, and in what order. Unless the appropriate format is followed exactly, Apollo will not understand the entry.

The agent's set has an important key labeled Enter. The Enter key is used to transmit information typed at the keyboard for computer processing. Until this key is pressed, the information is not transmitted.

Apollo commands are entered by typing the correct format, using the appropriate field identifier or command code, then pressing Enter.

CITY PAIR AVAILABILITY

Apollo has a comprehensive data base containing all United Airlines flights, as well as flights scheduled by other participating carriers. On request, Apollo will display a listing of flight schedules between any two designated points. This listing is referred to as **City Pair Availability,** or **CPA.** To display city pair availability, three things must be known:

- The travel date
- The city pair
- The estimated or desired departure time

Copyright © 1990 by Glencoe/McGraw-Hill Educational Division. All rights reserved.

Entering the Travel Date

Unless the travel date is specified, Apollo will display only flights scheduled for the current day. Most reservations are for future dates, and flight schedules are subject to change. Therefore, it is important to specify the exact travel date when requesting a flight schedule. The date is entered as a code, with the day entered as one or two digits and the month as a three-letter abbreviation. For example, the 17th of July is entered as 17JUL. The 3rd of December may be entered as either 3DEC or 03DEC.

Entering the City Pair

Remember that some cities are served by multiple airports. The choice of airport code usually depends on passenger preference. If the passenger requests a particular airport, the appropriate airport code should be used. Otherwise, the city code is used to display availability for all airports in the vicinity.

Entering the Departure Time

The estimated or desired departure time should always be entered, unless the passenger is specifically searching for the earliest flight. Times are entered as codes, omitting the punctuation marks and abbreviating A.M. as A and P.M. as P. For example, 8:30 A.M. is expressed as 830A, and 11:00 P.M. is entered as 1100P. The double zero may be omitted, as in 11P.

Displaying Availability

The Apollo code for availability is the letter A. The following command format is used to request city pair availability:

Format:

A<Date><City Pair><Departure Time>

Example:

A10MAYSFOMIA8A

Availability:	A
Travel date:	10MAY
City pair:	SFOMIA
Departure time:	8A

If a departure time is omitted, Apollo will assume an 8:00 A.M. departure. After typing the appropriate codes, complete the command by pressing the Enter key.

Example

A plant manager is planning a trip from Miami to San Francisco. He would like to fly on September 13, departing around ten o'clock in the morning.

Travel date:	13SEP
From:	MIA
To:	SFO
Departure time:	10A

Using the correct date code, city pair, and time code, the following entry would be used to find out what flights are available for your client:

A 13SEP MIA SFO 10A

Copyright © 1990 by Glencoe/McGraw-Hill Educational Division. All rights reserved.

Here, spaces have been inserted in the entry for illustration. When the entry is typed at the keyboard, the spaces should be omitted in the interest of speed. Thus, the entry would actually be made at the Apollo keyboard as follows:

```
A13SEPMIASFO10A
```

The estimated departure time may be entered either as 10A or 1000A.

Interpreting the Availability Display

Apollo responds by displaying a table of available flights for the designated city pair (Figure 2–1). Each line is numbered on the extreme left.

Carrier   The first column lists the carrier for each flight. In the example, line 1 is a United flight, and line 4 shows a Pan Am flight. Each airline is indicated by a two-letter code—the carrier code. UA is the carrier code for United Airlines, and PA is the code for Pan Am.

Flight Number   The second column lists the flight number. Line 1 in the example is United flight 485, and line 4 is Pan Am Flight 897. The flight number may consist of from one to four digits.

Seats Per Class   To the right of the flight number appear several columns showing the number of seats available in each class of service. On United flight 485, there are four first class (F) seats, four coach (Y) seats, and no seats offered at the super-saver fare (B). Other classes may be shown in the display as well, including seats offered at M and Q discounted fares.

Four is the maximum number of seats Apollo will display in each class of service for an off-line flight. If there are fewer than four seats available, Apollo will

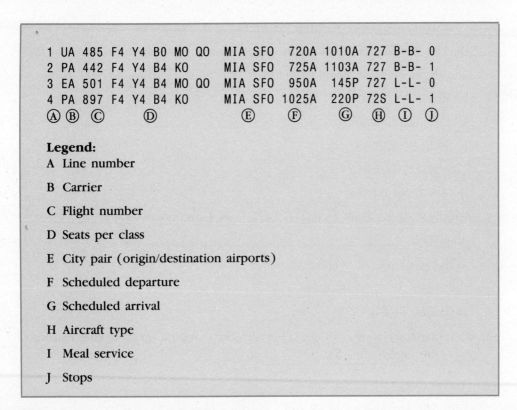

```
1 UA 485 F4 Y4 B0 MO QO   MIA SFO   720A  1010A 727 B-B- 0
2 PA 442 F4 Y4 B4 KO       MIA SFO   725A  1103A 727 B-B- 1
3 EA 501 F4 Y4 B4 MO QO   MIA SFO   950A   145P 727 L-L- 0
4 PA 897 F4 Y4 B4 KO       MIA SFO  1025A   220P 72S L-L- 1
Ⓐ Ⓑ Ⓒ          Ⓓ              Ⓔ     Ⓕ      Ⓖ   Ⓗ Ⓘ  Ⓙ
```

Legend:

A Line number

B Carrier

C Flight number

D Seats per class

E City pair (origin/destination airports)

F Scheduled departure

G Scheduled arrival

H Aircraft type

I Meal service

J Stops

Figure 2–1   The City Pair Availability display.

Copyright © 1990 by Glencoe/McGraw-Hill Educational Division. All rights reserved.

show zero seats. Only on United Airlines flights, Apollo will show the exact number of seats available, to a maximum of nine seats per class. Thus, on any carrier except UA, the number of seats in any class will appear as either four or zero. But on a UA flight, the number of seats may be any number between zero and nine.

City Pair   To the right of the seat inventory Apollo shows the codes for the "from" and "to" airports (city pair). If either city has more than one major airport, the corresponding airport code appears.

Flight Times   The two columns to the right of the city pair show the departure time and arrival time for each flight. For example, United flight 485 is scheduled to depart from Miami at 720A and arrive in San Francisco at 1010A.

Aircraft   The column to the right of the flight times gives the type of aircraft used in each flight. For instance, the flight in line 4 is a 727 Stretch Jet (72S). All airline reservation systems recognize a three-letter code for each aircraft type.

Meal Service   To the right of the aircraft code is shown the type of meal service provided in each class of service (technically, only the meal service in the first three classes of service is actually given). Common meal codes include B for breakfast, L for lunch, D for dinner, and S for snack. If no meal service is provided, no meal code will appear in this column.

Stops   To the right of the meal code is shown the number of stops made by the flight en route to the destination airport. In the example availability display (Figure 2–1), Pan Am 897 makes one stop between Miami and San Francisco.

CHECK-IN: A STUDY AID

Write the correct answer to each problem.

1. Select by circling the letter for the correct entry to display availability on the 22nd of August from Miami to Dallas–Ft. Worth, leaving around 8:00 in the morning.

   a. 22AUGMIADFW8A

   b. AUG22MIADFW8A

   c. A22AUGMIADFW8A

   d. AAUG22MIADFW8A

2. Write the correct entry to display availability based on the following coded information. *A12JUNPHXDEN7A*

   Travel date: 12JUN

   City pair: PHXDEN

   Departure time: 7A

3. Write the correct entry to display availability based on the following information. *A18SEPLAXDEN10A*

   Travel date: 18th of September

   City pair: Los Angeles to Denver

   Departure time: 10:00 A.M.

Copyright © 1990 by Glencoe/McGraw-Hill Educational Division. All rights reserved.

4. What entry would display availability on flights from New York-LaGuardia to Nashville on February 6, departing around 3:00 in the afternoon?

   A6FEBLGABNA3P

5. Write the correct entry to display availability on April 16 from St. Louis to Cleveland, leaving around 9:30 in the morning.

   A16APR STL CLE930A

6. Assume Apollo displays the city pair availability below:

```
1 AA 558 F4 Y4 B4 M4 Q4 STL CLE 1000A 1223P 72S L-L- 0
2 TW 422 F4 Y4 B4 M4 Q4 STL CLE 1100A  125P 727 S-S- 0
3 AA 120 F4 Y4 B4 M4 Q4 STL CLE  155P  415P 727 S-S- 0
4 UA 530 F9 Y9 B9 M9 Q9 STL CLE  225P  448P 727 S-S- 0
5 ML  34 Q4             STL CLE  245P  503P DC9 ---- 0
```

   a. One of the flights in the table above is a United Airlines flight departing around 2:30 P.M. What time does that flight arrive in Cleveland?

      _448P_

   b. What is the flight number of the flight that arrives at about 5:00 P.M.?

      _ML 34_

   c. What carrier operates a flight that departs at 11:00 A.M.?

      _TW_

   d. What type of meal service is provided on the flight that departs at 10:00 A.M.? _Lunch_

   e. What type of aircraft is used by the TWA flight?

      _727_

   f. What time does United 530 arrive in Cleveland?

      _448 p_

   g. How many stops are made by United 530 between St. Louis and Cleveland? _0_

   h. How many seats are available in Q class on the American flight that departs around 2:00 P.M.? _4_

Copyright © 1990 by Glencoe/McGraw-Hill Educational Division. All rights reserved.

To display flights for the return trip (i.e., for the "opposite" city pair), the following format is used:

Format:

A*O<Return Date>/<Departure Time>

Example:

A*O10MAY/5P

Availability:	A
Return flights:	*O
Return date:	10MAY
Slash:	/
Departure time:	5P

Remember to complete the command by pressing the Enter key.

For same-day return flights, the date may be omitted. For example, to display availability for return flights departing about 8:00 P.M. on the same day as the outbound segment, the following entry would be used:

A*O/8P

If a return flight is desired on a different date, insert the date code before the departure time.

Example

Assume you have just obtained an availability display for a certain city pair, and you now wish to request availability of return flights on the 12th of July, leaving around 6:00 P.M. The following entry may be used:

A*O12JUL/6P

Additional Flights

Apollo will display a maximum of seven flights in each table. However, in many cases, there are more than seven flights between the designated cities. To display additional flights, the following entry may be used:

Format:

A*

This entry may be used only when an availability table has already been displayed. Each time the entry is input, Apollo will display the next seven flights scheduled for the specified city pair until all the flights have been displayed.

Alternate Time

After city pair availability has been requested, additional availability may be displayed at a specified alternate departure time. To request an alternate time, simply add the time code, as in the following:

Format:

A*<Alternate Time>

Example:

A*5P

Copyright © 1990 by Glencoe/McGraw-Hill Educational Division. All rights reserved.

When this entry is made, Apollo will display availability for flights departing around the specified time (in the example, around 5:00 P.M.).

Alternate Date

After city pair availability has been requested, an alternate date can be specified by entering the following format:

Format:

    A*<Alternate Date>

Example:

    A*21MAY

Apollo will respond by displaying availability on the new date, using the same city pair requested in the most recent availability entry.

Alternate Date and Time

A single entry may be used to change both the date and time in an availability display, as follows:

Format:

    A*<Alternate Date><Alternate Time>

Example:

    A*21JUL5P

Apollo will respond by displaying availability on the new date and at the new time, using the same city pair as previously requested.

Original Availability

To redisplay the original availability table, i.e., the one first displayed for the current city pair, the following entry may be used:

Format:

    A*R

When this entry is made, Apollo will display the first flight schedule displayed for the current city pair.

Examples

Assume you are checking availability for a client who is planning a trip from Seattle, Washington, to Honolulu, Hawaii, on the 18th of September. Your client expresses a preference to depart around 8:00 A.M. The following entry would be used to display availability:

    A18SEPSEAHNL8A

Copyright © 1990 by Glencoe/McGraw-Hill Educational Division. All rights reserved.

Apollo responds as follows:

```
1NW  87 F0 Y0 B0 SEA HNL  810A 1208P 747 B-B- 0
2UA  67 F0 Y0 B0 SEA HNL  845A 1243P D10 B-B- 0
3DL 122 F0 Y0 B0 SEA LAX  900A 1112A 727 S-S- 0
4DL 312 F0 Y0 B0     HNL 1258P  350P D10 L-L- 0
5UA  35 F0 Y0 B0 SEA HNL 1005A  236P 747 L-L- 1
```

Observe the two Delta flights in lines 3 and 4. In this example, Delta 122 flies from Seattle to Los Angeles, where passengers connect to Delta 312 continuing on to Honolulu. The "from" city in line 4 is omitted, because it is the same as the "to" city in line 3. Apollo uses this method to indicate connecting flights.

Suppose your client inquires about flights leaving later in the day. To obtain additional availability, the following entry may be used:

A*

Apollo responds by displaying additional flights for the same city pair and date:

```
1AS  82 F4 Y4 B4 Q4 SEA SFO  550P  740P 72S D-D- 0
2CO   3 F4 J4 Y4 B4     HNL  845P 1100P D10 D-D- 0 X35
3UA 847 F9 Y9 B9 M9 SEA LAX  450P  655P 72S S-S- 0
4UA  23 F9 J9 Y9 B9     HNL  800P 1040P 747 D-D- 0
5DL 712 F4 Y4 B4 M4 SEA LAX  440P  704P 73S S-S- 0
6CO   1 F4 J4 Y4 B4     HNL  800P 1040P 747 S-S- 0
```

Observe that all the flights in the example above are connections. Alaska 82 originates in Seattle and connects in San Francisco to Continental 3, which completes the connection to Honolulu. United 847 connects in Los Angeles to United 23 for the final leg. Delta 712 also connects in Los Angeles to Continental 1.

Next, your client inquires about return flights. The party would like to return on the 26th of September, departing around 1:00 P.M. To display return availability, the following entry may be used:

A*026SEP/1P

Copyright © 1990 by Glencoe/McGraw-Hill Educational Division. All rights reserved.

Apollo responds by displaying return flights for the specified date and time:

```
1HA   22 F4 Y4 B4 M4   HNL SEA  125P   940P  L10 L-L- 0
2NW   86 F4 Y4 B4 Q4   HNL SEA  110P   929P  D10 L-L- 0
3UA   32 F9 Y9 B9 M9   HNL SEA 1245P   903P  D10 L-L- 0
4DL1560 F4 Y4 B4 M4    HNL LAX  120P   823P  D10 L-L- 0
5DL 951FN4YN4BN4MN4        SEA  941P  1159P  72S S-S- 0
```

Observe that the city pairs in the new availability display above are reversed, indicating return flights from Honolulu to Seattle. Note the class designations for Delta 951 in line 5; each class code ends with the letter N, indicating night travel. On this flight, passengers receive a reduced fare in each class.

Let us assume your client inquires about alternate flights departing one day earlier, about 9:00 A.M. The following entry may be used to change the date:

A*25SEP/9A

Apollo responds by displaying availability for the previous day, using a departure time of 9:00 A.M. :

```
1DL1552  F0 Y0 B0 Q0   HNL LAX 915A   418P  D10 B-B- 0
2DL1703  F0 Y0 B0 Q0       SEA 455P   706P  72S D-D- 0
3UA 812  F0 Y0 B0 H0   HNL LAX 900A   509P  747 B-B- 0
4UA 696  F4 Y0 B0 H0       SEA 620P   851P  72S D-D- 0
5UA  32  F9 Y9 B9 M9   HNL SEA 1235P  852P  D19 L-L- 0
```

CONNECTIONS

As shown in the previous examples, connections involving more than one city or airport are shown in the availability table as separate flights. The connecting city is shown as the destination in the first flight, but is omitted from the connecting flight. The line for the connecting flight thus shows only the destination city. Apollo will show connections involving from one to four legs. All airline reservation systems use this method to indicate connecting flights involving more than one leg.

Displaying Connections

Apollo can display availability with connections via a specified city. To request a connecting city, add the code for the connecting city to the end of the basic entry, as in the example on the next page.

Copyright © 1990 by Glencoe/McGraw-Hill Educational Division. All rights reserved.

A20OCTATLABQ9A DFW

A space is shown here for clarity, but when the entry is typed at the keyboard the space should be omitted.

Example

Assume you wish to request availability on the 17th of July from Portland, Oregon to Pittsburgh, connecting through Chicago departing around 7:00 A.M. with a minimum connecting time of 120 minutes. The following entry may be used to display the flights:

A17JULPDXPIT7AORD120

Response:

```
1 NW   46 F4 YO MO   PDX ORD  735A    100P  72S  B-B-  0
2 US  148 Y4              PIT  210P    425P  D9S  S-S-  0
3 UA  142 F9 Y9 BO   PDX ORD  750A    125P  D10  B-B-  0
4 UA  124 F9 Y9 BO        PIT  215P    432P  72S  S-S-  0
5 NW   58 F4 Y4 MO   PDX ORD  330P   1103P  727  L-L-  1
6 UA  408 F9 Y9 BO        PIT  109A    510A  737  S-S-  0
```

Changing the Boarding or Destination City

When availability has already been requested for a particular city pair, a different boarding city can be specified by entering A*B followed by the code for the origin city. For example, to change the current availability display for flights originating in St. Louis, the following simple entry may be used:

A*BSTL

Apollo uses the same date and time as the most recent availability request, but uses St. Louis as the origin city.

Availability can be redisplayed with a different destination city, by entering A*D and the code for the destination city, as in the following example:

A*DLGA

A number of other options may be also be used with the basic city pair availability entry, including a specified arrival time, class of service, or carrier. The agent can also request direct and nonstop flights only, omitting connections from the display altogether.

Copyright © 1990 by Glencoe/McGraw-Hill Educational Division. All rights reserved.

CHECK-IN: A STUDY AID

Write the correct answer to each problem.

1. What is the correct entry to display same-day return flights leaving around 9:00 P.M.? _____ A*0/9P _____

2. Select by letter the correct Apollo entry to request return flights on May 5, leaving around 7:00 P.M.

   a. A5MAY7P

   b. A*R7MAY5P

   c. A*05MAY5P

   d. A*05MAY/7P

3. Write the correct entry to display return flights on February 14th, leaving around 5:00 in the afternoon. _____ A*014FEB/5P _____

4. Mr. Carlton will be traveling from Miami to Cleveland on July 6th, and would like to leave around 10:00 in the morning.

   a. What entry would you use to display availability?

   _____ A6JUL MIA CLE 10A _____

   b. He would like to return on the same day, about 6:00 P.M. What entry would you use to display return flights?

   _____ A*0/6P _____

5. Ms. Emerson will be traveling from Los Angeles to Dallas-Ft. Worth on the 3rd of August. She would like a flight around 7:00 A.M.

   a. What entry would you use to display availability?

   _____ A 3AUG LAX DFW 7A _____ Your client would like a seat in first class, but none are available in the current display. What entry would you use to display more flights?

   _____ A* _____

   b. Assume Apollo has displayed only connections in the table. Your client would rather have a direct flight. What entry would you use to display the original availability table? _____ A*R _____

6. The Tingle family is planning a Hawaiian holiday. They plan to travel from Seattle to Honolulu on September 8th. They would like a flight departing around 9:00 in the morning.

   a. What entry would you use to display availability?

   _____ A8SEP SEA HNL 9A _____

Copyright © 1990 by Glencoe/McGraw-Hill Educational Division. All rights reserved.

b. The Tingles will be returning on September 21st, leaving Honolulu around 2:00 P.M. What entry would you use to display return flights?

_____

MORE ON AVAILABILITY

Availability by Arrival Time

Typing A before the time code tells Apollo to display availability by arrival time, instead of departure time. As an example, assume you wish to display availability on the 22nd of October from Seattle to Honolulu, for flights arriving around 4:00 P.M. The following entry may be used:

A22OCTSEAHNLA4P

Response:

```
1DL 122 F4 Y4 B4 Q4   SEA LAX  900A 1112A 727 S-S- 0
2DL 312 F4 Y4 B4 Q4       HNL 1258P  350P D10 L-L- 0
3UA  35 F9 Y9 B9 M9   SEA HNL 1005A  236P 747 L-L- 1
4AS  82 F4 Y4 B4 Q4   SEA SFO  550P  740P 72S D-D- 0
5CO   3 F4 J4 Y4 B4       HNL  845P 1100P D10 D-D- 0 X35
```

Observe that Apollo's response lists flights arriving in Honolulu closest to the specified time (4P). In line 5, note the code X35 displayed to the right of the stops column. The X signifies that the flight does not operate on certain days—in this case, on Wednesdays (3) and Fridays (5). Each day of the week is represented by a number, beginning with 1 for Monday and concluding with 7 for Sunday.

Availability by Class of Service

A class of service may be specified in the availability entry, as in the following example:

A/B/12DECCLESTL

Response:
1TW 745 B4 CLE STL 1250P 120P DC9 S-S- 0

Apollo displays the first flight with an available seat in the specified class (B).

Availability by Carrier

The availability entry may include a specified airline carrier as in the following example:

A18SEPSEAHNL9A‡DL

Copyright © 1990 by Glencoe/McGraw-Hill Educational Division. All rights reserved.

Response:

```
1DL 122 FO YO BO SEA LAX   900A 1112A 727 S-S- 0
2DL 312 FO YO BO     HNL 1258P   350P D10 L-L- 0
```

Note that Apollo's response includes only flights operated by the specified carrier (DL).

NONSTOP/DIRECT FLIGHTS

The option /D may be added to basic city pair availability entry to limit the display to nonstop and direct flights as in the following example:

    A18SEPSEAHNL9A/D

Response:

```
1NW  87 FO YO BO SEA HNL   810A 1208P 747 B-B- 0
2UA  67 FO YO BO SEA HNL   845A 1243P D10 B-B- 0
3UA  35 FO YO BO SEA HNL  1005A  236P 747 L-L- 1
```

Apollo's response includes only nonstop and/or direct flights. If additional availability is requested, Apollo will display connections.

CHECK-IN: A STUDY AID

I. *Write the correct word or phrase that belongs in the blank(s).*

1. The basic __Sign on__ entry is used to identify the agent and gain access to the computer.

2. Any agent's set that has been left on and not used for ___3___ hours is automatically signed off.

3. If a travel date is not specified, Apollo will display flights for __TODAY on CURRENT DAY__

Copyright © 1990 by Glencoe/McGraw-Hill Educational Division. All rights reserved.

4. The Apollo command code for availability is ___A___.

5. Apollo will display a maximum of ___4___ seats in each class of service for an off-line flight; if fewer seats are available, Apollo will display ___0___.

6. On United flights, Apollo will show ___EXACT___ seats available, to a maximum of ___9___ per class.

7. The meal code S indicates that the meal service consists of ___SNACK___.

8. Typing _____ before the time tells Apollo to display flights according to arrival time, rather than departure time.

9. The date March 6th may be entered as either ___6 MAR___ or ___06 MAR___.

10. The time 3:00 P.M. may be entered as either ___3P___ or ___300P___.

II. *Write the correct entry to modify the availability display based on the following information.*

1. Display additional availability. ___A*___

2. Display additional availability and change departure time to 3:00 P.M.
___A*3P___

3. Display additional availability and change travel date to the 16th of July.
___A*16JUL___

4. Display additional availability and change travel date to the 5th of August.
___A*5AUG___

5. Display the availability table originally obtained.
___A*R___

6. Display additional availability and change travel date to the 19th of June.
___A*19JUN___

7. Display additional availability and change time to 9:00 P.M.
___A*9P___

8. Display opposite availability at 6:00 P.M. on the same day as the previous availability display. ___A*O/6P___

9. Display opposite availability on the 19th of July at 2:00 P.M.
___A*O19JUL/2P___

10. Display additional availability. ___A*___

Copyright © 1990 by Glencoe/McGraw-Hill Educational Division. All rights reserved.

III. *Write the correct Apollo format for each of the following availability requests:*

1. Display availability on the 12th of March from Cincinnati to Ft. Lauderdale departing around 8:00 A.M. using Atlanta as a connecting point.

A12MAR CVG FLL 8A ATL

2. Display availability on the 25th of April from Anchorage to Albuquerque for the 9th of August departing around 1:00 A.M. via San Francisco with two hours to connect. A25APR ANC ABQ

2.0 A7W

3. Redisplay availability for the same city pair and date, changing the departure city to Seattle. A✳BSEA

4. Redisplay the original availability display.

A✳R

5. Display availability on the 16th of January from Los Angeles to Honolulu, arriving around 3:00 P.M. A16JAN LAX HNL /3P

6. Display availability on the 24th of August from New Orleans to Chicago, departing around 11:00 A.M. in B class. A1B24AUG MSY CHI 11A

7. Display availability in Q class on the 12th of July from Orlando to Greensboro, departing around 8:00 A.M. A/Q/12JUL MCO GSO 8A

8. Display availability on the 11th of February from Milwaukee to St. Louis departing around 6:00 A.M. on Continental. A11FEB MKE STL 6P FCO

Copyright © 1990 by Glencoe/McGraw-Hill Educational Division. All rights reserved.

CHAPTER 3
SELLING AIR SPACE

CHAPTER OBJECTIVES

At the end of the chapter, you should be able to perform the following tasks:

- Sell air space from a city pair availability display.

- Interpret an air segment.

- Identify the status/action code for a confirmed segment.

- Sell a connection from a city pair availability display.

- Waitlist a seat request on a sold-out flight in an availability display.

- Identify the status/action code for a waitlisted segment.

- Place a seat request on the priority United Airlines waitlist.

- Sell space directly on a specified off-line or UA flight.

- Waitlist seats directly on a specified flight.

- Book an open segment using the direct-sell format.

- Record an air segment booked directly with an off-line carrier.

- Record a surface (arnk) segment in the passenger itinerary.

Problem

An actress must travel from Los Angeles to a movie location in Miami. She would like to fly first class on a flight that departs at 7:00 A.M., but the first-class section is sold out. A seat is available in first class on a later flight departing at 10:30 A.M. She prefers the earlier flight, but will accept the later departure as a last resort.

Apollo Solution

Waitlist a seat in first class on the 7:00 A.M. flight, and sell a confirmed reservation in first class on the 10:30 A.M. flight. In this chapter, you will learn how to sell air space and waitlist seat requests, both from availability and on specific flights.

HOW TO SELL AIR SPACE

When a passenger reservation is booked on the computer, one or more seats are said to be sold. The act of booking seat reservations is called selling airline space. If the requested seats are not available, the reservations may be placed on a waitlist. If other passengers holding confirmed seats should later cancel their reservations, the waitlisted seats may be confirmed.

The Apollo command code to sell airline space is 0, also called the **segment key.**

SELLING FROM AVAILABILITY

When an availability table is displayed, seats may be sold for any flight listed in the table. This process is called "reference selling" and is the simplest method of booking airline space. The following format is used to sell from availability:

Format:
    0<Seats><Class><Line>

Example:
    01Y1

Sell:	0
Seats:	1
Class:	Y
Line:	1

34

Copyright © 1990 by Glencoe/McGraw-Hill Educational Division. All rights reserved.

The segment code 0 is input first, followed by the number of seats, the class of service requested, and the line number in the availability table corresponding to the desired flight. Complete the command as usual by pressing the Enter key.

Entering the Number of Seats

The number of seats may not exceed the number shown in the display in the requested class of service. In general, a maximum of four seats may be sold for an off-line flight, unless zero seats are shown in the availability display. Up to nine seats may be booked on a UA flight, unless the actual number shown in the display is less.

If you attempt to sell more than the maximum number, the seats will be booked on a request basis, and the reservations will not be confirmed until the carrier accepts the seat request.

Entering the Class

The class code must be one of the valid classes of service shown in the availability display—usually F first class, Y coach, M match fare, Q discounted fare, or B super-saver fare. The number of seats requested must not exceed the number shown in the requested class, unless the seats are to be waitlisted.

Entering the Line Number

The line number refers to the number in the extreme left column on each line of the availability table.

Example

Shown below is a partial availability display for flights between SFO and ORD on the 17th of July, leaving around 10:00 A.M. Assume your client would like to reserve three seats in coach on American Airlines 214.

```
1 AA 182 F4 Y4 B4 M4   SFO ORD 1000A   355P D10 L-L- 0
2 AA 214 F4 Y4 B4 M4   SFO ORD 1215P   615P D10 L-L- 0
3 AA 222 F4 Y4 B4 M4   SFO ORD  100P   705P 747 L-L- 0
4 UA 128 F9 Y9 B9 M9   SFO ORD  240P   841P D10 D-D- 0
```

Solution

AA 214 is the flight shown in line 2 of the sample display. Up to four seats are available to sell. Using the class code Y for coach, the following data is required to sell the space:

Number of seats: 3
Class: Y
Line: 2

Copyright © 1990 by Glencoe/McGraw-Hill Educational Division. All rights reserved.

The entry is typed as follows:

03Y2

Response:

1 AA 214Y 17JUL SFOORD SS3 1215P 615P

Apollo responds to the Sell entry by booking an itinerary segment.

ITINERARY SEGMENTS

The term *itinerary* refers collectively to all the flights booked for a passenger, including all departing and return flights, as well as any connections. Each flight in the itinerary is listed on a separate line, called a **segment**. Besides air segments, the itinerary may also include auxiliary segments—e.g., car rental or hotel reservations.

The air segment is illustrated in Figure 3–1. As shown in the illustration, each segment is numbered. Apollo automatically assigns the segment number based on the order in which the flight was booked. The segment in the example is segment 1, indicating the first flight in the passenger itinerary.

Each air segment includes the carrier, flight number, class, and travel date of the reservation. After the date, Apollo shows the city pair. If the city pair includes a city with multiple airports, the correct airport code—not the city code—will be shown. To the right of the city pair Apollo displays the number of seats preceded by an action code.

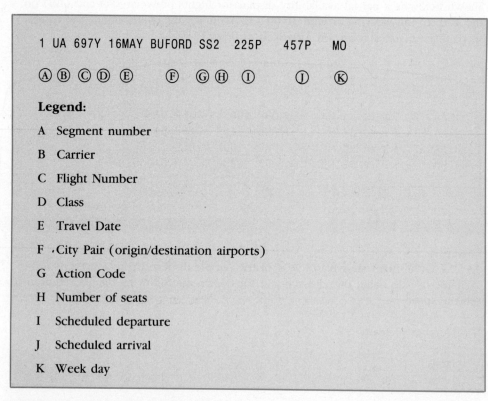

Figure 3–1 The itinerary segment line

Copyright © 1990 by Glencoe/McGraw-Hill Educational Division. All rights reserved.

STATUS/ACTION CODES

In the example segment, the code SS (Sell/Sell) indicates that the space is sold, signifying that the reservation will be confirmed as soon as the passenger record is saved. Whenever space is sold, the computer normally responds with SS if the seats are available. If the number of seats requested exceeds the maximum, the computer may respond with the action code NN (Need/Need), indicating that the seats will be requested, but the reservations will not be confirmed until they are accepted by the airline.

Each air segment also includes the flight times. The flight in the example segment departs at 2:25 P.M. and arrives at 4:57 P.M.

SELLING CONNECTIONS

To sell a connection, make the entry to sell the first leg, then add the class and line number of the second leg. Remember to complete the command by pressing the Enter key.

Example
Assume you wish to sell one of the connections in the partial availability screen below.

```
1 HP1257 Y4 K0 M0   ABQ PHX     700A  805A  73S ---- 0
2 HP1026 Y4 K4 M4       TUS 8   845A  920A  73S ---- 0
3 HP 599 Y4 K4 M4   ABQ PHX     840A  945A  73S ---- 0
4 HP1027 Y4 K4 M4       TUS 8  1015A 1055A  73S ---- 0
```

The availability display shows two connections. One begins in line 1, and the other in line 3. Each connection is actually two flights. For instance, the flight in line 1 travels from Albuquerque (ABQ) to Phoenix (PHX), where the passenger must change planes for a connecting flight to Tucson (TUS). Each flight of a connection is referred to as a leg.

To sell one coach seat on the connection beginning in line 1, the following entry may be used:

01Y1Y2

Remember to press the Enter key to complete the entry.

Three segment connections may be sold in the same manner, as in the following entry:

01Y4Y5Y6

Copyright © 1990 by Glencoe/McGraw-Hill Educational Division. All rights reserved.

CHECK-IN: A STUDY AID

Write the correct answer to each of the problems below.

1. Select by letter the correct entry to sell three first-class seats on a flight in line 2 of the availability display. _____ B _____

   a. 0F32

   b. 03F2

   c. 02F2

   d. 02F3

2. Study the following entry, then answer the questions below.

   03Y2

   a. In what class is the airline space being booked?

   _____ Y _____

   b. How many seats are being sold? _____ 3 _____

   c. What line number in the availability display lists the flight on which the seats will be booked? _____ 2 _____

3. Refer to the partial availability table below to answer the questions that follow.

   ```
   1 UA 671 F9 Y9 B9 Q9 M9 ORD TPA  745A  920A 72S S-S- 0
   2 EA 230 F4 Y4 B4 Q4 M4 ORD TPA  835A 1003P 72S S-S- 0
   3 DL 650 F4 Y4 B4 Q4 M4 ORD TPA 1219P  150P 727 S-S- 0
   4 UA 201 F9 Y9 B0 Q0 M0 BUF ORD  120P  255P 72S D-D- 0
   ```

   a. What entry would sell four seats in Y class on the flight that arrives about 3:00 P.M.? _____ 04Y4 _____

   b. What entry would sell two seats in B class on Eastern 230? _____ 02B2 _____

   c. What entry would sell one seat in first class on the flight that departs about noon? _____ 01F3 _____

4. Study the following itinerary segment to answer the questions below.

   1 UA 477F 13JUL MSPORD SS3 700A 802A   WE

Copyright © 1990 by Glencoe/McGraw-Hill Educational Division. All rights reserved.

a. In what class of service have the seats been booked?

_____ F _____

b. How many passengers are traveling together in the party?

_____ 3 _____

c. On what week day will the party be traveling?

_____ WE _____

d. From what city does the flight depart? ___ MSP _____

e. What time is the flight scheduled to arrive at the destination airport?

_____ 802 _____

5. Write the correct entry to sell one seat in first class on a two-leg connection
beginning in line 3. ___ 01F3F4 _____

6. Write the correct entry to sell three seats in B class on a two-leg connection
beginning in line 2. ___ 03B2B3 _____

7. Assume you just obtained the following availability table:

```
1 UA 900 F9 Y0 B0 M0 Q0 ORD LGA 1000A 1247P 727 B-B- 0
2 PM 456 A0                 HVN  145P  215P DHT ---- 1
3 TW 322 F4 Y0 B0 V0 K0 ORD LGA 1030A 121P 72S L-L- 0
4 PM  25 A4                 HVN  215P  315P PAG ---- 0
```

Note that the second leg of both connections has only one class of service,
A. Write the correct entry to sell one seat on the first connection that has at
least one seat available on both legs. ___ 01F3A4 _____

8. Write the correct entry to sell two seats in Y class on a flight in line 4, and K
class on a flight in line 5. ___ 02Y4K5 _____

9. Write the correct entry to sell four seats in Q class on both legs of a connection beginning in line 3. ___ 04Q3Q4 _____

Copyright © 1990 by Glencoe/McGraw-Hill Educational Division. All rights reserved.

WAITLISTED SEGMENTS

When a flight is sold out and the waitlist is open, the seat request may be placed automatically on the waitlist. If passengers holding confirmed seats cancel their reservations, the request may clear the waitlist.

Example

Assume you have just obtained the following availability display:

```
1 UA 941 F4 YO MO BO    SFO PHX 1055A 1245P 727 L-L- 0
2 US 509 YO BO VO       SFO PHX 1220P  232P M80 L-L- 0
3 US 244 YO BO VO       SFO PHX  125P  332P 727 S-S- 0
4 UA 385 F4 YO MO BO    SFO PHX  140P  352P 727 S-S- 0
5 US 815 Y4 B4 V4       SFO PHX  320P  515P M80 S-S- 0
```

Your client requests a seat in coach on a flight leaving as close to 11:00 A.M. as possible. All the flights except US 815 are sold out in coach. Assume your client would like to be waitlisted in coach on the USAir flight in line 2.

The following entry may be used to waitlist one seat in coach on USAir flight 509:

    01Y2

Response:

    1 US 509Y 18NOV SFOPHX LL1 1220PP 232P

Observe that the status/action code LL appears in the itinerary segment before the number of seats, indicating that the requested flight is sold out and the space has been waitlisted.

Just in case the seat request fails to clear the US waitlist, a confirmed reservation should also be booked on the USAir flight in line 5. The following entry may be used to book the alternate space:

    01Y5

Your client's itinerary would now appear as follows:

    1 US 509Y 18NOV SFOPHX LL1 1220P   232P
    2 US 815Y 18NOV SFOPHX SS1 320P   515P

Segment 1 shows the waitlisted seat on USAir 509. The action code LL signifies that the seat request will be placed on the waitlist. Segment 2 is the confirmed reservation on USAir 815. If the request clears the UA waitlist, you will be able to confirm the waitlisted UA segment and cancel the USAir segment.

When a waitlisted segment and a confirmed segment are booked in the same itinerary, the waitlisted segment should always be booked first.

Copyright © 1990 by Glencoe/McGraw-Hill Educational Division. All rights reserved.

CHECK-IN: A STUDY AID

Write the correct availability entry for each situation.

1. Display availability on the 13th of June from Denver to Milwaukee around 9:30 A.M. _____ A13JUNDENMKE930A

2. Display more availability. _____ A*

3. Display original availability. _____ A*R

4. Sell two seats in Q class on a flight in line 3 of the availability table.

   _____ 02Q3

5. Display return availability on the 17th of July around 4:00 P.M.

   _____ A*O17JUL4P

6. Waitlist two seats in Q class on a two-leg connection beginning in line 5.

   _____ 02Q5Q6

7. Sell two seats in Y class on a flight in line 2.

   _____ 02Y2

SELLING SPACE ON A SPECIFIED FLIGHT

Seats may also be sold on a specified flight without an availability display, if the flight number and departure date are already known. Selling air space on a specified flight is called direct selling. The action code NN is used to direct-sell, as shown in the following format:

Format:

   0<Carrier><Flight><Class><Date><City Pair>NN<Seats>

Example

Assume you wish to book two seats on Delta 650 in first class on the 27th of August from Tampa, Florida, to Chicago. The list below breaks down the information needed to book the air space.

Carrier:	DL
Flight Number:	650
Class:	F
Travel date:	27AUG
City pair:	TPAORD
Seats:	2

Based on this data, the following entry may be used to direct-sell the seats:

```
0 DL 650 F 27AUG TPAORD NN2
```

Copyright © 1990 by Glencoe/McGraw-Hill Educational Division. All rights reserved.

Here, spaces have been included in the entry for clarity. When the entry is typed at the keyboard, the spaces should be omitted, as follows:

    0DL650F27AUGTPAORDNN2

Response:
    1 DL 650F 27AUG TPAORD SS2   100P   231P

Apollo responds by booking the flight segment and adding the status/action code, class, and flight times.

SELLING SPACE ON UA FLIGHTS

If the requested flight is a United Airlines flight, the carrier code UA may be omitted. For example, to book one coach seat on UA flight 142 on the 3rd of December from Portland, Oregon, to Chicago-O'Hare, the following entry may be used to direct-sell the air space:

    0 142 Y 3DEC PDXORD NN1

The spaces which are shown here for clarity should be omitted when the entry is typed at the keyboard. If you omit the carrier code, Apollo will assume that United (UA) is the requested carrier.

Examples of Direct-Sell Entries

Off-line

    0AS105Y02APRLAXSEANN1

Sell:	0
Carrier/flight number:	AS 105
Class:	Y
Travel date:	02APR
City pair:	LAXSEA
Number needed:	NN1

On-line

    0289F17JUNLGAORDNN2

Sell:	0
Carrier/flight number:	UA 289 (carrier code omitted)
Class:	F
Travel date:	17JUN
City pair:	LGAORD
Number needed:	NN2

Copyright © 1990 by Glencoe/McGraw-Hill Educational Division. All rights reserved.

CHECK-IN: A STUDY AID

Write the answer to each of the following problems.

1. Use the direct-sell entry to sell airline space based on the following information. _O DL 810 Y 21 MAY IND DFW NN 2_

Carrier/flight number:	Delta 810
Class:	Y
Travel date:	May 21
From:	Indianapolis
To:	Dallas-Ft. Worth
Number of seats:	2

2. What entry would direct-sell AA flight 535 in M class on the 3rd of December from New York-LaGuardia to Buffalo, requesting one seat?

   O AA 535 M 3DEC LGA BUF NN 1

3. Write the correct direct-sell entry to book one seat in B class on Northwest flight 124 on the 5th of September from Minneapolis to Chicago. _SPEC. ARPT_

   O NW 124 B 5SEP MSP ORD NN 1

4. What entry would book three seats in first class on TWA flight 103 on the 22nd of April from Albuquerque to San Francisco?

   O TW 103 F 22APR ABQ SFO NN 3

5. What entry would book four seats in M class on United 285 on the 14th of January from Washington National Airport to Chicago-O'Hare?

   O UA 285 M 14JAN DCA ORD NN 4

WAITLISTING BY FLIGHT NUMBER

To waitlist with a direct-sell entry, substitute the action code LL for NN. For example, to waitlist two Y seats on Northwest flight 918 on the 16th of April from Milwaukee to Miami, the following entry would be used:

    O NW 918 Y 16APR MKEMIA LL2

The spaces inserted here for clarity should be omitted when the entry is typed at the keyboard, and should appear as follows:

    ONW918Y16APRMKEMIALL2

Copyright © 1990 by Glencoe/McGraw-Hill Educational Division. All rights reserved.

On UA flights, seat requests may be placed on a priority waitlist using one of two status/action codes.

PB   UA Priority Waitlist (normal)
PC   UA Priority Waitlist (within 24 hours)

Unless the flight departs within 24 hours of the booking, PB is used to waitlist the UA seat request as follows:

```
0923Y21JUNLGAORDPB2
```

OPEN SEGMENTS

A common application for the direct-sell format is booking open segments. Occasionally a client will desire a ticket for an itinerary which includes a segment without a specified flight or departure date. For example, a passenger may book a round-trip without knowing the exact date of the return. For this situation, an open segment is inserted in the itinerary.

To book an open segment, use the standard direct-sell entry, but substitute the word OPEN in place of the flight number. The status/action code NO (No action) is used to request an open segment.

Example

Assume that a client wishes to travel round-trip from SFO to PIT. He would like to return on a TWA flight, but cannot confirm exactly his return. Assuming one seat is desired, the open segment may be booked as follows:

```
0 TW OPEN Y PITSFO NO1
```

The spaces inserted here for clarity should be omitted when the entry is typed at the keyboard and should appear as follows:

```
0TWOPENYPITSFONO1
```

(In this example, it is assumed that the outbound segment has already been booked.)

Direct Bookings with Off-Line Carriers

On occasion, a travel agent may need to book air space directly with an off-line carrier, rather than through Apollo. In most situations, bookings are made by phone, but to record the segment in the traveler's itinerary, a special direct-sell entry is made.

The status/action code BK (Book) is used to record a segment booked directly with an off-line carrier, as in the following example:

```
0DL548F22SEPDFWATLBK2
```

Copyright © 1990 by Glencoe/McGraw-Hill Educational Division. All rights reserved.

The segment will be recorded in the passenger itinerary, but a message will not be sent to the off-line carrier (unless the segment is later canceled). Optionally, an asterisk * followed by the airline agent's initials or sine may be added to the end of the entry as follows:

```
0HA892V13OCTHNLLIHBK2*TR
```

To indicate a waitlisted segment booked directly with an off-line carrier, use the status/action code BL to record the segment in the passenger itinerary.

SURFACE SEGMENTS

Surface segments—travel by land or sea—may not be booked in an air itinerary. When the boarding point of an air segment is not the same as the destination in the previous air segment, an arnk segment (arrival not known) must be inserted in the itinerary to maintain continuity.

For example, assume you are making reservations for a client who will be traveling from ORD to MIA on an Eastern flight. Your client will take a cruise ship from MIA and return from St. Thomas, Virgin Islands (STT), to Chicago. Thus, the itinerary will include two air segments: one from ORD to MIA, and another from STT to ORD. To maintain continuity, an arnk segment must be inserted between the two air segments.

The arnk segment signifies that the trip is interrupted by another form of transportation, usually surface (ground or sea). The following command is used to record an arnk segment in an Apollo itinerary:

Format:
  Y

On older Apollo keyboards, a key labeled ARNK is used to indicate a surface segment. This key, when pressed, produces the character Y. On any Apollo keyboard, an arnk segment may also be entered by typing Y and pressing Enter.

Example

Assume you are making flight reservations for a client who will be traveling from Milwaukee to Des Moines on July 1st. Your client will rent an automobile in Des Moines to make sales calls between Des Moines and Omaha. In Omaha, he will catch a return flight to Milwaukee on July 8.

The itinerary should include an arnk segment between the Milwaukee–Des Moines flight and the Omaha–Milwaukee return flight. The following itinerary illustrates this principle:

```
1 NW   47Y  01JUL  MKEDSM SS2   910A    1010A    MO
2 ARNK
3 NW  197Y  08JUL  OMAMKE SS2   720P     750P    MO
```

An arnk segment is required whenever the boarding point of an air segment is different from the destination of the preceding air segment.

Copyright © 1990 by Glencoe/McGraw-Hill Educational Division. All rights reserved.

CHECK-IN: A STUDY AID

Write the correct answer to each of the following problems.

1. What two-letter action code is used to waitlist seats on an off-line flight with a direct-sell entry? _____ LL _____

2. Select by circling the letter for the correct entry to waitlist two coach seats on USAir 952 on the 12th of June from St. Louis to LaGuardia.

   a. 0952Y12JUNSTLLGALL2

   b. 0US952Y12JUNSTLLGANN2

   c. 0US952Y12JUNSTLLGAPB2

   d. 0US952Y12JUNSTLLGALL2

3. Write the correct entry to waitlist one passenger in Q class on AA 612 on the 5th of December from Dallas to Philadelphia.

   _____ 0AA612Q5DECDFW PHL LL1 _____

4. What is the correct entry to waitlist one passenger in F class on the UA priority waitlist (beyond 24 hours) for flight 659 on the 10th of July from GRR to ORD? 0659F10JUL GRR ORD PB 2
   or 0UA659 etc

5. Write the correct entry to waitlist three seats in Y class on United 198 on the 13th of April from San Francisco to Honolulu, on the UA priority waitlist (within 24 hours). 0198Y13APR SFO HNL PC 3

6. What term is used to describe a segment inserted in an itinerary to maintain continuity for pricing, when the destination of one air segment is different from the origin of the next air segment? _____ ARNK _____

7. What entry will enter the type of segment described in question 6 above in the passenger itinerary? _____ Y _____

Copyright © 1990 by Glencoe/McGraw-Hill Educational Division. All rights reserved.

8. Assume you booked a flight directly by phone with KX and reserved two seats in Y class on flight 516 from Jacksonville, Florida (JAX), to Grand Cayman (GCM) on the 20th of July. What entry will record the direct booking in the passenger itinerary? _0KX516Y20JUL JAX GCM BK2_

9. Make the entry to waitlist four seats in Y class on Delta 751 on the 3rd of April from SAV to FMY. _0DL751Y3APR SAV FMY LL4_

10. What entry would waitlist three seats in K class on Delta 229 on the 12th of March from Nassau to Houston (IAH)? _0DL 229K12MAR NAS IAH LL3_

Copyright © 1990 by Glencoe/McGraw-Hill Educational Division. All rights reserved.

CHAPTER 4
PASSENGER NAME RECORDS

CHAPTER OBJECTIVES

At the end of this chapter, you should be able to perform the following tasks:

- Identify the five mandatory parts of a passenger name record, or PNR.

- Name four optional parts of a PNR.

- Explain the use of the Name field, Phone field, Ticketing field, and Received field.

- Retrieve a PNR from storage.

- Enter the passenger name in a PNR.

- Record the agency phone and passenger contact phones in a PNR.

- Code ticketing information in a PNR.

- Enter Received information in a PNR.

- Redisplay the current record.

- End the transaction and save the PNR.

Copyright © 1990 by Glencoe/McGraw-Hill Educational Division. All rights reserved.

Problem

A mother planning a Hawaiian vacation for her family decides on a three-flight connection from Des Moines to Lihue, Kauai, via San Francisco and Honolulu. The same cities will be used for the return. The reservation, along with essential information about the travelers, must now be entered and saved in the CRS.

Apollo Solution

Build a passenger name record (PNR). In this chapter, you will learn how to build a complete PNR containing the passenger itinerary and the Name, Phone, Ticketing, and Received entries.

CREATING PASSENGER NAME RECORDS (PNRs)

If you have ever called an agent to make flight reservations, you are familiar with a series of questions requesting certain information about the traveler. The information typically includes the names of all the passengers, a residential or business telephone number, and other data. These data items represent the information required to create a Passenger Name Record, or PNR.

The PNR is a computer record of every reservation made for an airline passenger. Each PNR has five mandatory parts:

1. Number of passengers and their names
2. Contact telephone number(s)
3. Ticketing information
4. Received information
5. Itinerary

Each part that contains data about the passenger is referred to as a *field*. Each field has a name that identifies the information stored in the field. The passenger data fields include a Name field, Phone field, Ticketing field, and a Received field. The portion of the PNR that contains flight information is called the *Itinerary field*.

Name Field

The Name field consists of one or more name items. Passenger names are grouped together by last name. All passengers who have the same last name are listed in a collective name item. A PNR can contain one or more name items, for example, parties with different surnames.

Copyright © 1990 by Glencoe/McGraw-Hill Educational Division. All rights reserved.

Phone Field

The Phone field contains telephone numbers where the passenger can be contacted. The travel agency phone number is also included in every PNR.

Ticketing Field

The Ticketing field has information or advice about passenger ticketing, such as the date on which tickets will be issued.

Received Field

The Received field contains a record of the person who requested the reservation—the passenger, a secretary, or spouse.

Itinerary

The Itinerary consists of one or more air segments. Each segment represents a confirmed, requested, or waitlisted reservation on a designated flight. The segment line includes the carrier, flight number, class, travel date, city pair, number of seats, the status of the reservation, and the flight times.

These five parts of every PNR must be included in every passenger reservation and are called the **mandatory fields.** Apollo will not accept the PNR for permanent storage if any of the above fields has been left blank. The data may be entered in any order, but each must be entered using the proper format. Since Apollo recognizes an entry by the format, it will reject the entry if it is typed incorrectly. After gathering all the information for the five mandatory fields, the agent saves the record and sends it to the computer for permanent storage. This process is called ending the transaction.

Occasionally the agent may erase the work area without saving the data currently held in the area. This feat is accomplished by ignoring the transaction (discussed on page 52).

Figure 4-1 illustrates a completed PNR containing all the mandatory parts, or data fields.

```
1.1HEGARDT/E MR
1 UA 460Y 12SEP SFOSAN HK1   700A   954A   MO
FONE-ORDAS/312 555-1202-TERRY
ORDR/312 555-3210
TKTG-TAU/10SEP
```

Figure 4–1 Example of a completed PNR.

Copyright © 1990 by Glencoe/McGraw-Hill Educational Division. All rights reserved.

OPTIONAL PNR DATA

Besides the mandatory data described, the PNR may also include optional information, such as:

- Remarks
- Other service information
- Special service requests
- Billing address

Remarks Field

The Remarks field permits free-form text to be entered in the PNR, usually to communicate information to other travel agents, or as a reminder to take some future action.

OSI

Other Service Information (OSI) is used to send a message to airline personnel regarding some aspect of the passenger reservation. An OSI message does not require any response or action on the part of the airline personnel.

SSR

A Special Service Request (SSR) is used to request a service that is not normally provided to passengers, such as special meal requests, wheelchair service, or pets on board. Each type of SSR service has a special code that is used to request the service. Unlike an OSI message, an SSR request requires response or action by the airline.

The PNR has a special field, General Facts, for OSI and SSR entries.

CREATING A PNR

A PNR is created by entering information into the data fields. The five mandatory fields—Name, Phone, Ticketing, Received, and Itinerary—must be completed before Apollo will accept the PNR for permanent storage. Each field has an **identifier**—a code consisting of one or more letters, numbers, or symbols used to enter data into that field. For example, the identifier for the Name field is the Name key, which, when pressed, produces the character N: . To enter a passenger's name in the Name field, the agent presses the Name key (or types N:), then enters the name. The field identifier tells Apollo what field to use for storing the data.

Saving a PNR

The PNR is saved with the command to "end transaction." To end a transaction, the agent types the letter E and presses the Enter key. Some Apollo keyboards have a key labeled ET, which can be used also. Either method may be used to end a transaction, thereby saving the record and sending it to the computer for permanent storage.

Ignoring a PNR

If you do not wish to complete the record, ignore the PNR, by typing the letter I and pressing the Enter key. Some Apollo keyboards have a key labeled IGN, which may be used instead, but either method is acceptable.

Copyright © 1990 by Glencoe/McGraw-Hill Educational Division. All rights reserved.

Occasionally, a PNR may be "routed" to a special storage area—a *queue*—for further processing or special attention, instead of being ended in the usual fashion. You will learn how to work with queues later in this book.

Retrieving a PNR

A PNR which has been previously saved may be retrieved from computer storage and placed in the agent's work area. When a record has been retrieved, it may be changed or updated before being saved again.

A PNR in the work area must be ended or ignored before another record can be displayed. Any time a record is created or changed, an entry must be made to the Received field, to note the person who requested the reservation or change.

One way to retrieve a PNR from storage is by passenger name. The * key, which Apollo refers to as the Display key, is used to retrieve PNRs. The following is the simplest format for retrieving a PNR:

Format:
   **–<Passenger Name>

Example:

   **-PEABODY

   Display: **
   Dash: –
   Last name: PEABODY

Remember to press the Enter key after typing the complete command.

Apollo responds to the retrieve entry by searching for the passenger's record and, locating it, places it in the agent's work area. The PNR will appear on the display screen as follows:

```
1.2PEABODY/T MR/C MRS
1 UA   181Q 14JUL SFOHNL HK2  1000A   244P     MO
2 UA   189Q 22JUL HNLSFO HK2   330P 1155P      SU
FONE-SFOAS/415 555-5821-JAN
   B/415 555-5515
   R/415 555-0900
TKTG-TAU/30JUN
```

You will learn what each item means in the remainder of this chapter.

NAME ENTRIES

The basic name entry contains the number of passengers traveling under the same surname, along with the surname, initials, and identifying titles of each. The Name code N: is entered to begin the name entry. The basic name entry for a party of one passenger has the following format:

Copyright © 1990 by Glencoe/McGraw-Hill Educational Division. All rights reserved.

Format:

    N:<Last Name>/<First Name or Initial>

Example:

    N: LINDBERGH/C

Field identifier:	N:
Last name:	LINDBERGH
Separator:	/
Initial:	C

If the passenger is not an adult male, a title should be added to the entry, as in the following example:

    N: KELLER/R MS

The title serves to identify the gender and general age category of the passenger, and any special occupation, as in the case of a military or religious title. If no title is used, Mr. is assumed.

Titles for Use in Name Entries

MR	Mr. (optional for adult males)
MRS	Mrs.
MS	Ms. (females over 12, marital status unknown)
MSTR	Master (males under 12)
MISS	Miss (females under 12)
DR	Doctor
REV	Reverend
BR	Brother
FR	Father
PFC	Private First Class
SGT	Sergeant
LT	Lieutenant
CAPT	Captain
GEN	General

Other titles used include Congressman, Sister (religious orders), and Mlle (Mademoiselle).

For international travel, the passenger's complete name should always be entered in the PNR as it appears in the traveler's passport.

MULTIPLE PASSENGERS WITH THE SAME LAST NAME

When the name entry is to designate more than one passenger with the same last name, the number of passengers must be included as follows:

    N: 2GREENBERG/L MR/R MRS

Example

Assume the passenger, Mr. E. Hegardt, is traveling alone. The following entries are all correct:

Copyright © 1990 by Glencoe/McGraw-Hill Educational Division. All rights reserved.

```
N: 1HEGARDT/E MR
N: HEGARDT/E MR
N: HEGARDT/E
```

Suppose the reservations are for Mr. E. Hegardt and Mrs. C. Hegardt. The initial and title of each passenger would be separated from the other by a slash, as follows:

```
N: 2HEGARDT/E MR/C MRS
```

In this case, the number (2) is mandatory because more than one passenger is traveling under the same surname.

Now suppose the Hegardts will be traveling with their son, David. The title MSTR for master is used to identify a male child under the age of 12 as follows:

```
N:-3HEGARDT/E MR/C MRS/D MSTR                    TYPO
```

Guidelines for Name Entries

1. Determine the number of people traveling under the same surname.
2. Separate the first initial from the surname with a slash / .
3. Identify each passenger who is not an adult male with a title. Include a space between the initial and title.
4. Separate each initial and title from the others with a slash / .
5. Verify the exact spelling of the passenger's surname.
6. The airlines prefer family members to be entered in the following order: husband, wife (unless not accompanied by her husband), and children in descending age.

Multiple Name Entries

On the Apollo keyboard, a special key labeled **End-Item** produces the character ‡ and is used to string entries together. One use of the End-Item key is to combine multiple name entries with a single press of the Enter key. For example, assume you want to enter the names for Mr. C. and Mrs. R. Forrest along with those for Mr. A. and Mrs. B. Tree. The entries may be combined as follows:

```
N: 2FORREST/C MR/R MRS‡N: 2TREE/A MR/B MRS
```

Observe that this entry is actually two separate name entries connected by ‡ (End-Item).

Examples of Valid Name Entries

```
N: CARSON/LARRY
N: 1CHANDLER/T MR
N: 2BLOOMFIELD/M MR/A MRS
N: 4BEAMAN/R MR/T MRS/A MSTR/T MISS
N: DORMAN/HARRY SGT
N: 2MEESE/K REV/L MRS
N: 3GOLDSTEIN/F DR/A MRS/G MS
N: JUDSON/C MR‡N: MASTERS/A MR
```

Copyright © 1990 by Glencoe/McGraw-Hill Educational Division. All rights reserved.

MISCELLANEOUS NAME ENTRIES

Other information is entered in the Name field to identify travelers and to print information on a ticket, i.e., reference numbers, the age of an unaccompanied minor, and other remarks. To add miscellaneous information, use an asterisk * to separate the basic name entry from the information.

Examples

A passenger ID number may be entered along with the name:

    N:WIGGINS/CARL*65432

The name of an unaccompanied minor should be entered with the code UM followed by two digits indicating the child's age:

    N:RIGGINS/JULIE MISS*UM06

The age must always be entered as two digits, with a leading 0 if necessary.

CHECK-IN: A STUDY AID

Write the correct name entry for each situation.

1. What code is used to enter a passenger name?

   _____ N: _____

2. Mr. T. Moorehead will be traveling alone. What entry would you use to enter the passenger name in the PNR? N: MOOREHEAD /T

3. Mr. Arthur Clemson and his wife, Julie, will be traveling together. What entry would you make in the Name field? N:2 CLEMSON /ARTHUR /JULIE MRS

4. The Lionel family is planning a vacation. The parents, William and Martha, will be traveling with their 10-year-old son, James, and 6-year-old daughter, Elizabeth. Write the correct Name field entry. N:4 LIONEL /WILLIAM /MARTHA /JAMES MJR /ELIZABETH MISS

5. Dr. Charles Morris is scheduling a trip. His wife, Eleanor, and 16-year-old daughter, Tina, will be accompanying him. Write the correct Name field entry. N:3 MORRIS /CHARLES DR /ELEANOR MRS /TINA MRS

6. Sgt. William Chambers is traveling on furlough. Write the correct Name field entry. N: CHAMBERS /WILLIAM SGT

7. Bailey Simpson and his wife, Gloria, are planning a trip with their 5-year-old daughter Sharon. What entry would you use in the PNR Name field? N:3 SIMPSON /BAILEY /GLORIA /SHARON MISS

8. A 7-year-old boy, Glenn Lehman, will be traveling unaccompanied. Write the correct entry for the Name field. N: LEHMAN /GLENN MSTR*UM 07

9. Write the Name field entry for Reverend Arthur Coleman. N: COLEMAN /ARTHUR REV

Copyright © 1990 by Glencoe/McGraw-Hill Educational Division. All rights reserved.

PHONE ENTRIES

The Phone field is a mandatory item on every PNR. The travel agency's phone is entered first, and must appear on every PNR. The Phone key P: is the identifier for the Phone field. The basic phone entry has the following format:

Format:

P:<City><Location>/<Area Code>–<Phone>

Example:

P:SFOB/415 555-0198

Field identifier:	P:
City code:	SFO
Location indicator:	B
Slash:	/
Area code:	415
Phone number:	555-0198

In the entry above, the location indicator B is used for a client business phone.

Example

Assume the travel agency's phone number in Los Angeles is (213) 555–0218. The location indicator AS is used to identify the telephone number as the agency phone. The booking agent's name should be included in the agency phone entry:

P:LAXAS/615 555-0218-CHARLIE

The phone location indicators are summarized below.

Location Indicators

AS	Agency
B	Business
R	Residence
H	Hotel (with room extension)

Guidelines for Phone Entries

1. Enter the agency phone first and include it in every PNR.
2. Enter the remaining contact phones in the following order: business phone, residence, or hotel phone.
3. Be sure to include the phone location indicator, city code, and area code.
4. When entering the agency phone, include your name as the agent responsible for the booking.

Examples of Valid Phone Entries

P:BOSAS/617 555-0917 TERRY
P:INDB/317 555-0091
P:SFOR/415 555-0998
P:STLH/314 555-5102X542

Copyright © 1990 by Glencoe/McGraw-Hill Educational Division. All rights reserved.

When more than one traveler is included in the same PNR, each business phone and home phone should be identified by the name of the respective passenger. For example, assume that a PNR includes two travelers, Mr. L. Glenn and Mr. C. Rose. Mr. Glenn's business phone is entered as follows:

    P:MSPB/612 555-3461-GLENN

CHECK-IN: A STUDY AID

Write the correct phone entry for each situation.

1. What code is used to enter information in the Phone field?

   P:

2. Assume you are working for a travel agency in New York City with a phone number of (212) 555–0067. Write the correct phone entry.

   P: NYCAS/212 555-0067 TERRY

3. Suppose you are creating a PNR for Mr. Murray. His home phone in Miami is (305) 555–1632. How would you enter the phone number in the PNR?

   P: MIAR/305 555-1632

4. Assume you are creating a PNR for a client whose business phone in Los Angeles is (213) 555–3307. What entry would you use to record the phone number in the PNR? *P: LAXB/213 555 3307*

5. Ms. Jameson is staying in a Phoenix hotel. The phone number is (602) 555–4767, and her room extension is 440. Write the correct Phone field entry.

   P: PHXH/602 555-4767 X440

6. Write the correct entry to record a travel agency phone number in San Diego of (619) 555–7001. *P: SANAS/619 555-7001*

7. What entry would you use to record a client's residence phone in San Francisco of (415) 555–1134? *P: SFOR/415 555-1134*

8. Write the correct Phone field entry for a business phone in Indianapolis of (317) 555–7095. *P: INDB/317 555-7095*

9. Write the correct entry for a hotel phone in St. Louis of (314) 555–3677, extension 213. *P: STLH/314 555-3677 X213*

10. Write the Phone field entry for a travel agency phone in San Jose, California of (408) 555–6241. *P: SJCAS/408 555-6241 TERRY*

Copyright © 1990 by Glencoe/McGraw-Hill Educational Division. All rights reserved.

TICKETING ENTRIES

The information entered in the Ticketing field depends on the ticketing arrangements requested by the passenger. For example, if tickets will be printed on a future date, the ticketing date is entered. The identifier for the Ticketing field is the TKT key T: . The basic ticketing entry has the following format:

Format:

    T:<Ticketing Code>/<Date>

Example:

    T: TAU/18MAY

Field identifier:	T:
Ticketing code:	TAU
Slash:	/
Ticketing date:	18MAY

In the example above, the code for a future ticketing date TAU requires a slash / before the date.

Ticketing Codes

TAU	Future ticketing date
TAW	Future ticketing date (in-house account only)
TL30	Pickup at the UA airport counter 30 minutes prior to departure

Examples

Assume a client makes flight arrangements with your agency and requests ticketing on the 21st of June. The code TAU is entered in the Ticketing field:

    T: TAU/21JUN

In a TAU entry, a slash / is always included before the date.

This action causes the PNR to appear in an electronic holding area (the ticketing queue) on the specified future date. Optional information may be added to the entry as in the following example:

    T: TAU/21JUN/PSGR WL PUP 2P

In this entry, a comment is included as a reminder that the passenger will pick up the ticket at 2:00 P.M. on the future ticketing date.

Now assume that instead of issuing the tickets from the travel agency, your client would like to prepay the ticket for pickup at the airport. The advice code TL30 may be used to arrange for ticketing at the United Airlines airport counter at least 30 minutes prior to departure:

    T: TL30/PTA

The code PTA signifies a prepaid ticket advice.

Examples of Valid Ticketing Entries

    T: TAU/29JUL
    T: TLLAX/AA10A/12MAY
    T: TL30/PTA

Copyright © 1990 by Glencoe/McGraw-Hill Educational Division. All rights reserved.

CHECK-IN: A STUDY AID

Write the correct Ticketing field entry for each situation.

1. What code is used to enter information into the Ticketing field?
   _____T:_____

2. What ticketing advice code is used for a time limit for pickup at the airport?
   _____T:TL30_____

3. What three-letter advice code is used to show that tickets will be issued on a future date? _____TAU_____

4. Write the complete Ticketing field entry to show that tickets will be written on the 19th of July. T:TAU/19JUL_____

5. Write the complete Ticketing field entry for tickets to be picked up at the airport 30 minutes prior to departure. T:TL30_____

6. Assume you are creating a PNR for Mr. Thompson. Your client would like his airline tickets on the 23rd of April. What entry would you make in the PNR Ticketing field? T:TAU/23APR_____

7. Suppose you are booking flight reservations for Mr. and Mrs. Burlingame. Your clients would like to pick up their tickets at the United airport counter 30 minutes before departure. What entry would you make in the Ticketing field?
   _____T:TL30_____

RECEIVED ENTRIES

The Received entry is a mandatory item on every PNR. The field identifier for the Received field is the RECD key R: . The Received entry has the following format:

Format:
   R:<Text>

Example:

   R: P

   Field identifier: R:
   Text: P

The Received entry is used to record the party who placed the air reservation. In this example, the abbreviation P stands for passenger, denoting that the passenger made his or her own reservations. Entering the Received information is often referred to as receiving the record.

Copyright © 1990 by Glencoe/McGraw-Hill Educational Division. All rights reserved.

Assume that the reservation was requested not by the passenger, but by his secretary. The abbreviation SECY or SEC is commonly used to indicate received from secretary as in the following entry:

    R: SECY

If the reservation is requested by the passenger's wife, the abbreviation MRS may be used in the Received field as follows:

    R: MRS

Suppose the PNR is for more than one name item, and one of the passengers, Mr. Thomas, requested the reservation. In this case, the title and surname would be used in the entry:

    R: MR THOMAS

REDISPLAYING THE PNR

As information is entered into the various PNR fields, the data is held temporarily in the agent's work area. Within this agent assembly area the computer rearranges the data to create a standardized record. This rearranging takes place automatically whenever the record is redisplayed by means of the following entry:

    *R

Apollo responds by displaying the fields in the agent's work area which presently contain data. The Name, Phone, and Ticketing fields may appear as in the following example:

```
1.2WOODWARD/J MR/M MRS
NO ITIN
FONE-LAXAS/213 555-4343-TERRY
LAXR/213 555-9767
TKTG-TAU/18SEP
```

Observe that this record does not yet contain an itinerary. The Received field is not displayed, even though it contains information.

ENDING THE TRANSACTION

When all mandatory entries have been made in the new PNR, the agent ends the transaction and stores the record. This action is produced by typing E and pressing Enter (or pressing the ET key).

When the transaction is ended, a six-character code, the record locator, is added to the PNR. In addition, the current date and time are stamped on the record.

Copyright © 1990 by Glencoe/McGraw-Hill Educational Division. All rights reserved.

Following is an example of how the mandatory fields, including the itinerary, are displayed in a PNR after it has been ended and retrieved:

```
 1.2WOODWARD/J MR/M MRS
1EA 502Y 05OCT   LAXATL HK2 1135A   635P    MO
2EA  89Y 14OCT   ATLLAX HK2  350P   504P    WE
FONE-LAXAS/213 555-4343-JAN
LAXR/213 555-9767
TKTG-TAU/3OCT
```

CHECK-IN: A STUDY AID

I. *Write the correct Received entry for each situation.*

1. What code is used to enter information in the Received field?

    _____ R:_____

2. What abbreviation is used to indicate that the passenger made his or her own flight reservations? _____ R:P_____

3. Assume you are creating a PNR for a client whose flight reservations were made by his secretary. Write the complete Received entry.

    _____ R:SECY_____

4. Suppose you are creating a PNR for Sgt. Chambers. The reservations were re-quested by Pvt. Hollander. What entry would you make in the Received field?

    _____ R:PVT HOLLANDER___

5. Mr. and Mrs. Burrows will be traveling together. Mrs. Burrows made the flight arrangements. Write the correct entry for the Received field.

    _____ R:MRS_____

6. Mr. Turner calls to schedule flight reservations. He will be traveling alone. What entry would you make in the Received field?

    _____ R:P_____

7. Mr. and Mrs. White are planning a vacation with their two children. Mrs. White made the travel arrangements. Write the correct Received entry.

    _____ R:MRS_____

Copyright © 1990 by Glencoe/McGraw-Hill Educational Division. All rights reserved.

8. Mr. Carlson will be traveling to a convention; Ms. Greene made his flight reservations for him. Write the correct entry for the Received field.

_____R : MS GREENE_____

II. Write the word or phrase that belongs in the blank(s).

1. The initials PNR stand for ___PASSENGER___
   _____NAME_____ ___RECORD___ .

2. A PNR has five mandatory fields:
   a. ___NAME___
   b. ___PHONE___
   c. ___RCVD___
   d. ___TKTNG___
   e. ___ITINERARY___ .

3. Passenger names are grouped together by ___N :___ .

4. The ___T :___ field contains information or advice about passenger ticketing.

5. The ___R :___ field contains a record of the person who requested the reservation.

6. The optional ___□ : 5___ field permits free-form   P67
   text to be entered in the PNR.

7. ___□ : 3 OSI___ is used to send a message to airline   P68
   personnel regarding some aspect of the reservation.

8. ___□ : 3 SSR___ is used to request a special service,   P70
   such as a special meal or wheelchair assistance.

9. The ___OSI___ field is used for messages and   P68
   requests to airline personnel.

10. The ___E___ key is used to end the transaction and save the PNR.

11. The command to redisplay all parts of the current record is
    ___*R___ .

Copyright © 1990 by Glencoe/McGraw-Hill Educational Division. All rights reserved.

CHAPTER 5
SUPPLEMENTARY DATA

CHAPTER OBJECTIVES

At the end of the chapter, you should be able to perform the following tasks:

- Enter the client billing address in a PNR.
- Encode information in the Remarks field.
- Identify situations for OSI entries.
- Enter an OSI message.
- Identify situations for SSR entries.
- Make the SSR entry.
- Identify common SSR codes for United Airlines and off-line carriers.

Copyright © 1990 by Glencoe/McGraw-Hill Educational Division. All rights reserved.

Problem

You are making travel arrangements for Mr. and Mrs. Trainer, who will be flying cross country. Your clients will be billed for tickets by credit card. However, both passengers are elderly and will require assistance with boarding and deplaning. Mrs. Trainer, who is arthritic, requires a wheelchair, although with help she is capable of ascending and descending stairs. Mr. Trainer is under a physician's orders to eat only meals with low sodium.

Apollo Solution

Enter the client billing address in the Address field, send an OSI message to advise the airlines that the passengers are elderly, and use SSR entries to request wheelchair assistance for Mrs. Trainer and a low-sodium meal for Mr. Trainer. In this chapter, you will learn various uses of the Remarks field, and discover how to handle a variety of situations requiring OSI and SSR entries.

SUPPLEMENTARY DATA FIELDS

The term **supplementary data** refers to additional information which is often required to complete a PNR. Three fields are used for this purpose:

- Address
- Remarks
- General facts

The Address field is used for the client's name and address; the Remarks field is used to record general information about the PNR; and the General Facts field is used to communicate a message or service request to airline personnel.

Client Address

A special field is used for the client's name and address. The field identifier for the Address field is W- as follows:

Format:

W–<Client Name>□<Address Line 1>□<Address Line 2>Z/<Zip>

Example:

W-WORLDWIDE SALES CO□1234 INDUSTRIAL DR□SANTA ROSA CA Z/95401

66

Copyright © 1990 by Glencoe/McGraw-Hill Educational Division. All rights reserved.

Address field:	W-
Agency name:	WORLDWIDE SALES CO
Separator:	☐
Address line 1:	1234 INDUSTRIAL DR
Separator:	☐
Address line 2:	SANTA ROSA CA
Zip:	Z/95401

Punctuation is not necessary. Observe that each line is separated by ☐. The Address field must contain a minimum of two lines and a maximum of five.

Remarks Entries

The Remarks entry is used to record any free-form text, and abbreviations are frequently used. The field identifier ☐: 5 is used to enter information in the Remarks field. The basic Remarks entry has the following format:

Format:
☐:5<Text>

Example:

☐: 5CLI WL PUP TKTS

The text portion of the entry is largely free-form and may consist of up to 69 characters, abbreviated for conciseness.

Examples
Assume you are creating a PNR for a client who will be traveling abroad. You have advised the passenger of documents required for international travel. The abbreviation ADVD DOCS is often used for this purpose:

☐: 5ADVD DOCS

The Remarks field is also commonly used to record a fare quoted to a client, as in the following entry:

☐: 5QTD 139.00 FARE ON 12JUL

In the example above, the abbreviation QTD is used for quoted. There are no hard and fast rules governing the use of abbreviations in the Remarks field, but remember that the meaning should be clear to anyone else who may consult the PNR.

CHECK-IN: A STUDY AID

Write the correct answer to each problem.

1. What field is used to record free-form text in the PNR?

   ___REMARK___ What code is used to enter

   information in this field? ___☐:5___ _____

Copyright © 1990 by Glencoe/McGraw-Hill Educational Division. All rights reserved.

2. What field is used to record the client address?

_____ −W _____ What code is used to enter information in this field? _____

3. In the client address, what code is used to separate the name and each line?

_____

4. Write the entry to record the following address in a PNR:

    Microtech

    4004 Park Street

    Palo Alto, CA 94305

_____

_____

5. Write the entry to record the following remark in a PNR: MAIL TKTS.

_____

6. Suppose you are booking reservations for a client who will be traveling abroad. You have advised your client about documents required for international travel. What entry would you make in the PNR Remarks field?

_____

7. Write the entry to record the following remark in a PNR: QTD 149.00 FARE/ 12SEP. _____

8. Assume you quoted a fare of $89.00 on the 3rd of May. How would you note this fact in the Remarks field? _____

9. Write the entry to record the following remark in a PNR: CALL TO PUP TKTS.

_____

10. Write the entry to enter the following client billing address in the PNR:

    Thompson Drilling Co.

    PO Box 16002

    Syracuse, NY 13203

_____

_____

OTHER SERVICE INFORMATION

Other Service Information (OSI) passes along information of an advisory nature to airline personnel. For example, if the passenger is elderly or is a physically handicapped, airline personnel should be advised by an OSI message. The entry does not normally require specific action or a reply from the airline. OSI entries are commonly used to:

Copyright © 1990 by Glencoe/McGraw-Hill Educational Division. All rights reserved.

1. Note passenger language problems
2. Note passengers with physical handicaps
3. Inform the airline of infant travel
4. Record children's ages
5. Advise the airline of a VIP traveling
6. Advise the airline of a special courier
7. Note emergency travel
8. Indicate elderly travelers
9. Indicate first-time travelers
10. Send general advisory information
11. Cross-reference a PNR to another PNR

OSI Entries

The OSI entry has the following basic format:

Format:

□:3OSI<Carrier> <Message>

Example

Assume you are creating a PNR for a very important passenger, the president of ABM Corporation, who will be traveling on a Delta flight. The following entry may be used:

□:3OSI DL VIP PRES OF ABM CORP

Abbreviations are commonly used as illustrated above. In this example, VIP is used to indicate a very important passenger. There are no hard and fast rules governing abbreviations used in OSI messages, but consistency and clarity are important. Whenever possible, official OSI/SSR abbreviations should be used. The free-form text can be up to 55 characters maximum.

To indicate all carriers in the itinerary, use the code YY in place of the carrier code as in the following example:

□:3OSI YY TRVL W/INF

In this example, the OSI message will be sent to all carriers in the passenger itinerary. The abbreviation in this entry indicates that the passenger is traveling with an infant.

Examples of OSI Entries

□:3OSI YY SPEAKS SPANISH ONLY
□:3OSI CO FIRST TIME TRAVELER
□:3OSI DL ELDERLY TVLR

Copyright © 1990 by Glencoe/McGraw-Hill Educational Division. All rights reserved.

CHECK-IN: A STUDY AID

Write the correct OSI entry for each situation.

1. What code is used for an OSI message? _____

2. What code refers to all carriers in the itinerary?

_____

3. Assume you are creating a PNR for a passenger who is deaf. What entry would you use to send an OSI message to Delta Airlines?

_____

4. Suppose you are making flight reservations for a client who will be traveling on a United flight. Your client will be traveling with an infant. Write the entry to send an OSI message to the airline. _____

5. What entry would you use to send an OSI message to inform American Airlines personnel that a passenger is a VIP (president of Acme Aircraft)?

_____

6. What entry will notify all off-line carriers in the itinerary that the passenger speaks Japanese only? _____

7. Assume you are creating a PNR for a passenger whose itinerary includes a flight on UA. Mrs. Harper will be traveling with an infant. Write the correct OSI entry for this passenger. _____ Assume Mrs. Lamson is a first-time traveler. Write the correct OSI entry.

_____

8. Assume you are creating a PNR for a first-time traveler. Write the correct OSI entry for all carriers in the itinerary. _____

SPECIAL SERVICE REQUESTS

Special Service Requests (SSR) are sent to UA or to another airline to request a special type of service. For example, if a passenger requests a special meal or requires a wheelchair, an SSR request is sent to the airline. The following situations require an SSR entry:

1. Special meal requests
2. Wheelchair service or other handicapped needs
3. Bassinet
4. Personal assistance (e.g., for elderly or handicapped)
5. Approval of pet transportation
6. Off-line seat requests

Whereas the OSI entry merely passes along information, an SSR request results in specific action by the airlines.

Copyright © 1990 by Glencoe/McGraw-Hill Educational Division. All rights reserved.

SSR Entries

The SSR entry has the following basic format:

Format:

　□:3SSR<Code> <Carrier> NN<Number> <Segment Description>

Example:

　□: 3SSR WCHR AA NN1 AISLE AA202Y12JULSFODFW

The spacing is optional in this field. If the request applies to all carriers in the itinerary, the multiple-carrier code YY is used. The segment description should include the carrier, flight, class, departure date, and city pair exactly as they appear in the itinerary.

Most items or services are identified with a four-character SSR code.

SSR Codes

WCHR	Wheelchair (passenger can ascend/descend stairs)
WCHS	Wheelchair (passenger cannot ascend/descend stairs)
WCHC	Wheelchair (passenger completely immobile)
BLND	Assist blind passenger
DEAF	Assist deaf passenger
NSST	Seat requested in no-smoking section
SMST	Seat requested in smoking section
UMNR	Assist unaccompanied minor
AVIH	Live animal in cargo hold
PETC	Pet in cabin compartment
OTHS	Other service
XBAG	Excess baggage
BSCT	Bassinet
BIKE	Bicycle
BULK	Bulky baggage
CBBG	Cabin baggage
DIPL	Diplomatic courier
EMER	Emergency travel
EXST	Extra seat
FRAV	First available
FRST	First-time traveler
FRAG	Fragile baggage
GPST	Group seat request
MASS	Meet and assist
RQST	Request seat

Examples

Suppose you wish to request a wheelchair for a passenger who will be traveling on the following air segment:

　1 UA 917Y 13APR ORDSFO HK1　355P　615P　MO

Let us say your client is not capable of walking up stairs, but can walk to his seat. The SSR code for this situation is WCHS. Based on this information, the following entry may be used to request wheelchair service:

　□: 3SSR WCHS UA NN1 UA 917Y13APRORDSFO

Copyright © 1990 by Glencoe/McGraw-Hill Educational Division. All rights reserved.

In this entry, the spaces between each item are optional. In fact, all the spaces will be removed when the entry is accepted so that only the typed characters appear in the General Facts field as follows:

```
GFAX - 1. SSRWCHSUANN1UA917Y13APRORDSFO
```

For clarity, an underscore character _ may be typed instead of a blank space between the important items as illustrated below:

☐: 3SSRWCHS_UA_NN1_UA917Y13APRORDSFO

Examples of SSR Entries

☐: 3SSRBLNDDLNN1DL1489Q23DCECMSYORD

☐: 3SSR_OTHS_NN1_TW_INDSTL_SURFBOARD_IN_HOLD

Special Meal Requests

The SSR entry is used to request meals for passengers with special dietary restrictions, personal requirements, or religious preferences. Only official meal codes are used:

Meal Codes

BBML	Baby food meal
CSML	Children's meal
HNML	Hindu meal
KSML	Kosher meal
MOML	Moslem meal
NSML	No-salt meal
ORML	Oriental meal
SFML	Seafood meal
SPML	Special meal
VGML	Vegetarian meal

Example

☐: 3SSR KSML NW NN1 NW672F17FEBSEAORD

When a kosher meal is requested on UA flights, beef or chicken may be specified. If the number of meals requested is less than the number of travelers in the PNR, the passenger's name should be included.

Example

Assume you are making flight arrangements for two passengers, Mr. and Mrs. Hartpence. Mr. R. Hartpence is on a restrictive diet and requests a low-salt meal on a Continental flight from PHX to DEN. Based on this information, the following entry may be used to send the meal request:

☐: 3SSR NSML CO NN1 CO340Y13JULPHXDEN-MR

Copyright © 1990 by Glencoe/McGraw-Hill Educational Division. All rights reserved.

Unaccompanied Minors

Assistance for unaccompanied minors is requested with an SSR entry. The request code UMNR is used to indicate an unaccompanied minor. Preceding the segment description, type the letters UM, and the age of the child. On UA flights, three separate SSR entries are required—one for the unaccompanied minor, and two for the sending and receiving parties. The SSR code CTCH is used for both sender and receiver.

Example

Assume you are making flight arrangements for a divorcée who will be sending her 10-year-old son unaccompanied on a United flight to visit his father. The following entry may be used to request assistance from UA:

☐: 3SSR UMNR UA NN1 UM10 822Y25SEPLAXSEA

On UA flights, OSI entries should also be made to communicate the phone, address, and name of the responsible adults. The OSI/SSR code CTCH is used to indicate the catching parties as follows:

☐: 3OSI UA CTCH/213 555-8124/6245 OAK ST LAX-MS C THOMAS

☐: 3OSI UA CTCH/206 555-1092/812 PINE ST SEA-MR L BRENNAN

In this example, Ms. C. Thomas of Los Angeles is the sender, and Mr. L. Brennan of Seattle is the receiver.

CHECK-IN: A STUDY AID

I. *Write the correct SSR code.*

_____ Unaccompanied minor

_____ Pet in cabin

_____ Deaf passenger

_____ Blind passenger

_____ Smoking seat

_____ No-smoking seat

_____ Wheelchair (passenger can walk up stairs)

_____ Wheelchair (passenger must be carried)

_____ Wheelchair (passenger can walk to seat)

_____ Meet and assist

_____ Other service

Copyright © 1990 by Glencoe/McGraw-Hill Educational Division. All rights reserved.

II. *Write the correct off-line meal code.*

_____ Vegetarian

_____ Kosher

_____ Special

_____ Baby food

_____ Hindu

_____ Seafood

_____ No-salt

III. *Write the correct SSR entry for each situation.*

1. What code is used to send a Special Service Request (SSR) to airline personnel? _____

2. Assume you are booking flight reservations for an elderly client who will require a wheelchair but is capable of ascending stairs. Your client will be traveling on Continental 303 in Y class on the 12th of June from Denver to Dallas. What entry would you use to request wheelchair service?

   _____

3. Suppose you are creating a PNR for a client who will be traveling on UA 183 in Q class on the 25th of July from Seattle to Honolulu. Your client requests kosher meals for himself and his wife. What entry would you use to request the meals? _____

4. Assume you are making air reservations for a client who will be traveling on Delta 899 in Y class on the 3rd of September from Atlanta to Miami. Your client would like to carry a cat in a portable pet kennel aboard the flight. Write the correct entry to request the pet-in-cabin service.

   _____

5. Write the correct entry to request wheelchair service for a totally incapacitated client who will be traveling on TWA 303 in K class on the 18th of January from Denver to Des Moines. _____

Copyright © 1990 by Glencoe/McGraw-Hill Educational Division. All rights reserved.

6. Assume you are making travel arrangements for a child, age 9, who will be traveling unaccompanied on United 232 in Y class on the 12th of March from San Francisco to Miami. The sender is Ms. T. Gray and her phone number is (415) 555-2098; her address is 805 Elm St, Oakland, California. The receiver is Mr. A. Palmer, whose phone is (315) 555-3887; his address is 223 N 57th Pl, Miami. Write the correct SSR entries for this situation.

a. _____

b. _____

c. _____

Copyright © 1990 by Glencoe/McGraw-Hill Educational Division. All rights reserved.

CHAPTER 6

MODIFYING THE ITINERARY

CHAPTER OBJECTIVES

At the end of the chapter, you should be able to perform the following tasks:

- Retrieve a PNR by passenger name.
- Display a PNR by departure date and passenger name.
- Retrieve a PNR by flight, departure date, originating point, and passenger name.
- Retrieve a PNR by record locator number.
- Cancel a segment, a string, or a range of segments.
- Cancel and rebook with one entry.
- Insert a segment in the itinerary.
- Insert and book with one entry.
- Identify and interpret common status/action codes.
- Change segment status.
- Demonstrate an understanding of how to handle common segment status changes.

Copyright © 1990 by Glencoe/McGraw-Hill Educational Division. All rights reserved.

Problem

You previously made travel arrangements for several members of a college basketball team traveling to a distant city for a road game. Because of a schedule change by the league, the game has been postponed until an open date three weeks later.

Apollo Solution

Cancel the trip and rebook the flight reservations on the same flights three weeks later (subject, of course, to availability). In this chapter, you will learn several different techniques for retrieving a PNR and making changes (or edits) to the air itinerary.

In previous chapters, you learned how to create and save passenger name records (PNRs), and how to enter supplementary data. In this chapter, you will discover how to retrieve a PNR from storage and make changes in the itinerary.

RETRIEVING A PNR

After a PNR has been saved, it may be retrieved and displayed at any time. The Display key * is used for this purpose. The basic format to retrieve a PNR from storage is as follows:

Format:

**–<Last Name>

Example:

**-FROST

Only the last name is required in this entry, but the selection can be narrowed by including the first name or initial.

Example

Assume you previously created a PNR for a client, Edward Cummings. Mr. Cummings calls your agency to check on the status of his flight reservations. The following entry may be used to retrieve your client's PNR:

**-CUMMINGS/EDWARD

Copyright © 1990 by Glencoe/McGraw-Hill Educational Division. All rights reserved.

Apollo responds by retrieving the PNR from storage and placing the record in your work area. The contents of the PNR will be displayed on your CRT screen.

Examples of Name Retrieval

```
**-KLINGINSMITH
**-JOSLYN/J
**-HARCOURT/T MR
```

SIMILAR NAME LIST

Frequently, more than one passenger with the same last name will have a PNR stored in the Apollo database. In this situation, a Similar Name List will be displayed, giving the names and travel dates of the PNRs with the most similar names. Each record is numbered, starting at 1. Accessing PNRs from the list is quite simple: Locate the correct PNR and enter the number corresponding to the desired record.

Example

Assume you wish to retrieve the PNR for a passenger named Smith, using the following entry:

```
**-SMITH
```

Instead of displaying the PNR, Apollo displays a Similar Name List as follows:

```
1    SMITH/CLIFORD    15APR      2    SMITH/JOHN      24MAR
3    SMITH/RICH       24MAR      4    SMITH/D MR      22MAR
5    SMITH/JOHN       22MAR      6    SMITH/S MRS     04APR
7    SMITH/ROY        13APR      8    SMITH/SUE MS    12MAY
9    SMITH/MARSHA     22MAR     10    SMITH/MARSHA    24MAR
```

Assume that the Smith you are looking for is Rich Smith, who will be departing on March 24 (record 3). The PNR may be retrieved with the following entry:

```
*3
```

Apollo responds by retrieving the record, placing it in the work area, and displaying the contents on the screen.

Retrieving by Departure Date

To narrow the selection, the departure date may be included in the entry as follows:

Format:
```
**<Departure Date>–<Name>
```

Example:
```
**24MAR-SMITH/M
```

Copyright © 1990 by Glencoe/McGraw-Hill Educational Division. All rights reserved.

Retrieve: * *

Date: 24MAR

Name: -SMITH/M

Retrieving UA Records

Besides PNRs booked for clients of the travel agency, Apollo also provides access
to reservations booked directly with United Airlines. However, a reservation
booked by one agency cannot be accessed by a different agency.

To retrieve a PNR booked directly with UA, the following format is used:

Format:
    *<Flight>/<Date><Origin>-<Name>

Example:

    *374/10AUG DFW-MICHAELS/F

The space inserted here for clarity should be omitted when the entry is typed at
the keyboard, as follows:

    *374/10AUGDFW-MICHAELS/F

The entry above retrieves a PNR for passenger F. Michaels departing on UA flight
374 on the 10th of August.

Retrieving by Record Locator

Any PNR can be retrieved by the six-character record locator assigned by Apollo
when the record is created. The following format is used:

Format:
    *<Record Locator>

Example:

    *A2QWR5

DISPLAYING ALL OR PART OF THE PNR

At any time a PNR is in the agent's work area, all or part of the record may be
displayed on the screen. The Display key * is used with a qualifying letter or code
to specify the portion to be displayed.

*R	Display record
*I	Display itinerary
*N	Display Name field
*P	Display passenger data fields
*PO	Display OSI information
*PP	Display Phone field
*PR	Display Remarks field
*PS	Display SSR information
*PW	Display Address field
*T	Display Ticketing field

Example

Assume you are working with a PNR. To display only the passenger data fields,
excluding the names, the following entry may be used:

Copyright © 1990 by Glencoe/McGraw-Hill Educational Division. All rights reserved.

To display only the itinerary, the following entry may be used:

*I

As long as the PNR remains in the agent's work area, all or part may be redisplayed as often as required.

The display is further limited with the following options:

*IA   Display air segments only
*IC   Display car rental segments only
*IH   Display hotel segments only

CHECK-IN: A STUDY AID

Based on the information given, write the correct entry to retrieve the PNR of each client.

1. Passenger Templeton. _____

2. Passenger Greene. _____

3. Passenger Norman. _____

4. R. Hurt. _____

5. Mrs. L. Silverstein. _____

6. Mr. F. Brodervic. _____

7. Passenger Thiessen departing on August 12. _____

8. Passenger Broderick departing on July 17. _____

9. Passenger Kleinman departing on AA 567 on the 18th of June from Phoenix.

_____

10. Passenger Gleason departing on UA 64 on the 11th of January from Denver.

_____

11. Record locator number T7KJ4H. _____

12. Write the correct entry to display the following portions of the current PNR:

_____ All fields, including itinerary

_____ Itinerary only

_____ Passenger data fields only

_____ OSI information

_____ SSR information

_____ Phone field only

_____ Name field only

Copyright © 1990 by Glencoe/McGraw-Hill Educational Division. All rights reserved.

13. Write the entry to display the PNR for passenger Lee, departing on the 13th of June. _____

14. Assume Apollo responds as follows:

```
1   LEE/ARNOLD     13JUN   2   LEE/BARRY      13JUN
3   LEE/B MR       13JUN   4   LEE/RICHARD    13JUN
5   LEE/TERI MRS   13JUN   6   LEIGH/LOIS MS  13JUN
```

Let's say you're looking for the record for Richard Lee. What entry would display the PNR? _____

15. Assume you wish to display a PNR with the record locator number VB73QK. What entry would you use? _____

CANCELING A SEGMENT

On occasion, a segment previously booked in a passenger itinerary must be canceled. For example, the client may change his mind about the departure date or alter his travel plans. The X key is used to cancel an itinerary segment as follows:

Format:
    X<Segment Number>

Example:
    X2

Apollo responds with the following message:

    NEXT REPLACES 2

The numeral 2 refers to the canceled segment number. You must next book a new segment to replace the canceled one, or redisplay the record or itinerary. If you redisplay the record *R or redisplay the itinerary *I without booking a new segment, the computer will delete the canceled segment and renumber any succeeding segments.

Example of Canceling

Let's say you previously booked flight reservations for a client, J. Thielman. Mr. Thielman calls to cancel the flight in the first segment of the itinerary. The first step is to retrieve the PNR as follows:

    **-THIELMAN/J

Assume the PNR is displayed on the screen. To cancel the first segment in the itinerary, you would use the following entry:

Copyright © 1990 by Glencoe/McGraw-Hill Educational Division. All rights reserved.

X1

Apollo responds as follows:

    NEXT REPLACES 1

If new reservations are booked now, the new air segment will replace segment 1. Let's say that Mr. Thielman does not want to book a replacement flight at this time. To renumber the remaining segments of the itinerary, the record is redisplayed as follows:

    *R

(Alternatively, only the itinerary may be displayed, with the entry *I.)

Whenever a PNR is created or changed, a notation must be made of the person who requested the reservation or change. The Received entry is made as follows:

    R: P

In this example, the letter P is used to indicate that the change was received from passenger. The final step is to end the transaction and return the record to storage as follows:

    E

Example of Canceling and Rebooking

Now suppose a different client, Ms. Hatcher, asks you to rebook a flight in her PNR. Let's say the passenger was previously booked for a roundtrip from Boston to Philadelphia, and now Ms. Hatcher would like to take a different return flight (segment 2). After displaying the PNR, cancel the return flight with the following entry:

    X2

Apollo responds as follows:

    NEXT REPLACES 2

The next air segment you book will replace the canceled segment 2. Suppose Ms. Hatcher requests a seat in coach on 697 on the 23rd of April. Using the direct-sell entry, the canceled segment may be rebooked as follows:

    0697Y23APRPHLBOSNN1

Remember to redisplay the record or itinerary and enter the Received-From information, before ending the transaction.

Canceling and rebooking can be handled in one entry, using the / key. For example, to cancel segment 3 and rebook two seats on UA 1268 in Q class on the 24th of October (from SEA to SFO) the following entry may be used:

    X3/01268Q24OCTSEASFONN2

If the requested flight is not available, an availability display will appear (the segment will remain canceled).

Copyright © 1990 by Glencoe/McGraw-Hill Educational Division. All rights reserved.

Rebooking the Same Flight and Class

To rebook the same flight and class on a different date, a simpler format may be used:

Format:

X<Segment>/0<Date>/<Class>

Example:

X1/025OCT/Q

This entry cancels segment 1 and rebooks the canceled flight, using the same flight number, on the 25th of October in Q class.

Canceling and Rebooking from Availability

In most cases, ascertaining the flight number and available classes of alternative flights requires an availability display. Request city pair availability before canceling the segment, then use the following format:

Format:

X<Segment>/<Sell Entry>

Example

Assume your client has previously made the following flight arrangements:

```
1 UA 156Q 12JAN ORDPHL HK1   655A   951A
2 UA 162Q 16JAN PHLORD HK1   410P   505P
```

Your client would like to cancel the outbound segment and rebook another flight around noon on the 12th of January.

The first step is to display availability for the new departure date as follows:

A12JANORDPHL12N

Assume that Apollo displays the flight schedules, and your client decides on a flight in line 3. Now cancel the outbound segment and rebook the new flight at the same class (Q):

X1/01Q3

Canceling Multiple Segments

More than one segment may be canceled at one time. To cancel selected multiple segments, separate the segment numbers with an End-item ‡. For example, to cancel segments 1 and 3, the following entry may be used:

X1‡3

Always identify the lowest segments first, canceling in chronological order.

If the multiple segments are consecutive, identify the first and last segments, separated with a dash -. For example, to cancel segments 1 through 4, the following entry may be used:

X1-4

Observe that the entry above has the identical effect of entering X1‡2‡3‡4.

Copyright © 1990 by Glencoe/McGraw-Hill Educational Division. All rights reserved.

Canceling the Itinerary

To cancel the entire air itinerary, the following entry may be used:

Format:
    XA

The A stands for air, commanding Apollo to cancel all air segments in the itinerary.

CHECK-IN: A STUDY AID

Write the correct answer to each problem.

1. What code is used to cancel an air segment in a passenger itinerary?

   _____

2. What entry would cancel the third segment in an itinerary?

   _____

3. What entry would cancel the return segment of a two-segment round-trip?

   _____

4. What entry would cancel the outbound segment in a round-trip itinerary?

   _____

5. What entry would you use to cancel the entire itinerary in a PNR?

   _____

6. Assume a PNR has the following itinerary:

```
1 AA 324Y 13APR BOSPVC HK1   700A   751A    MO
2 TW 204Y 15APR PVCBOS HK1   410P   500P    WE
```

   Your client decides to stay a day longer. What entry will cancel the return

   segment? _____

7. Assume a PNR has the following itinerary:

```
1 NW 460Y  03JUN  STLMSY  HK2   720A   810A    MO
2 DL 849Y  09JUN  MSYSTL  HL2   400P   540P    SU
3 DL1641Y  09JUN  MSYSTL  HK2  1040P  1130P    SU
```

Copyright © 1990 by Glencoe/McGraw-Hill Educational Division. All rights reserved.

Here, your clients are waitlisted for the return on a 4:00 P.M. flight and confirmed on a late night flight. The requested seats on Delta 849 fail to clear the waitlist.

a. What entry will cancel the waitlisted segment?

_____

b. What entry would cancel the outbound flight and rebook the same flight and class on the 5th of June? _____

8. Assume a PNR has the following itinerary:

```
1 AA   459D  22SEP  BDLORD  HK5   1240P  205P   TH
2 CO    26Y  22SEP  ORDDEN  HK5    225P  417P   TH
3 TW   388M  26SEP  DENPIT  HK5   1205P  449P   MO
4 TW    99M  26SEP  PITBDL  HK5    610P  726P   MO
```

a. What entry would cancel the Pittsburgh-Hartford segment and rebook TWA 22 in Y class on the same date? _____

b. What entry would cancel the Continental segment and rebook United 309 in M class on the same date? _____

c. What entry would cancel both TWA segments without rebooking?

_____

d. What entry would cancel only the American segment without rebooking?

_____

e. What entry would cancel the American segment and both TWA segments without rebooking? _____

f. What entry would cancel the entire itinerary?

_____

INSERTING AFTER A SEGMENT

On occasion, a new air segment must be inserted after a designated segment. The / key is used to insert a new segment in an itinerary as follows:

Format:
    /<Segment to Follow>

Example:
    / 2

Copyright © 1990 by Glencoe/McGraw-Hill Educational Division. All rights reserved.

The segment to follow is the existing segment in the itinerary after which the new segment should appear. Apollo responds with the following message:

```
NEXT FOLLOWS 2
```

The numeral 2 refers to the segment after which the new segment will appear.

Example
Assume a PNR is currently displayed on your CRT screen, and you want to insert a new segment in the itinerary. The new segment should appear first. In this case, the segment to follow is 0, so the following entry would be used to insert the new segment:

```
/0
```

A new air segment must be booked to be inserted after segment 0. Assume your client would like two coach seats on CO 252 on the 23rd of October from San Francisco to Denver. Using the direct-sell entry, the new segment may be booked as follows:

```
0CO252Y23OCTSFODENNN2
```

Remember to redisplay the record or itinerary and enter the Received information before ending the transaction.

Inserting and Booking

The insertion and booking may be handled in one entry, using the ‡ key. In the example above, the following entry may be used instead of two separate entries:

```
/0‡0CO252Y23OCTSFODENNN2
```

Usually it is more practical to display availability prior to inserting a new segment, then insert and book in one entry as follows:

```
/3‡02Y3
```

Inserting an Arnk Segment

To insert an arnk segment in an existing air itinerary the following format may be used:

Format:
    /<Segment>‡Y

Example:
    /4‡Y

Copyright © 1990 by Glencoe/McGraw-Hill Educational Division. All rights reserved.

CHECK-IN: A STUDY AID

Write the correct entry for each situation below.

1. What key is used to insert a new segment in an itinerary?

_____

2. Make the correct entry to insert a new segment based on the information given:

    a. Insert after segment 2 _____

    b. Insert after segment 1 _____

    c. Insert as segment 1 _____

    d. Insert after segment 5 _____

3. Write the correct entry to insert after segment 3 and book two seats in B class on AA 253 on the 9th of January from Milwaukee to Omaha.

_____

4. Write the entry to insert after segment 1 and book two seats in Q class on the flight in line 5 of the availability display. _____

5. What entry will insert before segment 1 and book one seat in Y class on US 314 on the 15th of April from St. Louis to Syracuse (SYR)?

_____

6. Assume the following availability screen is displayed:

```
1  AA  558 F4  Y4 B4  M4 Q4   STL CLE  1000A  1223P  72S  L-L-  0
2  TW  422 F4  Y4 B4  M4 Q4   STL CLE  1100A   125P  727  S-S-  0
3  AA  120 F4  Y4 B4  M4 Q4   STL CLE   155P   415P  727  S-S-  0
4  UA  530 F9  Y9 B9  M9 Q9   STL CLE   225P   448P  727  S-S-  0
5  ML   34 Q4               STL CLE   245P   503P  DC9  ----  0
```

What entry will insert after segment 2 and book one seat in B class on UA 530? _____

CHANGING SEGMENT STATUS

When a flight reservation is requested or waitlisted, but not confirmed, it may become necessary to change the status of the air segment—for example, if the seat request clears the waitlist or is confirmed by the airline. The period . key (CSS on some keyboards) is used to change segment status. The CSS entry has the following basic format:

Copyright © 1990 by Glencoe/McGraw-Hill Educational Division. All rights reserved.

Format:

.<Segment><Status>

Example:

. 1HK

Note that the period . is the same as the CSS key. The entry above is used to update a previously waitlisted (KL) or requested segment (KK) to a confirmed segment.

Example

Assume you previously booked the following itinerary for a client:

```
1 DL 818Y 13APR PHLBOS HL2 1010A 1116A    MO
2 US 969Y 17APR BOSPHL HK2  645A  755A    FR
```

The seats in segment 2 are confirmed, as indicated by the status code HK, meaning Holding Confirmed. In segment 1, the status code KL indicates that the seats were previously waitlisted but have since been confirmed.

After confirming the reservation with your client, you would then change the segment status to HK (Holding Confirmed). The following entry is used to change the segment status:

. 2HK

Whenever a PNR is changed or updated, a Received-From entry must be made. Let's say you notified the passenger's wife before changing the status of the waitlisted segment. The following entry could be used for the Received-From field:

6MRS

Now end the transaction to save the changes.

Apollo Status/Action Codes

BK	Booking confirmed (entered when a segment is booked directly with an off-line carrier, usually by phone)
DL	Deferred from waitlist (requires cancellation and re-waitlisting)
GK	Guaranteed group booking (off-line carriers only)
HK	Holding Confirmed status
HL	Holding Waitlisted status
HN	Have requested (no reply received)
IN	If not holding, need (used to re-request space on off-line carriers when the possibility exists that a reservation is already held)
IX	If holding, cancel (used to cancel space on off-line carriers obtained directly by the client)
KK	Confirmed by carrier (used to confirm requested space on off-line carriers)
KL	Confirmed from waitlist
LL	List/List (used to waitlist UA and off-line segments)
MO	Manual override (car, hotel, Apollo direct-sell)
NN	Need/Need (used to request space on off-line carriers)
NO	No action (open segment)
PA	UA priority waitlist (emergency travel)
PB	UA priority waitlist (normal)

Copyright © 1990 by Glencoe/McGraw-Hill Educational Division. All rights reserved.

PC	UA priority waitlist (24 hours)
PD	UA priority waitlist (active until 24 hours before departure)
PN	Pending need (no reply received)
RR	Reconfirm (international flights only)
SB	Passenger boarded stand-by
SC	Schedule change (replacement segment appears in the itinerary; confirm to client and change segment status to HK)
SS	Sell/Sell (segment will be confirmed)
UC	Unable to confirm (off-line carriers)
UN	Unable to sell (followed by suggested replacement segment)
US	Unable to sell (have waitlisted)
UU	Unable/Unable (off-line flight is sold out)
WK	Was confirmed (segment should be canceled)
WL	Was waitlisted (segment should be canceled)
YK	Cancel confirmed segment

HANDLING STATUS CHANGES

Some status/action codes do not require any action on the part of the booking agent. Others, however, are critical to the passenger reservation and require special action or handling.

Confirmations

KK and KL indicate confirmation of previously requested but unconfirmed, space.

When more than four seats are booked on an off-line carrier, or on an airline not represented in the Apollo database, the code NN appears in the itinerary segment. If the space is confirmed by the off-line carrier, the segment status is updated to KK and the record is placed in an electronic "holding tank" called the **confirmation queue.**

When a waitlisted segment with PB or PC clears the waitlist, Apollo updates the status to KL and places the record in a **waitlist confirmation** queue.

When KK or KL appears in a flight segment, notify the traveler to verbally confirm the reservation, then change the segment status to HK.

Declined Space Requests

On occasion, space requested on an off-line carrier will be declined because the flight is completely sold out. In addition, sudden or unexpected changes in flight schedules may affect confirmed space as well as waitlisted seats on both off-line and UA flights.

When an off-line carrier declines to accept space requested in an NN segment, Apollo updates the segment status to UC, UN, US, or UU. When any of these codes appears in a segment, cancel the segment and offer your client an alternative flight.

UA Schedule Changes

When a UA schedule change occurs, Apollo automatically cancels any corresponding air segments in existing PNRs, then attempts to rebook the best alternative flight. The code SC appears in the new suggested segment to indicate a schedule change. When this situation occurs, call the client to confirm the substitute reservation, then change the segment status to HK.

Copyright © 1990 by Glencoe/McGraw-Hill Educational Division. All rights reserved.

CHECK-IN: A STUDY AID

Write the correct answer to each problem.

1. What key is used to change the status of a segment in a passenger itinerary?

   _____

2. When a seat request has cleared the waitlist, what status code appears in the previously waitlisted segment? _____

3. When a seat request has been confirmed by an off-line carrier, what status code appears in the segment? _____

4. When a confirmed segment has been canceled because of a UA schedule change, what status code appears in the previously booked segment?

   _____

5. Write the correct meaning of each status code.

   UU _____

   WK _____

   WL _____

   DL _____

6. Write the correct CSS entry for each situation:

   a. Change the status of segment 3 to HK: _____

   b. Change the status of segment 5 to HK: _____

   c. Change the status of segments 1 and 3 to HK:

   _____

7. Assume a PNR shows the following itinerary:

   ```
   1 DL 549Y 12JAN PHLATL KL2   650A   852A   MO
   2 DL 939Y 12JAN ATLNAS HK2  1121A   110P   MO
   3 DL 441Y 20JAN NASATL HK2   225P   448P   TU
   4 DL 615Y 20JAN ATLPHL HK2   645P   730P   TU
   ```

   Here the Philadephia-Atlanta leg is confirmed from the waitlist. What entry would you use to update the segment status?

   _____

Copyright © 1990 by Glencoe/McGraw-Hill Educational Division. All rights reserved.

CHAPTER 7
MODIFYING THE PNR

CHAPTER OBJECTIVES

At the end of the chapter, you should be able to perform the following tasks:

- Change or delete data in the Name field, the Phone field, and in the Remarks and Ticketing fields.
- Reduce the number in a party.
- Divide the PNR.
- Divide multiple passengers from a PNR.

Copyright © 1990 by Glencoe/McGraw-Hill Educational Division. All rights reserved.

Problem

You previously made flight arrangements for two executives, Mr. Crenshaw and Ms. Lawson, traveling together to a sales meeting. Mr. Crenshaw has now decided to depart a day later. Both passengers' home phone numbers are shown in the PNR.

Apollo Solution

Divide the PNR so that each passenger has a separate record, then cancel and rebook Mr. Crenshaw's outbound flight. Delete Mr. Crenshaw's home phone from Ms. Lawson's PNR, and delete Ms. Lawson's from Mr. Crenshaw's. In this chapter, you will discover how to change information contained in the passenger data fields, reduce the number in a party, and divide the PNR.

CHANGING THE PASSENGER NAME

Data stored in various PNR fields can be added to, deleted, or changed at any time the PNR is in the agent's work area. The CHNG key, which produces the characters C: , may be used for any of these purposes.

Changes to a passenger data field are initiated by pressing CHNG (or typing C:), then typing the item number (e.g., name item 1 or 2), and the field identifier. The remainder of the entry consists of new data. To master the technique of changing passenger data, let us begin by exploring the procedure for changing passenger names.

The Apollo command to change the Name field entry has the following format:

Format:

C:<Name Item>N:<New Data>

Example:

C: 1N: JOHNSON/H

The new name entry should be entered exactly as it will appear in the PNR. If there is only one name item, the item number (1) may be omitted, as in the following example:

C: N: JOHNSON/H

Copyright © 1990 by Glencoe/McGraw-Hill Educational Division. All rights reserved.

If more than one passenger is involved in the name change, the number must be included, as in making an original name entry.

Example

Suppose you are working with a PNR in which the Name field appears as follows:

```
1.1HOFFMAN/G       2.1CARLYSLE/A MS
```

Let's say that Ms. Carlysle will not be accompanying Mr. Hoffman after all, and Ms. Teri Petersen will be traveling in her place. The following entry could be used to change the second name item:

```
C:2N:PETERSEN/T MS
```

The record may be redisplayed at any time with the following command:

```
*R
```

When the PNR is redisplayed, the Name field will now appear as follows:

```
1.1HOFFMAN/G       2.1PETERSEN/T MS
```

Example of Multiple Passengers with the Same Last Name

Assume the first name item in a PNR appears as follows:

```
1.2WHITE/T/A MRS
```

Let's say the surname should be spelled Whyte instead of White. The following entry may be used to change the name item:

```
C:1N:2WHYTE/T/A MRS
```

Be sure to include the number of persons traveling together under the same surname, as in the original name entry.

Deleting a Name Item

To delete a name item, simply leave the new name portion of the entry blank. For example, the following entry would delete the entire second name item:

```
C:2N:
```

In effect, this entry simply changes the specified name item to blank spaces, thereby erasing the entire item.

Examples of Name-Change Entries

```
C:N:BURR/M MR
C:1N:SILVERSTEIN/P MS
C:1N:1GRANGER/L
C:1N:3BRUER/S/R MRS/S MSTR
C:2N:2BELL/G MR/N MRS
```

Copyright © 1990 by Glencoe/McGraw-Hill Educational Division. All rights reserved.

Other Name-Change Entries

Besides passenger names, other information in the Name field may also be added or changed. The following format will add or change a passenger ID number in the Name field:

Format:

C:<Item>N:*<ID Number>

Example:

C: 1N: *1234567

Observe that the name entry itself is unchanged; only the passenger ID number is being changed (or added).

Changing the Phone Field

The Apollo format to change the Phone field is similar to that used for name changes, except that the identifier P: is used to indicate the field to be changed. The following format is used for changes to a Phone field entry:

Format:

C:<Phone Item>P:<New Phone Entry>

Example:

C: 3P: SFOR/415 555-0112-GREENBAUM

The phone item corresponds to the phone number you want to change.

Example

Assume you are working with a PNR in which the Phone field appears as follows:

FONE-LAXAS/213 555-8019-TONY
LAXB/213 555-6662
LAXR/213 555-0091

Let's say you want to change the home phone (item 3) to LAXR/213 555-0091. The following entry may be used:

C: 3P: LAXR/213 555-0091

Be sure to include the location indicator, as in the original phone entry.

Deleting a Phone Number

To delete a phone number, simply leave the new phone number portion of the entry blank. For example, the following entry would delete the third item from the Phone field:

C: 3P:

Examples of Phone-Change Entries

C: 2P: 602-555-8876-B
C: 2P:

Copyright © 1990 by Glencoe/McGraw-Hill Educational Division. All rights reserved.

Besides name and phone entries, other passenger data fields may also be changed by means of the same technique. The following general format may be used to change an item in passenger data field:

Format:

    C:<Item Number><Field Identifier><New Data>

Example:

    C: 2 ☐: 5QTD 89.00 FARE/8FEB

The entry in the example above changes the second item in the Remarks field. If the field contains only one item, the item number (1) may be omitted.

Example

Assume you are working with the following PNR:

```
   1.1BARRAS/D MR
   1 CO 512Y 31JUL LAXMIA HK1   115P   920P    FR
   2 UA 742Y 34JUL MIALAX HK1   820A   144P    MO
   FONE-LAXAS/213 555-4404-TERRY
   LAXB/213 555-1008
   TKTG-TAU/30JUL
   RMKS-CLI WL PUP TKTS/2P
```

Let's say Mr. Barras would like to pick up his tickets on the 28th of July. The following entry may be used to change the future ticketing TAU date in the Ticketing field:

    C: T: TAU/28JUL

Deleting Passenger Data

To delete a data item, simply leave the new data portion of the entry blank. For example, the following entry may be used to delete the first remark in a PNR:

    C: 1☐: 5

CHECK-IN: A STUDY AID

Write the correct entry to change passenger data for each situation.

1. What code is used to change a passenger data field?

   _____

2. Write the correct entry to change the second name item to Ms. R. White-head. _____

Copyright © 1990 by Glencoe/McGraw-Hill Educational Division. All rights reserved.

3. Write the correct entry to change the first name item to show Mr. G., Mrs. G., and Miss J. Heilman as the passengers. _____

4. Write the entry to delete the second name item.

_____

5. Write the entry to change the second phone item to a business number in STS of (707) 555–1006. _____

6. Write the entry to change the third phone item to a residential phone number in Memphis of (901) 555–9445. _____

7. What entry would delete the third phone item?

_____

8. What entry would delete the seventh remark?

_____

9. Assume the third item in the Remarks field should read as follows:

QTD 119.00 FARE/6JUN

What entry could you use to change the remark?

_____

10. Assume the following PNR is displayed:

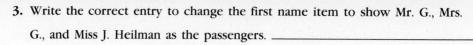

```
1.1 PAPPAS/MURRAY
1 UA 485F 12NOV MIASFO HK1 1245P  705P    MO
FONE - MIAAS/313 555-0978-TERRY
 MIAB/313 555-0987
 R/313 555-9876
TKTG - TAU/10NOV
```

Let's say the passenger's home phone should be entered as (313) 555–9876. Write the entry to change the phone. _____

REDUCING THE NUMBER IN A PARTY

PNRs are frequently created for clients traveling in a party. For example, executives from the same company may be traveling together, or family members or friends may be traveling on vacation. What happens when one of the passengers cancels?

One option might be to cancel the entire PNR and book a new itinerary for the remaining members of the party. This approach, however, has several disadvantages. First, rebooking would require that a completely new PNR be created.

Copyright © 1990 by Glencoe/McGraw-Hill Educational Division. All rights reserved.

Second, the air space may no longer be available at the same class or fare (or worse, might not be available at all).

A far better solution is to simply reduce the number in the party. The following format may be used for this purpose:

Format:
> C:–<New Number in the Party>

Example:
> C:-2

The entry is made by pressing the CHNG key C: and typing - followed by the new number in the party. In the example above, the party is reduced to two passengers.

Apollo responds by reducing the number of seats in all air segments in the itinerary. However, Apollo has no way of knowing which party member(s) to remove from the PNR. The Name field (and any other passenger data fields affected) must be changed to reflect the new party.

Example
Assume you previously created the following PNR, which is now in your work area:

```
 1.3MCGRAW/M MR/H MRS/A MS
1 DL 555Y 12JUL ATLPHL HK3 1215P  159P    MO
2 TW 393Y 18JUL PHLBOS HK3  517P  621P    SU
3 TW 325Y 25JUL BOSPHL HK3  903A 1005A    SU
4 DL 588Y 25JUL PHLATL HK3 1100A 1250P    SU
FONE-ATLAS/404 555-0075-JAN
 ATLR/404 555-2767
TKTG-TAU/10JUL
```

Let's say that the McGraw's teenage daughter, Adrienne, has decided to stay home. To reduce the number in the party, the following entry may be used:

> C:-2

Apollo responds with the following message:

> PTY NOW 2 STARTING AT 1

This is Apollo's way of telling you that it has reduced the party to two passengers, beginning with segment 1. If the itinerary is now displayed, the air segments will show two confirmed seats on all air segments in the itinerary:

Copyright © 1990 by Glencoe/McGraw-Hill Educational Division. All rights reserved.

```
*I
1 DL 555Y 12JUL ATLPHL HK2 1215P   159P   MO
2 TW 393Y 18JUL PHLBOS HK2  517P   621P   SU
3 TW 325Y 25JUL BOSPHL HK2  903A  1005A   SU
4 DL 588Y 25JUL PHLATL HK2 1100A  1250P   SU
```

However, the Name field still shows three passengers:

```
*N
1. 3MCGRAW/M MR/H MRS/A MS
```

Therefore, the next step is to change the Name field to show only Mr. and Mrs. McGraw as follows:

```
C: N: 2MCGRAW/M MR/H MRS
```

If the Name field is redisplayed, only Mr. and Mrs. McGraw will remain:

```
*N
1. 2MCGRAW/M MR/H MRS
```

The number of seats in the itinerary must be identical to the number of names remaining in the PNR. The same number of seats must be booked on all air segments in the itinerary.

The number in the party may only be reduced, never increased.

CHECK-IN: A STUDY AID

Write the correct entry to reduce the party for each situation.

1. What code is used to reduce the party? _____

2. Write the correct entry to reduce the party to one.

   _____

3. Write the correct entry to reduce the party to three.

   _____

4. What entry will reduce the party to two? _____

5. Assume a PNR has the following names:

```
1. 1BRADLEY/F MR
2. 1SIMON/F MR
3. 1PARKER/T MR
```

   Mr. Simon decides to stay behind. What entry would you use to reduce the party? _____

Copyright © 1990 by Glencoe/McGraw-Hill Educational Division. All rights reserved.

What entry will delete Mr. Simon's name? _____

6. Assume a PNR has the following names:

   1. 2GREENE/C MR/F MRS

   Mrs. Greene will not be traveling after all. What entry would you use to reduce the party? _____

   What entry would you use to change the Name field?

   _____

7. Assume a PNR has the following names:

   1. 3MURRAY/R MR/M MRS/T MSTR

   2. 1HEFLER/A MSTR

   Mrs. Murray decides to stay behind. What entry would reduce the party?

   _____

   What entry would you use to change the Name field?

   _____

DIVIDING THE PNR

Occasionally, one or more travelers in a multiple-passenger PNR may want to change flight itineraries. Rather than canceling the entire PNR and rebooking new itineraries, a simpler solution is to divide the PNR.

The Apollo command code to divide a PNR is DN. The entry has the following basic format:

Format:

   DN<Name Item>

Example:

   DN2

The name item refers to the passenger to be divided out. This entry divides the entire name item—i.e., all passengers traveling together under the same last name.

Dividing a PNR results in two separate records—one for the passenger who is divided out, and one containing the original (unchanged) flight plans of the remaining passengers.

To divide a PNR requires the following steps:

1. Divide out the party requesting the itinerary change. When the PNR is divided, the new record is automatically displayed.
2. Make the requested itinerary changes to the new record.
3. Make any other required changes (phone, ticketing, etc.).
4. Enter the Received information.
5. File the new PNR. (Do not end the transaction.) When the new PNR is filed, the original record is automatically redisplayed.
6. Make any required changes to the original record (phone, ticketing, etc.)
7. End transaction.

Copyright © 1990 by Glencoe/McGraw-Hill Educational Division. All rights reserved.

Example

Assume you previously created the following PNR, which is now in your work area:

```
  1.1WILLIAMS/R MS    2.1LEHMAN/C MRS
1 UA  81Y 19APR LAXSFO HK2   200P   310P        MO
2 UA 525Y 20APR SFOLAX HK2   755P   905P        TU
FONE-LAXAS/213 555-5250-JAN
  LAXB/213 555-7738
TKTG-TAU/17APR
```

Let's say that Mrs. Lehman has decided to depart on a different flight later in the day. To change her itinerary without also changing Ms. Williams' reservations, you must divide Mrs. Lehman from the PNR as follows:

DN2

Apollo responds by creating a new record for Mrs. Lehman in your work area. The new PNR is automatically displayed for changes:

```
  1.1LEHMAN/C MRS
1 UA  81Y 19APR LAXSFO HK1   200P   310P        MO
2 UA 525Y 20APR SFOLAX HK1   755P   905P        TU
FONE-LAXAS/213 555-5250-JAN
  LAXB/213 555-7738
TKTG-TAU/17APR
```

Mrs. Lehman's itinerary may now be modified according to her new travel plans.

Assume you have canceled and rebooked the outbound flight. You may want to cross-reference this record to the original PNR with an OSI message as follows:

□: 3OSIUA TCP2 W/WILLIAMS

The abbreviation TCP2 means "to complete a party of 2" with Williams.

The next step is to enter the Received information and file the new PNR. The File key (which produces the character 2) is used to file a record. The Received and File entries can be combined in one entry, using an End-Item ‡, as follows:

6P‡2

Apollo responds by filing the new PNR for Mrs. Lehman and redisplaying the original record:

Copyright © 1990 by Glencoe/McGraw-Hill Educational Division. All rights reserved.

```
 1.1WILLIAMS/R MS
1 UA  81Y 19APR M LAXSFO HK1   200P   310P       MO
2 UA 525Y 20APR T SFOLAX HK1   755P   905P       TU
FONE-LAXAS/213 555-5250-JAN
  LAXB/213 555-7738
TKTG-TAU/17APR
```

Observe that only Ms. Williams' name remains in the Name field. When the PNR is divided, Apollo automatically reduces the number of seats held in the itinerary. Before ending the transaction, you may want to cross-reference this record to the new PNR as follows:

□: 3OSIUA TCP2 W/LEHMAN

Dividing by Name Reference

To single out a particular passenger in a name item, include the complete name reference as in the following example:

DN1-3

This entry divides out the third passenger in the first name item, and does not affect other passengers.

Example

Assume a PNR contains the following passengers in the Name field:

1.3LEONARD/J MR/R MRS/C MSTR

Let's say that Mrs. Leonard would like to depart on an earlier date. To divide this passenger from the PNR, the following entry may be used:

DN1-2

As a general rule, divide out the passenger whose itinerary requires change.

Dividing Multiple Passengers

To divide out more than one passenger, separate the name or references with an End-Item ‡. For example, to divide all the passengers in name items 1 and 3, the following entry may be used:

DN1‡3

Example

Assume a PNR contains the following Name field:

1.3GUERRERA/J MR/S MRS/E MS

Let's say that Mrs. S. and Ms. E. will be taking a different itinerary. To divide these passengers, the following entry may be used:

DN1-2‡1-3

Copyright © 1990 by Glencoe/McGraw-Hill Educational Division. All rights reserved.

When a PNR is divided, any supplemental information in the Name field (e.g. an AAdvantage account number) is divided out along with the name.

CHECK-IN: A STUDY AID

Write the correct entry to divide the PNR for each situation.

1. What code is used to divide a passenger from the PNR?

_____

2. What code is used to file a divided PNR? _____

3. Assume a PNR has the following passengers in the Name field:

1.1MERITT/R MR

2.1GOULD/F MS

What entry would divide Ms. Gould from the PNR?

_____

4. Assume a PNR has the following passengers:

1.1SIMPSON/A MR

2.1CRENSHAW/K MS

3.1LEE/M MS

Ms. Lee wants to depart a day later. What entry would you use to divide the PNR? _____

5. Assume a PNR has the following passengers:

2.5SIMMS/H MR/G MRS/L MSTR/A MISS/L MISS

Mrs. G. will be departing a few days earlier. What entry would you use to divide the PNR? _____

6. Assume a PNR has the following passengers:

1.2FORREST/A MR/T MRS

2.2MERTZ/D MR/L MRS

Mrs. Forrest and Mrs. Mertz would like to depart a few days later and take a side trip. What entry would you use to divide this PNR?

_____

Copyright © 1990 by Glencoe/McGraw-Hill Educational Division. All rights reserved.

7. Assume a PNR has the following passengers:

1.4MCNAMARA/F MR/G MRS/L MS/W MS

Mrs. McNamara and the children have decided to depart three days later.

What entry would you use to divide this PNR?

_____

Copyright © 1990 by Glencoe/McGraw-Hill Educational Division. All rights reserved.

CHAPTER 8
APOLLO FARES

CHAPTER OBJECTIVES

At the end of the chapter, you should be able to perform the following tasks:

- Use the tariff display entry to display fares for all carriers from least expensive to most expensive.
- Obtain a tariff display for a specific carrier.
- Interpret the tariff display.
- Obtain a tariff display for a specific fare basis.
- Modify a tariff display.
- Display joint fares.
- Display availability with fares.
- Display a menu of fare rules pertaining to a given fare basis.
- Display the rule description from the menu.
- Display a fare rule without a tariff display.

Copyright © 1990 by Glencoe/McGraw-Hill Educational Division. All rights reserved.

Problem

Mrs. Klinginsmith, a divorcée in Chicago, wants to send her 11-year-old daughter to visit the child's father in Seattle. She asks you if a discounted child's fare is available. If not, what is the lowest available roundtrip fare? To obtain a discounted fare, must she purchase the ticket by a certain date?

Apollo Solution

Use the Tariff Display entry to display the lowest-to-highest normal and excursion fares on all carriers that provide service from Chicago to Seattle. (Unaccompanied minors do not normally qualify for a discounted child's fare.) Then display the fare rules for the fare basis in which your client expresses interest. In this chapter, you will learn how to display comparative fares of various airlines, fares for a particular carrier, and rules that govern excursion and other discounted fares.

ACCESSING APOLLO FARES

Most domestic and many international fares can be accessed from Apollo's enormous database of airline facts. To access fares, at least two things must be known: city pair and travel date. Technically, fares may be obtained without a travel date. But unless a date is specified, Apollo will display only fares for the current day (i.e., travel today). Most travelers inquire about fares for traveling on a future date. Because fares and schedules change frequently, it is essential to specify the exact date on which the passenger(s) will be traveling.

Examples of Valid Date Codes

22JAN	22nd of January
05MAR	5th of March
18JUL	18th of July
12DEC	12th of December

THE TARIFF DISPLAY

Most travelers who inquire about airline fares are shopping for bargains. Few passengers want to pay more than the lowest available rate for a particular class of service. Although many travelers prefer to fly on certain carriers, particularly

Copyright © 1990 by Glencoe/McGraw-Hill Educational Division. All rights reserved.

members of frequent-flyer programs, it is almost always beneficial to obtain a comparative display of all published fares in a specific market.

The basic tariff display entry is used to display a table of fares, from least expensive to most expensive, for all carriers who service a particular route (and whose fares are stored in Apollo's database). The tariff display entry has the following format:

Format:

$D<City Pair><Travel Date>

Example:

    $D ATLORD 18AUG

Tariff Display:	$D
City pair:	ATLORD
Travel date:	18AUG

The spaces inserted in the example for clarity should be omitted when the entry is typed at the keyboard, as follows:

    $DATLORD18AUG

The entry in the example above requests adult normal and excursion fares from Atlanta to Chicago-O'Hare for travel on the 18th of August.

Example

Assume that a passenger, Mr. Pennypincher, is planning a trip from Tampa Bay to San Francisco. He will be traveling on the 21st of July and would like the lowest possible fare. To display all published normal and excursion fares, the following entry may be used:

    $D TPASFO 21JUL

The spaces inserted here for clarity should be omitted when the entry is typed at the keyboard, as follows:

    $DTPASFO21JUL

Apollo responds by displaying the requested fares. Note that the third column displays one-way (OW) fares, and the fourth column displays roundtrip (RT) fares.

```
     TPA SFO NORMAL/EXCURSION VALID 12APR THRU 19OCT
     FARE BASIS         OW FARE      RT FARE        AIRLINES
  1  QE70P50              89.00      178.00 R       UA AA
  2  ME70NR              129.00      258.00 R       NW
  3  B                   149.00      298.00         NW
  4  Y                   415.00      830.00         UA AA NW
  5  F                   668.00     1336.00         UA AA
```

Copyright © 1990 by Glencoe/McGraw-Hill Educational Division. All rights reserved.

Apollo's response lists regular, discounted, or special fares for flights between the designated city pair. Observe the header line at the top of the tariff display, repeating the origin and destination cities. The remainder of the header gives the fare types which appear in the screen (normal and excursion) and the validity dates. In this example, the displayed fares are valid from the 12th of April through the 19th of October.

READING THE TARIFF DISPLAY

Each fare is shown on a separate line identified by a line number. The fare basis code appears first in each listing. One-way (OW) and roundtrip (RT) fares are given for each fare basis. Where only roundtrip travel is permitted, the code R appears after the roundtrip fare.

	Fare Basis	One-Way	Roundtrip	Carriers
1	QE70P50	89.00	178.00 R	UA AA
2	ME70NR	129.00	258.00 R	NW

The carrier codes on the extreme right refer to the airlines which offer each published fare. In the example above, the QE70P50 fare is valid only for roundtrip travel on United and American. All local domestic fares are quoted in U.S. dollars (not NUCs).

SPECIFYING A CARRIER

Apollo also has the capability of displaying both domestic local fares and joint fares, as well as some international fares on specific airlines. The following format is used to request a tariff display for a specific carrier:

Format:
$D<City Pair><Travel Date>*<Carrier>

Example:

$D SFOMIA 13JUL *CO

Fare Quote:	$D
City pair:	SFOMIA
Travel date:	13JUL
Separator:	*
Carrier:	CO

The spaces inserted here for clarity should be omitted when the entry is typed at the keyboard:

$DSFOMIA13JUL*CO

Requesting a tariff display results in a table of fares offered by the requested carrier in order from least expensive to most expensive.

Example

Assume a passenger calls your agency to inquire about fares from LAX to DFW. He would like to depart on the 13th of July and is interested in the lowest available fare on DL. The following information is required to obtain a tariff display:

Copyright © 1990 by Glencoe/McGraw-Hill Educational Division. All rights reserved.

City pair: LAXDFW
Travel date: 13JUL
Carrier: DL

Based on this information, the following entry will display the requested fares:

```
$DLAXDFW13JUL*DL
```

FARE CATEGORIES

Besides normal and excursion fares, other fare categories may also be obtained from Apollo. The term **fare category** refers to a combination of one or more fare bases which may appear in a tariff display. Each official fare category is identified by a three-letter code. For example, NLX refers to normal and excursion fares, and EXC signifies excursion-child fares.

The following list illustrates the official fare categories recognized by Apollo.

Fare Categories

1	EXA	Excursion-adult
2	EXB	Excursion-adult/child
3	EXC	Excursion-child
4	NLX	Normal/excursion-adult
5	NLA	Normal-adult
6	NLC	Normal-child
7	GRP	Group
8	ITB	Individual tour basis
9	SPL	Special
10	MIL	Military
11	SEN	Senior citizen

Observe that besides a three-letter code each fare category is also identified by a number.

To request a particular fare category for the tariff display, the following variation may be used:

Format:
    <Standard $D Entry>–<Fare Category>

Example:

```
$DATLDFW19APR-NLA
```

The example above requests normal adult fares (NLA). Either the three-letter code or the category number may be used to specify the type of fares. The example above may also be entered as follows:

```
$DATLDFW19APR-5
```

Category 5 signifies NLA (normal and adult) fares.

Copyright © 1990 by Glencoe/McGraw-Hill Educational Division. All rights reserved.

It is also possible to specify a booking code that further limits the tariff display. To indicate a booking code, use the following command format:

Format:

<Standard $D entry>–<Booking Code>*<Carrier>

Example:

$DATLDFW19APR-M*DL

When the example is entered, Apollo will display only M-class fares for travel on Delta.

SPECIFYING A FARE BASIS

On occasion, you may want to check if a specific fare basis is available on a future date. The following variation may be used to specify a specific fare basis:

Format:

<Standard $D Entry>□<Fare Basis>

Example:

$DSFOTYO12NOV□Y02

The example above requests the Y02 fare on flights from San Francisco to Tokyo for travel on the 12th of November.

CHECK-IN: A STUDY AID

I. *Write the word or phrase that belongs in each blank.*

1. If a travel date is not specified, Apollo will display fares for

   ___TODAY___.

2. The ___$D___ entry is used to display a table of fares, from least expensive to most expensive for all carriers.

3. If no fare type is specified, Apollo will display only

   ___NLX___ fares.

4. A ___JOINT___ is a throughfare for a connection involving different carriers (interline connection).

5. The restrictions that govern the various fares published in the airline tariffs are

   referred to as ___RULES___.

6. The date entered in a tariff display entry is the

   ___TRAVEL DATE B___

   a. Current date

   b. Departure date

   c. First date on which the fare is effective

Copyright © 1990 by Glencoe/McGraw-Hill Educational Division. All rights reserved.

7. A fare category may be entered either as a three-letter code or as a

_____CATEGORY #_____ .

8. Write the correct fare type code for each of the following:

_____NLC_____ Normal children's fares

_____NLA_____ Normal adult fares

_____EXA_____ Excursion adult fares

_____NLX_____ Normal and excursion adult fares

_____ITB_____ Individual tour basis

_____MIL_____ Military fares

II. *Refer to the tariff display to answer the questions below.*

```
   LGA MIA NORMAL/EXCURSION VALID 21OCT THRU 15APR
   FARE BASIS        OW FARE      RT FARE     AIRLINES
 1 QE7X30              96.00      198.00 R   PA
 2 QAP30              116.00      232.00 R   EA
 2 ME7                149.00      298.00 R   PA
 3 B                  149.00      298.00     EA
 4 Y                  198.00      396.00     EA PA
 5 F                  258.00      516.00     EA PA
```

1. What is the origin city? _____NYC - LGA_____

The destination? _____MIA_____

2. What carrier offers a $232.00 roundtrip fare on this route?

_____EA_____

3. What is the fare basis at the fare in question 2 above?

_____QAP30_____

4. What booking code would you use in question 2 above?

_____Q_____

5. What carrier offers a reduced one-way coach fare? — WRONG

_____PA IS EA_____

6. What is the one-way fare in M class on Pan Am? — WRONG

_____149_____

7. What is the normal adult roundtrip coach fare on Eastern?

_____396_____

Copyright © 1990 by Glencoe/McGraw-Hill Educational Division. All rights reserved.

III. *Write the correct Apollo format for each fare request.*

1. Display normal adult fares from Seattle to Dallas–Ft. Worth on the 13th of April. _$D SEA DFW13APR_

2. Display normal and excursion fares from Cincinnati to San Juan, Puerto Rico, on the 22nd of December. _$D CVG SJU 22 DEC_

3. Display excursion children's fares from Albuquerque to Chicago on the 3rd of July. _$D ABQ CHI 3JUL -EXC_

4. Display normal children's fares from Baltimore to St. Louis on the 17th of May. _$D BWI STL17MAY·NLC_

5. Display normal adult fares from Chicago to Boise, Idaho, on the 12th of June. _$DCHIBOI12JUN -NLA_

6. Display normal and excursion fares from Grand Rapids, Michigan, to New York-Kennedy International Airport on the 12th of March. _$DGRRJFK12MAR-NLX_

7. Display excursion adult and children's fares from Los Angeles to Portland, Oregon, on the 26th of April. _$D LAX POX 26APR EKB_

8. Display normal adult fares from Atlanta to Tulsa on the 5th of December. _$D ATL TUL5DEC -NLA_

9. Display excursion adult fares from Philadelphia to Cleveland on the 13th of May. _$D PHLCLE13MAY-EXA_

10. Display excursion children's fares from Birmingham, Alabama, to Los Angeles on the 22nd of July. _$DBHMLAX22JUL-EXC_

IV. *Write the correct Apollo format for each fare request.*

1. Display Delta's normal and excursion fares from New Orleans to Chicago on the 23rd of April. _____

2. Display Alaska Airlines' normal adult fare from Anchorage to Portland, Oregon, on the 14th of July. _____

3. Display United's normal children's fares from New York-LaGuardia Airport to Indianapolis on the 20th of October.

   _____

4. Display American's normal adult fare from Dallas–Ft. Worth to Memphis on the current date. _____

5. Display TWA's normal and excursion fares from Denver to Des Moines on the 7th of September. _____

6. Display the USAir excursion adult and children's fares from Pittsburgh to Ft. Lauderdale, Florida, on the 19th of August. _____

Copyright © 1990 by Glencoe/McGraw-Hill Educational Division. All rights reserved.

7. Display the American adult excursion fares from Boston to Los Angeles on the 8th of January. _____

8. Display the TWA normal children's fare from Philadelphia to Omaha on the 22nd of March. _____

9. Display Hawaiian Airlines' excursion adult fare from San Francisco to Honolulu on the 12th of October. _____

10. Display Eastern's excursion adult and children's fares from Miami to St. Thomas on the 5th of January. _____

JOINT FARES

A **joint fare** is simply a throughfare (a single amount) for a connection involving different carriers. Joints fares are based on mutual agreements between participating airlines. Prior to deregulation, joint fares for domestic travel were common, as were inter-airline connections. Because many airlines merged (or ceased operations), domestic joint fares all but disappeared. Nevertheless, some published joint fares are still available in some North American markets, particularly when small regional airlines are involved.

The following entry is used to request a display of domestic joint fares for connections in a specific city:

Format:
$D<City Pair><Connecting City><Date>

Example:

$DMKEDFWORD15MAY

The example above requests joint fares from Milwaukee to Dallas, for flights that connect in Chicago. No carrier is specified, so Apollo will display all joint fares offered by participating carriers.

Response:

```
 MKE DFW NORMAL/EXCURSION VALID 11JUL THRU 4AUG
 FARE BASIS        OW FARE      RT FARE       AIRLINES
 CONNECTING   ORD - JOINT FARES
 1 MJE14            178.50        357.00 R    UA-DL
 2 YJ               340.00        680.00      UA-DL
 3 FJ               510.00       1020.00      UA-DL
```

Apollo's response repeats the city pair in the header line and the connecting city on the line just above the fares. The joint fares apply only to the specified connecting city and for the participating carriers named.

Copyright © 1990 by Glencoe/McGraw-Hill Educational Division. All rights reserved.

To display a list of connecting points for stored joint fares, use the following format:

Format:

$D<City Pair>C

Example:

$DMKEDFWC

Response:

```
MKE DFW
  JOINT SINGLE CONNECTION CITIES
  CHI HOU IND
```

Apollo responds with a list of single-connection cities for which joint fares are available.

AVAILABILITY WITH FARE QUOTATION

When city pair availability has been displayed, a fare quotation may be obtained for any flight in the display.

Format:

$DL<Line>

Example:

$DL4

The line number refers to the line on the availability screen corresponding to the desired carrier and flight.

Example

Assume you are making arrangements for a client who will be traveling from Chicago to Sacramento, California, on the 22nd of June. He would like to depart about 8:00 A.M. City pair availability may be obtained with the following entry:

A22JUNORDSMF8A

Assume Apollo responds as follows:

```
1 AA 291  F4 Y4 B4 M4 Q4   ORD SMF   849A   102P M80 B-B- 1
2 UA 575  F9 Y9 B9 M9 Q9   ORD SMF  1008A  1216P 72S L-L- 0
3 AA 253  F4 Y4 B0 M0 Q0   ORD SMF   250P   521P M80 D-D- 0
4 AA 525  F4 Y4 B4 M4 Q0   ORD SMF   632P   903P M80 D-D- 0
5 DL1485 F4 Y4 B4 M4 Q4   ORD SMF   644P  1002P 72S D-D- 1
6 UA 839  F9 Y9 B9 M0 Q0   ORD SMF   654P   904P D8S D-D- 0
```

Copyright © 1990 by Glencoe/McGraw-Hill Educational Division. All rights reserved.

Let's say your client inquires about fares on the flight that arrives in Sacramento at 10:02 P.M. The following entry may be used to obtain a fare quotation:

$DL5

In this example, the desired flight (DL 1485) is listed in line 5 of the availability screen.

Response:

```
ORD SMF NORMAL/EXCURSION VALID 12APR THRU 19OCT
FARE BASIS        OW FARE     RT FARE      AIRLINES
1  ME90             169.00      338.00 R    DL
2  B                199.00      398.00      DL
3  Y                245.00      490.00      DL
4  F                369.00      738.00      DL
```

CHECK-IN: A STUDY AID

Write the correct Apollo format for each joint fare request.

1. Display joint fares from San Francisco to Sioux City, Iowa, via St. Louis on the 18th of November. _____

2. Display joint fares from Hartford to Kahului, Maui (Hawaii), via San Francisco on the 6th of December. _____

3. Display joint fares from Los Angeles to Baton Rouge via Dallas–Ft. Worth on the 5th of May. _____

4. Display joint fares from Newark to Sacramento, California, connecting via San Francisco on the current day. _____

5. Display joint fares from Raleigh-Durham, North Carolina, to Daytona Beach, Florida, on the 16th of January connecting in Atlanta.

_____

FARE RULES

The restrictions which govern the various fares published in the airline tariffs are referred to as **rules.** Competition among carriers has prompted the creation of a

Copyright © 1990 by Glencoe/McGraw-Hill Educational Division. All rights reserved.

diverse and complex assortment of discounted fares with a long list of rules. A rules display detailing the restrictions that apply to a given fare basis may be obtained whenever a tariff table is displayed. The Apollo command to request a rules display has the following format:

Format:

$V<Line Number>

Example:

$V5

The line number refers to the line in the tariff display corresponding to the desired fare.

Apollo responds to the fare rules request by displaying a menu, or index, of subjects. Each subject is identified by a number as indicated in the following list:

Menu Subject List

0	General information	9	Stopovers
1	Travel dates	10	Permitted combinations
2	Reservations/Ticketing	11	End-to-end combinations
3	Minimum stay	12	Accompanied travel
4	Maximum stay	13	Fare by rule
5	Flight applications	14	Other sales requirements
6	Day/Time applications	15	Surcharges
7	Seasonal applications	16	Deposits/Service charges
8	Prohibited travel dates		

When fare rules are requested, Apollo displays only the subjects which apply to the selected fare. To view a detailed description of a particular rule, the following entry is used:

Format:

$V/<Line>

Example:

$V/10

The line number refers to the line in the menu corresponding to the desired fare rule.

Example

Assume you have just obtained the tariff screen partially displayed below:

```
  BDL MSY NORMAL/ADULT      VALID 11APR THRU 12MAY
  FARE BASIS          OW FARE     RT FARE      AIRLINES
  1 MZ6                134.00      268.00       US
  2 QAP3               219.00      438.00       AA US
  3 BAP3               260.00      520.00       NW TW
  4 M                  320.00      640.00       TW
  5 Y                  403.00      806.00       AA TW US NW
```

Copyright © 1990 by Glencoe/McGraw-Hill Educational Division. All rights reserved.

Let's say your client inquires about the MZ6 fare on USAir. To display the menu of applicable rules, the following entry may be used:

    $V1

Response:

```
       ***** THESE SUBJECTS APPLY *****
             BDL/MSY/12MAY/□MZ6/*US
   0 GENERAL INFORMATION        2 RESERVATIONS/TICKETING
   6 DAY/TIME APPLICATION      10 PERMITTED COMBINATIONS
   15 SURCHARGES
```

Apollo's response indicates which rules are applicable to the requested fare. Let's say you wish to obtain an explanation of day and time restrictions. The following entry may be used to display the fare rule:

    $V/6

Response:

```
*DAY/TIME APPLICATION*
FARES APPLY FOR TRAVEL ON FLIGHTS THAT DEPART ON
SATURDAY.
***** THESE SUBJECTS APPLY *****
    0 GENERAL INFORMATION        2 RESERVATIONS/TICKETING
X   6 DAY/TIME APPLICATION      10 PERMITTED COMBINATIONS
   15 SURCHARGES
```

Apollo displays an explanation of the selected rule and redisplays the menu with an X next to the subject accessed.

Multiple Rule Explanations

Multiple rule subjects may be selected simultaneously as in the following examples:

$V/3‡6	Displays rules 3 and 6
$V/3-6	Displays rules 3 through 6
$V/2‡5-7	Displays rules 2 and 5 through 7
$V/ALL	Displays all rules

Copyright © 1990 by Glencoe/McGraw-Hill Educational Division. All rights reserved.

Specifying the Carrier

When a particular fare basis is offered by more than one airline on a route, the carrier must be specified when the rules menu is displayed. The following entry illustrates this technique:

    $V5*CO

Example

Assume you obtained the following tariff display:

```
     IAH OMA NORMAL/EXCURSION VALID 16JAN THRU 22FEB
     FARE BASIS          OW FARE      RT FARE        AIRLINES
     1 VHLE7NR             89.00      178.00 R       UA AA
     2 Q0E70X              99.00      198.00 R       NW
     3 B0E2P25            119.00      238.00 R       NW TW
     4 VHOE7NR            129.00      258.00 R       UA AA
     5 MPE70H             139.00      278.00 R       NW TW
```

Let's say your client inquires about the $278.00 roundtrip fare on TWA. This fare basis is offered by two carriers. To display the rules menu, the desired carrier must be specified as follows:

    $V5*TW

Response:

```
          ***** THESE SUBJECTS APPLY *****
               IAH/OMA/22FEB/□MPE70H/*TW
     0 GENERAL INFORMATION       2 RESERVATIONS/TICKETING
     3 MINIMUM STAY              7 SEASONAL APPLICATION
     10 PERMITTED COMBINATIONS   11 END TO END COMBINATIONS
     14 OTHER SALES REQUIREMENTS  16 DEPOSITS/SERVICE CHARGES
```

Displaying Fare Rules Without a Tariff Display

A tariff display does not necessarily have to be displayed before a fare rule can be obtained. The following entry may be used to display an explanation of a specific fare basis:

Format:
    $V<Origin>/<Destination>/<Date>/□<Fare Basis>

Example:

    $VSFO/MIA/10MAY/□QHHE70

Copyright © 1990 by Glencoe/McGraw-Hill Educational Division. All rights reserved.

Fare Rules:	$V
City Pair:	SFO/MIA
Departure Date:	/10MAY
Fare Basis:	/☐QHHE70

Separating each item with a slash / is mandatory in this entry.
A specified carrier may be included as follows:

`$VSFO/MIA/10MAY☐QHHE70/*TW`

Copyright © 1990 by Glencoe/McGraw-Hill Educational Division. All rights reserved.

CHAPTER 9

ITINERARY PRICING

CHAPTER OBJECTIVES

At the end of the chapter, you should be able to perform the following tasks:

- Price an itinerary at the full adult fare.

- Identify common passenger type codes.

- Price an itinerary using passenger type codes, with name selection, with segment selection, using a forced connection, by a specified fare basis or class, at the lowest available fare.

- Store pricing instructions for ticketing, and the form of payment.

- Store ticketing instructions.

Copyright © 1990 by Glencoe/McGraw-Hill Educational Division. All rights reserved.

Problem

A PNR in your work area has an itinerary with six air segments, including a three-segment connection. All flights have been booked in Q class. Your client asks for the total fare for the entire itinerary.

Apollo Solution

Use itinerary pricing to compute the total fare. In this chapter, you will learn how to "autoprice" an itinerary, or to price selected segments, passengers, and passenger types.

USING ITINERARY PRICING

Apollo has the capability of automatically computing the total fare or ticket price for almost any domestic air itinerary contained in a passenger record.* This automatic itinerary pricing function is called the basic fare quote.

When Apollo prices an itinerary, it takes into consideration any applicable fare rules and joint fare applications. Most domestic and some international itineraries can be automatically priced.

The Apollo command code for itinerary pricing is $B. The following format is used to price an itinerary:

Format:
    $B<Modifiers>

Example:

    $B

This example does not include any modifiers. It instructs Apollo to price the itinerary for all passengers in the PNR at the full-price adult fare on all air segments.

Example
Assume the following PNR is currently in your work area:

---

*The U.S. transportation tax is changed periodically. The fares and tax amounts in this textbook are based on an 8-percent tax, but the principles of fares, itinerary pricing, and ticketing remain the same regardless of the current tax rate.

Copyright © 1990 by Glencoe/McGraw-Hill Educational Division. All rights reserved.

```
   1.1FLORES/MARIA MS
   1 DL 791Y 12JUL BOSPHL HK1    830A  945A    TU
   2 DL 296Y 17JUL PHLBOS HK1    850A  959A    SU
FONE-PHLAS/215 555-1701-JAN
PHLB/215 555-6615
TKTG-TAU/10JUL
```

The completed PNR may be priced as follows:

$B

Apollo responds by calculating the total price for all air segments in the itinerary:

```
FARE  289.35    TAX   23.15    TOTAL  312.50
BOOKING: Y    FB: Y         RULE: DFR-1 2000
EFF: NONE                   EXP: NONE
PRICE APPLIES IF TICKETED BY: 15MAR
              289.35            23.15            312.50
SEG  1 DL  791 O Y  BOS PHL  146.75 Y
SEG  2 DL  296 O Y  PHL BOS  142.60 Y
```

Before proceeding, let's examine this response in detail. In the first line, Apollo gives the the base fare, tax, and total amount for each passenger. In the second line, the booking code identifies how the fare will be shown in the fare ladder at ticketing.

If the fare has an effective or expiration date, the dates will be shown on the line below the booking code. The next line gives the last ticketing date.

The fare ladder at the bottom of the display shows the itemized fare calculation. Observe that only base fares, excluding tax, are used in the fare calculation. The computer can only price air segments for carriers with fares stored in Apollo's database.

PRICING MODIFIERS

In the basic itinerary pricing entry, a modifier may be used to qualify the response. Pricing actions fall into the following general categories:

- Segment selection
- Name selection
- Passenger type
- Future ticketing date
- Lowest fare for class of service

Copyright © 1990 by Glencoe/McGraw-Hill Educational Division. All rights reserved.

Segment selection may be used to price a portion of the itinerary, and name selection may be used to calculate the price for a particular passenger in the Name field.

Pricing actions are requested by adding the correct modifier to the basic $B entry.

Apollo Pricing Modifiers

Segment selection:	S<Segment Number>
Name selection:	N<Name Item>
Passenger type:	*C<Child's Age>
Forced connection:	X
Ticketing date:	:<Date>
Lowest fare:	•

Example of Segment Selection

Assume you are working with a PNR which has the following itinerary:

```
1  AA  653Y  11NOV  JFKSJU  HK2    1135P    402P    FR
2  PQ  200S  12NOV  SJUSTT  HK2     615A    645A    SA
3  QY  300S  12NOV  STTSTX  HK2    1100A   1120A    SA
4  AA  626Y  21NOV  STXJFK  HK2     250P    553P    MO
```

In this example, two passengers will be traveling from New York to St. Thomas, Virgin Islands (STT), with a stopover in San Juan, Puerto Rico (SJU). They will continue on to St. Croix (STX) before returning to New York on a direct flight.

Let's say your client asks you for the price of the St. Thomas–St. Croix segment. Using modifier S, the following entry may be used to price the segment:

$BS3

This entry instructs Apollo to price only segment 3 of the itinerary (STT-STX).

Now let's say your client would like to know the price of the San Juan–St. Croix portion of the trip (segments 2 and 3). The following entry may be used to price the segments:

$BS2‡3

Observe that an End-item ‡ separates the segment numbers. The modifier S must always precede the first segment number. Segment selection in itinerary pricing follows the same principles as in canceling segments; thus $BS2-4 may be used to indicate a range of segments (from 2 through 4) for pricing.

Whenever a PNR contains two segments with the same routing, one must be selected for pricing. For example, assume a PNR contains the following itinerary:

Copyright © 1990 by Glencoe/McGraw-Hill Educational Division. All rights reserved.

```
1 UA 156Y  5JUL PDXORD HL1  735A  100P     MO
2 UA 156F  5JUL PDXORD HK1  735A  100P     MO
3 UA 141Y  9JUL ORDPDX HK1 1005A 1220P     FR
```

This example includes two duplicate segments on the outbound trip; the passenger is waitlisted in coach (Y) and confirmed in first class (F). This itinerary cannot be priced unless one of the duplicate segments is selected. To price the itinerary using the confirmed first-class segment, the following entry may be used:

$BS2‡3

Now let's say your client would like to know what the price will be if the coach seat request clears the waitlist. The following entry may be used to price the itinerary using the waitlisted coach segment:

$BS1‡3

Example of Name Selection

Assume you are working with a PNR which has the following Name field and itinerary:

```
1.2KNUTZ/R MR/L MRS    2.2BOLTZ/E MR/F MRS
1 AA 622Y 01JUN LAXDFW HK4  722A 1202P    WE
2 AA 333Y 15JUN DFWLAX HK4 1107A 1205P    WE
```

Let's say Mrs. Boltz calls to request the price of her ticket only. Using the secondary action code N, the following entry may be used to price the itinerary for the selected name item:

$BN2-2

The numbers in the pricing entry correspond to the desired passenger's position in the Name field. In this example, Mrs. Boltz is the second passenger in the second name item.

Now let's say your client requests the price for both Mrs. Knutz and Mrs. Boltz. The following entry may be used to price the itinerary for multiple names:

$BN1-2‡2-2

Observe that the End-Item ‡ separates the name items. The modifier N must precede the name selection.

Copyright © 1990 by Glencoe/McGraw-Hill Educational Division. All rights reserved.

CHECK-IN: A STUDY AID

Write the correct answer to each problem.

1. What is the basic command to price an itinerary at the normal full adult fare?

__$B__

2. Assume Apollo displays the following price:

```
FARE  394.45     TAX    31.55     TOTAL  426.00
BOOKING: Y  FB: Y               RULE: DFR-1 2000
EFF: NONE                       EXP: NONE
PRICE APPLIES IF TICKETED BY: 20OCT
        394.45              31.55              426.00
SEG  1 DL  142 O Y  MIA ORDY        Y
SEG  2 US  863 X Y  ORD DSM  394.45 Y
```

a. What is the base fare excluding tax? __394,45__

b. What is the tax amount? __31,55__

c. What is the total fare for this passenger? __426__

3. Write the correct passenger type code:

__C9 or C09__ Child age 9

__YM__ Military

__5D10__ Senior citizen

__MP50__ Mileage-plus 50–percent discount fare

4. Write the pricing modifier for each of the following pricing situations:

__X__ Price a forced connection

__S__ Price selected segments of the itinerary

__$BB0__ Price at the lowest available fare

__N__ Price selected passenger names

PASSENGER IDENTIFICATION CODES

The basic pricing entry $B uses full-price adult fares to price the itinerary. On occasion, the agent may want to specify an overriding passenger type. For example, children from 2 to 11 years of age qualify for children's fares on major carriers. (Remember that most adult excursion and other low discount fares are generally less expensive. Some airlines offer children's excursion fares priced somewhat lower than adult excursion fares.)

Copyright © 1990 by Glencoe/McGraw-Hill Educational Division. All rights reserved.

Other passengers may also qualify for special fares, such as military personnel and senior citizens. These types of passengers are indicated in the pricing entry by means of Passenger Identification Codes (PICs).

Passenger Identification Codes

*C<Age>	Child
*YM	Military
*GOV	Government
*SD10	Senior citizen
*SD10C	Senior citizen companion
*MP<Pct>	Mileage plus (frequent flyer)

It should be noted that Apollo does not have all the fares stored in its database to price itineraries for every possible passenger type.

Example of Pricing with PICs

Assume you wish to override the full-price adult fare in the itinerary and specify a military fare instead. Using the passenger type *YM, the following entry may be used:

$B*YM

When a PNR includes multiple passengers of different types (e.g., an adult and a child), a separate PIC must be specified for each non-adult passenger. For example, assume a PNR in your work area has the following passengers in the Name field.

1. 2TRAVIS/C MRS/A MISS

Let's say that you would like to price a ticket for Mrs. Travis at the full adult fare for the class in which the itinerary is booked, and book 6-year-old Adrienne at the children's fare. To price the itinerary, the following entry is required:

$BN1-1‡1-2*C6

In this entry, name selection is used to distinguish the party members by PIC. Mrs. Travis (name 1.1) does not require a PIC, since she is to be priced at the adult fare. The code *C6 identifies Miss A. (name 1.2) as a child of age 6.

Guidelines for Pricing with PICs

When pricing an itinerary using Passenger Identification Codes, remember the following guidelines:

1. If all passengers in the itinerary are to be priced at the adult fare, no PIC code is necessary. If no passenger type is specified, Apollo always uses adult fares to calculate the totals.
2. The PIC for pricing with the child's fare must include the child's age. Either one or two digits may be used to indicate the age (e.g., *C8 or *C10).

Copyright © 1990 by Glencoe/McGraw-Hill Educational Division. All rights reserved.

3. When traveling at a discounted fare, members of UA's Mileage Plus, Frequent Flyer program should be identified with *MP followed by the appropriate discount. The discount should be expressed as a percentage (e.g., *MP50).
4. Passengers traveling at a discounted senior citizen fare should be identified with *SD followed by the discount (e.g., *SD10).

FORCED CONNECTION

Let's take another look at the New York–St. Croix trip from a previous example.

```
1 AA 653Y 11NOV JFKSJU HK2   1135P   402P     FR
2 PQ 200S 12NOV SJUSTT HK2    615A   645A     SA
3 QY 300S 12NOV STTSTX HK2   1100A  1120A     SA
4 AA 626Y 21NOV STXJFK HK2    250P   553P     MO
```

When an itinerary includes a valid connection with a connecting time of less than four hours, Apollo attempts to use the published throughfare or joint fare for pricing. But on rare occasions, a connection exceeds the four-hour limit. To force Apollo to price the connecting segments using the throughfare, the modifier X may be used. The following entry may be used to force a connection for pricing:

WPX3

The number after the X refers to the segment at which the connection occurs. In this example, the connection occurs in segment 3; i.e., segment 3 should be priced as a continuance of the flight in segment 2.

FUTURE TICKETING DATE

A future date may be specified in a pricing entry to take advantage of anticipated fare changes. For example, to price an itinerary for ticketing on a future date of March 27, the following entry may be used:

$B: 27MAR

This entry will price the itinerary using fares which are valid on or after the designated future ticketing date.

EXAMPLE OF LOWEST FARE

On request, Apollo will use the lowest fare for a particular class of service, to price a confirmed itinerary. When the entry is made, Apollo will search for the lowest applicable fare for each segment and compute the price based on the indicated class. The itinerary, however, will not automatically be rebooked at the lower fares.

As an example, assume a PNR contains the following itinerary:

```
1 UA  87Y 18FEB DTWLAX HK2   515P   655P     MO
2 UA  82Y 22FEB LAXDTW HK2  1100A   555P     FR
```

Copyright © 1990 by Glencoe/McGraw-Hill Educational Division. All rights reserved.

Let's say you'd like to check the lowest available price for this itinerary in Y class. The following entry may be used to obtain the price:

$B.Y

A different modifier (PE) may be used to price an itinerary at the lowest fare based on rebooking/cancellation penalty. For example, to price at the lowest fare with a maximum 50 percent penalty, the following entry may be used:

$BPE50

This entry instructs Apollo to use the lowest available fares which have a rebooking/cancellation penalty no higher than 50 percent of the original ticket price.

CHECK-IN: A STUDY AID

Write the correct pricing entry for each situation.

1. Sgt. Harper qualifies for a military discount fare. What entry will price the itinerary? _$B*YM_

2. Assume a PNR contains the following passengers:

   1.2MITSU/T MRS/R MISS

   What entry could you use to price Mrs. T. at the full adult fare and Miss R., age 8, at the children's fare? _$BN1-1≠1-2*C8_

3. Assume you wish to price an itinerary for the following passengers:

   1.4CROWELL/T MRS/R MSTR/C MISS/D MISS

   Mstr. R. is age 10, Miss C. is 8, and Miss D. is 5. What entry would price Mrs. Crowell at the full adult fare and the remaining passengers at the children's fare?

   _$BN1-1≠1-2*C10≠1-3*C8≠1-4*C5_

4. What entry will price only segment 4 of an itinerary?

   _$BS4_

5. What entry will price only segments 1, 3, and 5?

   _$BS1≠3≠5_

6. Assume a PNR contains the following names:

   1.3RIVERS/T MRS/A MS/C MR

   How would you price the itinerary for Mrs. Rivers only?

   _$BN1-1_

   For Ms. A. and Mr. C. only? _$BN1-2≠1-3_

Copyright © 1990 by Glencoe/McGraw-Hill Educational Division. All rights reserved.

7. Assume a PNR has the following itinerary:

```
1 US   15B 08JUN LGAPIT HK4   745A 1003A    TU
2 US   85B 08JUN PITLGA HK4   250P  448P    TU
3 US  111B 15JUN LGAPIT HK4   455P  609P    TU
4 US  129B 15JUN PITLGA HK4   700P 1005P    TU
```

Here, on the outbound trip the connecting time in Pittsburgh exceeds 4 hours. How could you price the itinerary using the throughfare?

WPX1

8. Assume a fare change is anticipated. What entry could you use to price an itinerary for ticketing on a future date of August 18?

$B:18AUG

9. Write the correct entry to price segment 1 in Q class:

_$BS1□Q_

10. What entry will price segment 1 in Q class and segment 2 in M class?

_$BS1□Q'S2□M_ – _$20M_

11. How would you price an itinerary at the fare basis YE14?

_$B□YE14_

12. What entry will price an itinerary at the lowest available fare in Q class?

_$BB□Q_

13. What entry will price only segment 3 at the lowest available fare?

$BBS#/3   _$BBS_

STORED PRICING FOR TICKETING

The stored pricing entry T: $B provides Apollo with specific instructions on how to fare the itinerary when the passengers are ticketed. Whereas the $B entry merely calculates the itinerary price, T: $B both calculates and stores the price, thereby setting the PNR up for ticketing.

Format:

    T:$B<Modifier>

Example:

    T: $B

The example above is comparable to the $B entry; it prices the itinerary for all passengers in the PNR at the adult fare on all segments.

Copyright © 1990 by Glencoe/McGraw-Hill Educational Division. All rights reserved.

Example

Assume you are working with the following passenger record and wish to store the price for future ticketing.

```
1.1WALKER/SPENCER MR
1 US  65Y 17MAR PITMCI HK1   945A 1048A    TH
FONE-PITAS/412 555-2233-KEVIN
TKTG-TAU/15MAR
```

The stored pricing entry is made as follows:

    T: $B

Apollo responds by calculating and storing the total price for all air segments using adult fares.

```
FARE 239.81     TAX   19.19     TOTAL  259.00
BOOKING: Y   FB: Y           RULE: DFR-1 2000
EFF: NONE                    EXP: NONE
PRICE APPLIES IF TICKETED BY:  17MAR
              239.81        19.19        259.00
SEG  1 US  65 O Y PIT MCI 239.81 Y
```

Apollo stores the fare information in a special field of the PNR used for ticket authorization and fare quote information, called the ATFQ field. When the passengers' tickets are issued, Apollo will refer to the fare data stored in this field to price each ticket.

When the PBR is displayed, the ATFQ field appears as follows:

    ATFQ-OK/$B
    FQ-239.81/10.19/259.00 - 17MAR Y

The same modifiers used with a $B entry may also be used with stored pricing.

Examples of Stored Pricing Entries

T: $B*YM	Store price by passenger type
T: $BS1‡3	Store price with segment selection
T: $N1-1‡2-1	Store price with name selection

Copyright © 1990 by Glencoe/McGraw-Hill Educational Division. All rights reserved.

FORM OF PAYMENT

Before Apollo can ticket a PNR, the form of payment must be stored in the FOP (Form of Payment) field. The identifier for this field is F-. Payment by cash or check is identified by one of the following codes:

S	Cash
CK	Check

If a valid credit card is used to purchase the ticket, the credit card number is entered instead.

Examples of Form-of-Payment Entries

F-S	Cash
F-CK	Check
F-6002365418872/D995-SMITH	Credit card number with expiration date and cardholder name

If the form of payment has not been stored, the payment data may be included in a stored pricing (ATFQ) entry as follows:

T:$BFCK

If a form of payment has been stored, this entry will override FOP.

OTHER TICKETING INSTRUCTIONS

The stored pricing entry is also used to provide special ticketing instructions. When a ticket is issued, an invoice listing the passenger's itinerary and itemizing collectible charges is also generated. The modifier D may be used to designate only an itinerary/invoice, or only a ticket, to be printed as follows:

T:$BDID	Print itinerary/invoice only
T:$BDTD	Print ticket only

The modifier G is used for generic ticketing instructions, as illustrated in the following examples:

T:$BGF/FS	Free ticket
T:$BGIN	Omit dollar amount on printed itinerary
T:$BGIS	Print separate itinerary/invoice for each passenger

Copyright © 1990 by Glencoe/McGraw-Hill Educational Division. All rights reserved.

CHECK-IN: A STUDY AID

Write the correct stored pricing entry for each situation.

1. Write the entry to price an itinerary and store the pricing instructions.

$\underline{\hspace{2cm} T:\$B \hspace{2cm}}$

2. What entry will price an itinerary and issue an itinerary/ invoice without dollar amounts? $\underline{\hspace{1cm} T:\$BGIN \hspace{2cm}}$

3. Write the stored pricing entry for a free ticket.

$\underline{\hspace{2cm} T:\$BGF/FS \hspace{2cm}}$

4. How would you make a stored future pricing entry for segments 1, 3, and 5 of an itinerary? $\underline{\hspace{1cm} T:\$BS1F3F5 \hspace{2cm}}$

5. Assume a PNR contains the following names:

1.3TILLMAN/R MR/F MRS/A MISS $\underline{\hspace{0.5cm}}$ Need Age ?

a. Let's say you wish to price Mr. and Mrs. Tillman at the full adult fare and Miss A. at the children's fare. What entry would show the fare and the itinerary, and store instructions for ticketing?

$\underline{\hspace{1cm} T:\$BN1-1F1-2F1-3*C06 \hspace{2cm}}$

b. Assume you wish to price only segments 2, 3, and 4. What stored pricing entry would fare the selected segments for the Tillmans?

$\underline{\hspace{1cm} T:\$BS2F3F4 \hspace{2cm}}$

Copyright © 1990 by Glencoe/McGraw-Hill Educational Division. All rights reserved.

CHAPTER 10

DEMAND TICKETING

CHAPTER OBJECTIVES

At the end of the chapter, you should be able to perform the following tasks:

- Issue tickets for a retrieved PNR.
- Issue tickets without pricing instructions in the ATFQ field.
- Issue an itinerary/invoice.
- Store itinerary remarks.
- Print a message on the itinerary/invoice.

Copyright © 1990 by Glencoe/McGraw-Hill Educational Division. All rights reserved.

Problem

You previously made flight reservations for Mr. and Mrs. Tower who are traveling to St. Thomas—where they will board a cruise ship. Their tickets are scheduled to be written on the 17th of March. The Towers drop by a week early to pick up their tickets.

Apollo Solution

Instruct Apollo to issue the ticket on demand. In this chapter, you will learn how to issue tickets from a PNR.

THE DEMAND TICKETING PROCESS

On demand, Apollo can issue tickets automatically for most PNRs. If any changes or additions are needed, the PNR must be modified and ended before the ticket is issued. Before the basic ticketing entry is used, the pricing instructions must have been previously stored in the ATFQ field.

    The PNR has to be retrieved from storage and displayed in the agent's work area. The basic entry to issue tickets has the following format:

Format:

    HB:<Modifier>

Example:

    HB:

The example above does not include any modifier. This entry may be used to issue tickets from a retrieved PNR which has pricing instructions stored in the ATFQ field.

Example

Assume you previously created a PNR for a client, Ms. Gina Gaite, and now want to issue a passenger ticket. The first step is to retrieve the record as follows:

    **-GAITE

Copyright © 1990 by Glencoe/McGraw-Hill Educational Division. All rights reserved.

Response:

```
      1.1GAITE/GINA MS
       1 UA 990Y 22JAN SFOORD HK1     100A  950A        FR
     FONE-SFOAS/415 555-0102-ZELDA
     TKTG-TAU/11JAN
     ATFQ-OK/$BFAX3884757573737/D1289
     FQ-476.85/38.15/515.00 - 10DEC Y
```

The pricing instructions are stored in the ATFQ field. The OK indicates that you may proceed with ticketing.

If the form of payment has not been stored or is incorrect, the valid form must be included in the ticketing entry using the modifier F. For example, assume you just retrieved the following PNR for ticketing:

```
      1.1MCMUFFIN/ED MR
       1 EA 678M 21JUL ATLCMH HK1    950A  1113A        TH
     FONE-ATLAS/404 555-9989-CARLA
     TKTG-TAU/19JUL
     ATFQ-OK/$B□MAP3
     FQ-175.00/14.00/189.00 - 17JUL MAP3
```

Observe that the fare basis is stored in the ATFQ field, but the form of payment is not. Let's say Mr. McMuffin plans to pay for the ticket with a personal check. The following entry may be used to issue the ticket and indicate the form of payment:

HB: FCK

DEMAND TICKETING WITHOUT AN ATFQ FIELD

To issue a ticket when the PNR does not contain an ATFQ field, omit the colon : . The code HB instructs Apollo to price the itinerary without using the modifiers normally stored in the ATFQ field.

Example
Assume you just retrieved the following PNR for ticketing:

Copyright © 1990 by Glencoe/McGraw-Hill Educational Division. All rights reserved.

```
   1.2WHITFIELD/KYLE MR/CORA MRS
   1 AA 487Y 13DEC MCODFW HK2    845A 1018A      TU
  FONE-ORLAS/305 555-0909-JENNA
  ORLB/305 555-4999-MRS/R/305 555-3883
  TKTG-TAU/10DEC
```

No pricing instructions have been stored; thus, no ATFQ field appears in the record. Let's say your client will pay with cash. The following entry may be used to issue tickets:

    HBFS

OTHER TICKETING MODIFIERS

When no ATFQ field exists, modifiers for name selection and segment selection may be required in the demand ticketing entry. For example, suppose you want to ticket a PNR that has the following data in the Name field:

    1.3CARLSON/G MR/T MRS/L MSTR

Let's say you want to ticket only Mrs. T. and her son, Mstr. L., at this time. To include the name selection, the following entry may be used to issue tickets:

    HBN1-2‡1-3

To ticket only a portion of the passenger itinerary, include the segment selection. For example, if you want to ticket only segments 1 and 3, the following entry may be used:

    HBS1‡3

TICKETING REMARKS

A special PNR field, the Ticketing Remarks field, may be used to store invoicing instructions. When tickets are issued with an itinerary/invoice, Apollo refers to information in this field to print the documents.

Format:
    T–<Modifiers>

Example:
    T-SD

This entry tells Apollo to print separate invoices for each passenger in the PNR in chronological order. The Ticketing Remarks modifiers include the following examples:

Copyright © 1990 by Glencoe/McGraw-Hill Educational Division. All rights reserved.

SD	Separate invoices for each passenger by date
SA	Separate invoices for each passenger by product line
CD	Single invoice for all passengers by date
CA	Single invoice for all passengers by product line
IR	Print message on itinerary/invoice
ID	Itinerary only without dollar amount

Invoices generated by date are printed in chronological order. For invoices generated by product line, auxiliary segments such as hotel, tour, and car rental reservations are listed separately.

The modifier IR causes a printing remark or message to appear on the itinerary/invoice as in the following example:

```
T-IR-HAVE*A*GREAT*VACATION
```

In this entry, an * separates each word for spacing. Observe that a dash — is typed before the printing remark, which may consist of 42 characters maximum.

CHECK-IN: A STUDY AID

Write the correct demand ticketing entry for each situation.

1. What is the basic entry used to issue tickets for a retrieved PNR?

_____

2. Assume the ticketing instructions are not stored in the ATFQ field. Your client will purchase the ticket with a company check. What entry will issue tickets and include the form of payment information?

_____

3. Assume you wish to issue tickets and enter the form of payment as credit card account number AX622309867610032, expiring on 10-94. Write the correct entry to issue tickets.

_____

4. Assume you want to issue tickets for only segments 2 through 5 of an itinerary. What entry could you use for this purpose?

_____

5. What entry will issue a single itinerary/invoice for all passengers in the PNR by date? _____

6. What entry will issue separate itinerary/invoices for each passenger by product line? _____

7. What entry will issue an itinerary only, without the dollar amount? _____

_____

Copyright © 1990 by Glencoe/McGraw-Hill Educational Division. All rights reserved.

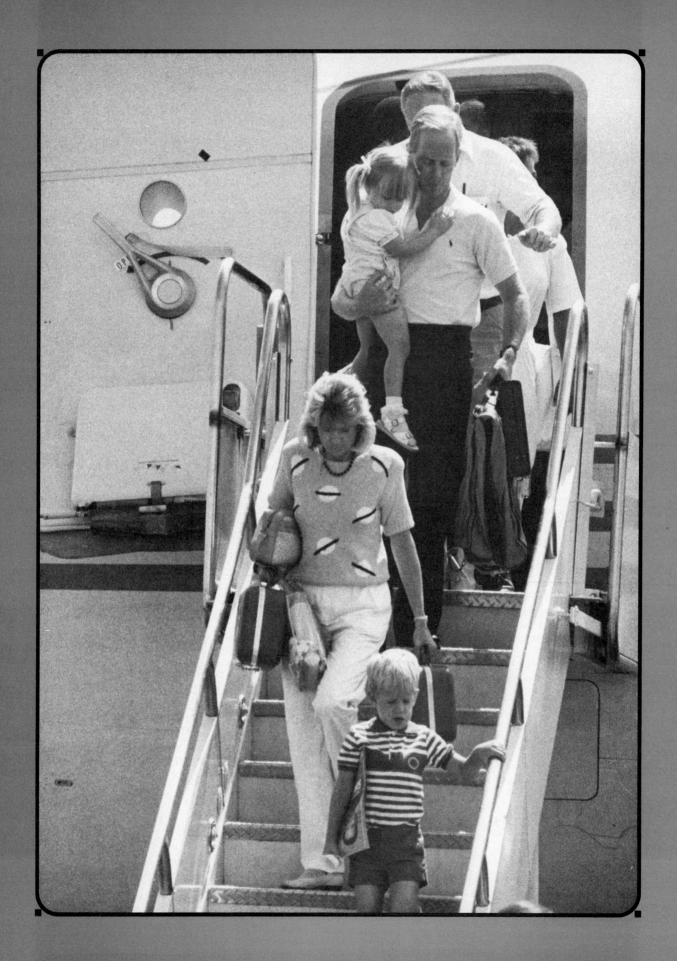

CHAPTER 11

MISCELLANEOUS ENTRIES:

SEAT ASSIGNMENTS AND QUEUES

CHAPTER OBJECTIVES

At the end of the chapter, you should be able to perform the following tasks:

- Identify the factors that affect passenger seating preference and selection.
- Request automatic seat assignment by zone and location.
- Assign specific seats on a designated segment.
- Display the seat map for a designated segment.
- Interpret the Apollo seat map codes.
- Display seat assignment information in a PNR.
- Cancel seat assignments.
- Enter the passenger's Mileage Plus, Frequent Flyer account number.
- Define the term *queue.*
- Identify important queues.
- Request a queue count.
- Access a queue.
- Suspend a PNR in a queue.
- Route a PNR to a queue.
- Initiate continuous queue ticketing.

Copyright © 1990 by Glencoe/McGraw-Hill Educational Division. All rights reserved.

Problem

You are making flight arrangements for Mr. Rush and Mr. Stein, who will be traveling to a convention. Your clients would like advance seat assignment with two aisle seats across from each other in the no-smoking section.

Apollo Solution

(1) Request automatic seat assignment for two seats in no-smoking, aisle across; or (2) display the seat map for your clients' flight and select two seats which meet the requirements. In this chapter, you will learn how to assign prereserved seats, verify flight information, and work with queues.

ADVANCE SEAT ASSIGNMENTS

Apollo permits travel agents to assign prereserved seats on UA flights and certain other carriers, up to six months prior to the departure date. On UA flights, advance boarding passes may be issued for the assigned seats.

In general, passenger seating depends on two factors: zone and location. Many flights (except designated no-smoking flights) have two basic zones: a smoking section (S) and a no-smoking section (N). In addition, there is a buffer zone between the smoking and no-smoking sections. A seat in one of these zones may have any of the following locations (depending on aircraft configuration):

- Aisle
- Window
- Center

Most clients have a definite preference for a particular zone and location. Seats may be assigned by one of two methods: automatic and specific.

Automatic Seat Assignment

The Apollo command code for the seat assignment function is 9S. If the preferred zone and location are supplied, Apollo will automatically assign a prereserved seat. The entry for automatic seat assignment has the following basic format:

Copyright © 1990 by Glencoe/McGraw-Hill Educational Division. All rights reserved.

Format:

    9S/<Seat Type>

Example:

    9S

The seat type refers to the zone and location preferred by the passenger. In the entry above, no seat type is specified, so Apollo will attempt to assign a window seat in the no-smoking section.

The following modifiers are used to indicate a different seating preference:

(None)	No-smoking, window
/A	No-smoking, aisle
/AA	No-smoking, aisle across
/X	Smoking, window
/XA	Smoking, aisle

The basic seat assignment entry, without a seat-type modifier, requests a window seat in the no-smoking zone. Other seat types are requested by adding the appropriate modifier.

Example

Assume you are working with an itinerary that involves three segments on UA flights. Your client would like an advance seat assignment on all segments. His preference is an aisle seat in the no-smoking section. The following entry may be used to request the seat assignment:

    9S/A

Now assume that two passengers are traveling, and they request aisle seats across from one another in the smoking section. The following entry may be used to assign the seats:

    9S/XAA

The basic seat assignment entry requests seats on all segments of the itinerary. A segment selection may be included in the entry as follows:

    9S/S3/XAA

Example

Assume a PNR with the following itinerary is in your work area:

```
1 UA 193Y  19MAR LGAHNL HK2   900A   440P    WE
2 HA 706Y  19MAR HNLOGG HK2   555P   622P    WE
3 HA 352Y  25MAR OGGHNL HK2  1145A  1224P    WE
4 CO · 2Y  25MAR HNLLGA HK2   100P  ‡529A    WE
```

Copyright © 1990 by Glencoe/McGraw-Hill Educational Division. All rights reserved.

Let's say you want to assign prereserved seating on the UA flight on segment 1. Your clients would like seats in the smoking section, with one seat at the window. The following entry may be used to assign the seats:

9S/S1/X

Apollo responds as follows:

```
    UA 193 Y 19MAR LGA HNL
01.  JONES‡R      HK  35C  SA
02.  JONES‡D      HK  35B  S
```

In this example, seat 35C (row 35, seat C) has been assigned to passenger R. Jones, and seat 35B has been assigned to D. Jones. Seat 35C is a smoking-section aisle seat (SA).

Specific Seat Assignment

To assign a specific seat, substitute the seat number in place of the seat type. For example, to assign seat 14C on segment 1, the following entry may be used:

9S/S1/14C

Multiple seats may be assigned in one entry as in the following example:

9S/S1/14ABC

This entry assigns seats 14A, 14B, and 14C. Observe that neither the zone nor the location need to be indicated when the seat number is specified.

To determine what seats are available on a particular flight, a seat map may be displayed. Seat maps are available for flights operated by United and Delta.

Seat Maps

A seat map is a chart showing the status of all the passenger seats on a particular flight. The arrangement of the seats depends on the configuration of the aircraft. For example, seats on 727 aircraft are arranged on both sides of a single aisle, whereas on wide-body planes (e.g., 747 or DC-10 aircraft), several center seats are located between two aisles.

To display the seat map for a segment in a PNR in your work area, use the following format:

Format:
9V/S<Segment>

Example:

9V/S1

The example above requests a seat map of the flight on segment 1. The seat map corresponds to the class of service booked on the indicated segment. If the

Copyright © 1990 by Glencoe/McGraw-Hill Educational Division. All rights reserved.

passengers are booked in first class on that segment, the map for the first-class cabin will be displayed. Otherwise, the coach cabin is displayed.

Response:

```
UA 220   18JAN DEN SEAT MAP *DC10*
      A    B    C    D    E    F    G    H    J
11   X   XA   XA   X    X    X   XA   XA   X
12   S    S   XA   X    X    S    S    S    S
13W  R    R    R    S    S    S    S    S    S
14W  N   NA   NA   N    N    N    S    S    S
15W  S   NA   NA   N    N    N   NA    S    S
```

Seat locations marked with R have already been reserved. The following codes may appear in the seat map:

X	Available/no-smoking
N	Available/smoking permitted
A	Available aisle seat
W	Over the wing
S	Saved (already reserved)
R	Reserved

Displaying Seat Information

Preassigned seat information does not automatically appear on the screen when a PNR is displayed. To view the information, the following entry may be used:

9D

Canceling Seat Assignments

Canceling an itinerary segment also cancels the seat assignment. However, it is also possible to cancel only the seat assignment without affecting the confirmed segment. To cancel all seat assignments in the itinerary, the following entry may be used:

Format:
9X

To cancel an assigned seat, add the segment and seat number as follows:

Format:
9X/<Segment>/<Seat Number>

Example:
9X/S1/23B

Copyright © 1990 by Glencoe/McGraw-Hill Educational Division. All rights reserved.

This entry cancels previously assigned seat 23B on segment 1, permitting a different seat to be assigned.

OFF-LINE SEAT REQUESTS

To request seats on carriers that do not offer direct seat assignment through Apollo, an SSR entry must be used. For example, the following entry requests an aisle seat in the smoking section:

```
3SSR NSST AS NN1 AISLE AS91Y13JUNANCSEA
```

The SSR codes NSST (no-smoking section seat) and SMST (smoking section seat) may be used in the off-line entry. The location is briefly described in the text portion of the entry (aisle or window).

FREQUENT FLYER ID NUMBERS

Members of United's Mileage Plus, Frequent Flyer program earn mileage credits for travel on UA flights. To enter a passenger's frequent flyer ID number, the following entry is used:

Format:
    MP*<ID Number>

Example:

```
MP*776655
```

This entry assures that the correct mileage will be posted to the member's Mileage Plus account.

In a PNR with multiple passengers, name selection may be included in the entry. For example, assume a PNR contains the following passengers in the name field:

```
1. 1THOMPSON/ARTHUR/CARLA MRS/TANYA MS
```

Let's say that Mr. Thompson is a Mileage Plus member, and his ID number is 838261. The following entry may be used to enter the frequent flyer number in the PNR:

```
MP*838261/N1-1
```

CHECK-IN: A STUDY AID

I. *Write the correct code or interpretation.*

1. Give the correct code for the following seating preferences:

_____ Aisle seat in no-smoking

_____ Window seat in smoking

Copyright © 1990 by Glencoe/McGraw-Hill Educational Division. All rights reserved.

_____ Two seats, aisle across, in no-smoking

_____ Aisle seat in smoking

2. Give the correct code for the following seats:

_____ Row 17, seat A

_____ Row 23, seat C

_____ Row 31, seat J

3. Give the correct meaning of the following seat map codes:

N _____

R _____

X _____

A _____

S _____

II. *Write the correct seat assignment code for each situation.*

1. What entry will request an aisle seat in the no-smoking section on segment 1? _____

2. What entry will request a window seat in the smoking section on segment 3?

_____

3. What entry will request a window seat in the no-smoking section on all segments in the itinerary? _____

4. What entry will assign seat 12A on segment 1?

_____

5. What entry will assign seat 23F on segment 5?

_____

6. Assume you wish to assign adjacent seats 9A, 9B, and 9C. Write the correct entry to assign the seats. _____

7. What entry could you use to display the seat map of the flight in segment 2?

_____

8. What entry would display the seat map on segment 1?

_____

9. What entry would display the seat map for United 268 on the 5th of February departing from Miami? _____

Copyright © 1990 by Glencoe/McGraw-Hill Educational Division. All rights reserved.

10. Assume the following partial seat map is displayed:

	A	B	C	D	E	F	G	H	J
11	S	XA	S	S	X	X	XA	XA	S
12	X	S	XA	X	X	S	S	XA	X
13W	R	R	R	S	S	S	S	S	S
14W	R	NA	NA	R	R	R	R	R	X

a. What two adjacent seats are available by a window?

_____

b. What window seat is available on the left side?

_____

c. What four adjacent seats are available in the center section of the compartment? _____

11. What entry will display seat assignment information contained in a PNR?

_____

12. Assume that seat 35C was previously assigned to a passenger on segment 2. What entry will cancel the seat assignment so that a different seat can be selected? _____

13. Assume a client requests an aisle seat in the no-smoking section on TS flight 1411 in Y class from HNL to OGG on the 17th of February. What SSR entry could you use to request the seat?

_____

14. Assume a PNR has the following names:

1. 1EVANS/BARRY   2. 1KLEINMAN/RICH

Mr. Kleinman's Mileage Plus account number is 500362. What entry would you use to enter his account number?

_____

QUEUES

The word *queue* is French for a waiting line; for example, a crowd of people standing in line at a theater box office is a *queue*. In the language of computers, a queue is a sequence of data awaiting display or processing.

To visualize a queue, imagine a stack of papers sitting in an "in" basket on an executive's desk. The sheet on top of the stack is first in the queue; remove it, and

Copyright © 1990 by Glencoe/McGraw-Hill Educational Division. All rights reserved.

the next sheet in the stack appears. Similarly, a queue holds a stack of records that may be accessed one after another.

Each queue in the Apollo reservation system has a unique number and function. The records in a queue all have some common trait that requires attention. For instance, PNRs with confirmations from the waitlist are placed in one queue, and PNRs affected by schedule changes are placed in another.

The number and function of each queue is shown in the following list:

Queue	Function
SPV	Supervisory message queue
MSG	General message queue
UTC	Unable to contact (PNRs suspended for a set interval)
LMCB	Left message to call back (PNRs suspended for a set interval)
0	URG (urgent confirmations/within 24 hours)
1	GEN (advance confirmations)
2	SEAT (alternate confirmations)
9	TAW (future ticketing date)
10	TAU (current day ticketing)
12	TL (tickler file for follow-up action)
15	GROUP
17	Waitlist confirmations
18	UA schedule change within 14 days (reservation protected)
19	UA schedule change (reservation not protected)
20	UA schedule change beyond 14 days (reservation protected)
22	UA schedule change beyond next major schedule change
33	Stored pricing
71	Interrupted airline service
80	Waitlist confirmations, discount fares

As suggested by the various functions, PNRs in a queue generally require some sort of action. For example, PNRs in queue 0 contain urgent confirmations requiring the agent to contact the passenger and change the segment status to HK. PNRs in queue 10 are scheduled to have tickets printed on the current date.

A record stored temporarily in a queue and awaiting action is said to be *on queue*. Accessing a queue and processing the records are referred to as "working a queue."

Before working queues, it is advisable to obtain a count of the records awaiting action. The queue count function is use for this purpose.

Queue Count

The Apollo command code to obtain a count of PNRs on queue is QC. To display a count for a specific queue, the following format may be used:

Format:
    QC/<Queue number>

Example:

    QC/10

This entry displays a count of all PNRs held in the current day ticketing queue.

Response:
    02APR ZC4
    PNR/Q10 36

Copyright © 1990 by Glencoe/McGraw-Hill Educational Division. All rights reserved.

The header line gives the date of the request and the agency's pseudo-city code. In this example, thirty-six PNRs are waiting in queue 10.

To obtain a count of records in all the queues, omit the queue number and use the following entry:

    QC/ALL

(For a branch location, include the pseudo-city code.)

Response:

```
02APR   ZC4
SPV - 0    MSG - 17    UTR - 0    LMT - 0    URG - 1    GEN - 1
Q10 - 36  Q22 - 4     Q40 - 20   Q41 - 96   Q42 - 33   Q43 - 37
Q44 - 11
```

In the example above, seventeen messages are contained in the general message queue (MSG). No records are assigned to the special UTR and LMT queues. Queue 10 has thirty-six records, and queue 41 has ninety-six.

Record counts for numbered queues may be obtained by queue selection as in the following example:

    QC6‡10

Accessing a Queue

The action code Q is used to sign into a queue and display the first record as follows:

Format:
    Q/<Queue Number>

Example:
    Q/1

When this entry is made, the first record in queue 1 will be displayed for processing.

If the queue is accessed from a branch office, the pseudo-city code must be added as follows:

    Q/CZ4/10

Working the Queue

When the record has been processed and the transaction is ended, the PNR is removed from the queue automatically and the next record is displayed. If the PNR is ignored, the record is placed automatically at the end of the queue, but is not removed.

After a queue has been accessed, only records in the queue may be processed. To perform other duties, the agent must exit from the queue as follows:

Copyright © 1990 by Glencoe/McGraw-Hill Educational Division. All rights reserved.

The last PNR remains in the work area until the transaction is ended or ignored.

To remove a PNR from the queue when no action has been taken, the following entry may be used:

QR

When the queue is worked, the following commands may be used to exit the queue:

QX‡E   Exit from queue and end last PNR
QX‡I   Exit from queue and ignore last PNR

Example

Let's say you wish to begin working the waitlist confirmations in queue 17. A queue count may be obtained as follows:

QC/17

Apollo displays the records waiting in queue 17:

02APR ZC4
PNR/Q17 2

Only two records await handling. The next step is to access the queue as follows:

Q/17

Apollo responds by displaying the first record for processing. Assume the PNR contains the following itinerary:

```
  1.1BARKER/HARRY/MARY MRS
1 DL 818Y 13APR PHLBOS KL2 1010A 1116A
2 US 969Y 17APR BOSPHL HK2  645A  755A
```

Here, the clients' seat request in segment 1 has cleared the waitlist, and Apollo has changed the segment status to KL. You should now contact your clients to confirm the reservation, then change the segment status to HK, as follows:

.1HK

Copyright © 1990 by Glencoe/McGraw-Hill Educational Division. All rights reserved.

Remember that a Received entry is required whenever a PNR is edited or modified. Let's say you spoke with Mrs. Barker. The following entry may be used to record the Received information and end the transaction:

R:MRS‡E

When the client cannot be contacted to confirm a reservation, the record may be placed on the UTC queue (unable to contact). If a message is left, the record may be placed on the LMCB queue (left message to call back). These special queues suspend the record for a set interval, after which the PNR reappears at the top of the original queue. The UTC queue commonly returns each PNR after 15 minutes. A PNR placed in the LMCB queue reappears in its original queue on the following morning.

The following entry may be used to set the UTC interval:

QI/15

This entry sets the interval to 15 minutes.

The current PNR may be placed in one of the special queues by the following entries:

QUTC   (Place PNR in UTC queue)
QLMCB   (Place PNR in LMCB queue)

When you have finished working the queue and want to return to your other duties, you may end the current PNR and exit as follows:

QX‡E

Routing PNRs to a Queue

Apollo automatically places certain PNRs on queue. On occasion, an agent may route a record to a particular queue for special handling. The following format may be used to place a PNR on a specific queue:

Format:
    QEP/<Queue Number>

Example:

QEP/41

This entry is commonly used to place a record in a queue reserved for internal use by the travel agency. For example, one queue might be used to route PNRs to a particular agent for handling.

Continuous Queue Ticketing

Queue 10 holds PNRs scheduled for ticketing on the current date. All of the records in this queue contain TAU entries with the current date. For example, on April 12, queue 10 will contain records with the following entry in the Ticketing field:

TKTG-TAU/12APR

Copyright © 1990 by Glencoe/McGraw-Hill Educational Division. All rights reserved.

On command, Apollo will continuously ticket all the PNRs on queue, using the price information stored in the ATFQ field. The following entry is used to initiate continuous queue ticketing:

Format:
HB:Q/<Queue Number>

Example:

HB:Q/10

Apollo will issue tickets for all PNRs in the queue.

To ticket from a branch office, the pseudo-city code may be included as follows:

HB:Q/CZ4/10

Manual Queue Ticketing

PNRs scheduled for current-day ticketing are placed automatically in queue 10. To issue tickets for PNRs with future ticketing dates, a different technique—manual queue ticketing—must be used.

Manual queue ticketing involves three basic steps:

1. Obtain a count of PNRs scheduled for future ticketing on the specified date.
2. "Orbit" the PNRs into a designated queue.
3. Initiate queue ticketing.

The first step is to count the number of PNRs with future ticketing dates. The command code ORC entry is used for this purpose as follows:

Format:
ORC/TAU/<Date>

Example:

ORC/TAU/15MAY

This example requests a count of PNRs with a TAU ticketing date of 15MAY.

A date range may also be specified in the entry as in the following example:

ORC/TAU/10MAY*24MAY

Observe that * separates the first and last dates in the range.

The second step is to place the future ticket orders in a designated queue. The command code ORB (on-line record bump) is used for this purpose:

Format:
ORB/TAU/<Date>–Q<Queue>

Example:

ORB/TAU/15APR-Q/36

This entry bumps PNRs with a TAU date of 15APR into queue 36. The actual queue designated for this operation is more or less arbitrary—every agency has its own preference.

A date range may also be specified as follows:

Copyright © 1990 by Glencoe/McGraw-Hill Educational Division. All rights reserved.

`ORB/TAU/18JUN*2JUL`

The final step is to initiate queue ticketing. To access queue 36, the following entry would be used:

`HB:Q/36`

This entry instructs Apollo to issue tickets for all the PNRs in the currently accessed queue.

Response:
`XQ0/36 QUEUE TICKETING ACTIVATED`

To interrupt automatic queue ticketing, the following entry may be used:

Format:
`HB:Q/<Number>/STOP`

Example:
`HB:Q/41/STOP`

Example
Assume that, because of a pending fare increase, you would like to ticket PNRs scheduled for ticketing on the 12th of February. An on-line record count shows nine PNRs with a TAU date of 12FEB. Let's say your agency uses queue 39 for manual queue ticketing. The following entry may be used to move the PNRs into the queue:

`ORB/TAU/12FEB-Q/39`

Apollo responds as follows:

`MOVED 9 TO Q 39`

Tickets may now be issued for all PNRs in the queue by the following entry:

`HB:Q/39`

CHECK-IN: A STUDY AID

Write the correct queue entry for each situation.

1. Obtain a count of records in queue 21. _____

2. Obtain a count of records in all queues. _____

3. Obtain a count of queues 3, 5, and 14. _____

4. Begin working queue 18. _____

5. Remove the current record from the queue. _____

6. Exit from queue and end record. _____

7. Exit from queue and ignore record. _____

Copyright © 1990 by Glencoe/McGraw-Hill Educational Division. All rights reserved.

8. Place current record on queue 36. _____

9. Activate continuous ticketing of all PNRs in the current queue.

   _____

10. Activate continuous ticketing of all PNRs in queue 10, without signing into the queue. _____

11. Remove all records from queue 37. _____

12. Obtain a record count of all PNRs with TAU ticketing dates of 23OCT.

   _____

13. Route PNRS with TAU ticketing dates of 22MAR to queue 43.

   _____

Copyright © 1990 by Glencoe/McGraw-Hill Educational Division. All rights reserved.

CHAPTER 12

CLIENT PROFILES

CHAPTER OBJECTIVES

At the end of the chapter, you should be able to perform the following tasks:

- Define the term *client profile*.
- Display a Business Account Record.
- Display a Passenger Account Record.
- Identify the line codes in a client profile.
- Move mandatory data lines from a client profile into a PNR.
- Move optional data lines from a client profile.
- Use a blind move to insert the agency phone from the Master Account Record into a PNR.
- Build and edit client profiles.

Copyright © 1990 by Glencoe/McGraw-Hill Educational Division. All rights reserved.

Problem

A company, Acme Manufacturing, utilizes the travel agency where you work for all its travel arrangements, and many Acme employees have occasion to travel. Building PNRs for these frequent travelers involves entering the same business phone, client billing address, and other data time after time.

Apollo Solution

Retrieve the client profile for Acme and transfer the required entries into the PNR. In this chapter, you will learn how to work with client profiles.

WORKING WITH CLIENT PROFILES

A client profile is a special computer record containing standard PNR entries for the travel agency's regular clients. Each profile contains frequently used entries for the Name, Phone, Remarks, and other data fields. Using a client profile greatly enhances the process of creating a new PNR. When a profile has been retrieved from storage, the PNR entries contained in the client profile can be moved into a new PNR currently being created.

Apollo has three levels of profiles:

1. Master Account Record (MAR)
2. Business Account Record (BAR)
3. Passenger Account Record (PAR)

Each Apollo agency has its own Master Account Record (MAR) containing the agency's name, address, and telephone number. Companies which book travel arrangements through the agency have separate Business Account Records or BARs. Individual passengers, including employees of client companies, have Passenger Account Records or PARs.

Working with profiles involves two basic steps:

1. Display the profile.
2. Move the selected data lines into the PNR.

160

Copyright © 1990 by Glencoe/McGraw-Hill Educational Division. All rights reserved.

DISPLAYING A BUSINESS ACCOUNT RECORD

161

Displaying
a Business
Account
Record

Each profile has a unique title, or ID code, up to 21 characters in length. The command to retrieve and display a profile has the following basic format:

Format:

    S*<Title>

Example:

    S*ACME

The example above retrieves a client record (BAR) titled ACME.

Example

Assume you are creating a PNR for a passenger who will be traveling on behalf of Sample Bars, Inc., one of your agency's regular clients. Let's say the title of your client's BAR is SAMPLE. The following entry would be used to display the client profile:

    S*SAMPLE

Apollo responds by retrieving the profile and displaying the data lines on the screen.

```
1N    SAMPLE BARS INC
2Y    P:LASB/702 555-5432
3O    W-2001 ODYSSEY BLVD□LAS VEGAS NV 89001
4O    F-AX6518717171213191/D995
5N    NET 30 DAYS
```

This profile contains the client business phone, billing address, and an optional form-of-payment entry. Observe that each line of the client profile is coded with a line number followed by a letter. The letter indicates the type of data contained in each line.

A profile may contain three types of data:

Y   Always used
O   Optional
N   Never used

PNR entries may be found in the lines coded Y or O. The lines bearing the code Y are always used in a PNR for this account. Lines bearing the code O contain optional data which may—or may not—be used in a PNR, depending on the situation. Lines coded N are informational only and are never used in a PNR.

If you are uncertain of a profile title, you can display a list of BARs by using the following entry:

Copyright © 1990 by Glencoe/McGraw-Hill Educational Division. All rights reserved.

Format:

SLB/<Initial>

Example:

SLB/T

The initial refers to the first letter of the desired title. The example above will display a list of BAR titles that begin with the letter T.

DISPLAYING A PASSENGER ACCOUNT RECORD

Whereas a BAR contains frequently used data for a company, a PAR contains data for a specific passenger. A PAR is retrieved with the following format:

Format:

S*<Title>-<Passenger Name>

Example:

S*ACME-SMITH

The example above retrieves a PAR for a passenger named Smith, who travels on behalf of Acme.

MOVING DATA LINES

When a profile has been displayed, data lines may be transferred from the client profile into the PNR with the following entry:

Format:

MV/<Optional Lines>

Example:

MV/

The entry in the example above does not include any optional lines. Therefore, Apollo will transfer only the mandatory lines Y. When one or more optional lines 0 are specified, Apollo will transfer all Y lines plus the specified 0 lines. No other type of data lines contained in a profile may be transferred to a PNR.

Transferring coded lines from a profile into a newly created passenger record is called moving data. This entry moves data from both the passenger's PAR and the company's BAR. To move data from one level without affecting data in another level, the following alternative entries may be used:

MVB/   Move all Y lines, BAR only
MVP/   Move all Y lines, PAR only

Example

Assume you are creating a PNR for a passenger named Hubbard, traveling on behalf of a frequent account, Mother's Cupboards. You happen to know that the BAR title is MOTHERS and that a PAR exists for this traveler. The first step is to display the client profile as follows:

S*MOTHERS-HUBBARD

Apollo responds by displaying the profile.

Copyright © 1990 by Glencoe/McGraw-Hill Educational Division. All rights reserved.

```
1N      MOTHER'S CUPBOARDS
2Y      N: HUBBARD/M MRS
3Y      P:LAXB/213 555-5544
40 ☐: 30SI YY OTHS GIVE HER POOR DOG A BONE
5N      USE ZD FOR CAR RENTAL
```

Let's say you want to move the passenger's name, business phone, and optional OSI message into the PNR. The following entry may be used:

    MVP / 4

Observe that line 4 is specified so that the optional 0 line will be transferred in addition to the mandatory Y lines. Apollo enters the data in the passenger record automatically, as if each entry had been manually inserted.

```
N: HUBBARD/M MRS
P: LAXB/213 555-5544
40 ☐: 30SI YY OTHS GIVE HER POOR DOG A BONE
*
```

The * indicates that Apollo has accepted the PNR data. Data lines may only be moved into a PNR once, unless the record has been ended or ignored.

Observe that, since MVP was used in the entry, only the data stored in the PAR was moved into the PNR.

MOVING MULTIPLE 0 LINES

To specify more than one optional 0 line to be moved, separate the line numbers with an End-Item ‡, as in the following example:

    MV / 4‡6

Whenever the basic MV entry is used, all lines coded Y are automatically moved into the PNR. To indicate a range of 0 lines, separate the first and last line with a dash -, as follows:

    MV / 4 - 6

This entry moves all mandatory Y data, plus optional lines 4, 5, and 6.

Copyright © 1990 by Glencoe/McGraw-Hill Educational Division. All rights reserved.

BLIND MOVES

Data from a MAR, BAR, or PAR can be moved automatically without retrieving the profile. This technique is referred to as a "blind" move. The modifier T is used to initiate a blind move:

```
MVT/CZ4‡*TERRY
```

This example moves all Y lines from the agency MAR and adds the agent's name to the end of the phone entry. Here, the agency's pseudo-city code is entered to identify the MAR. Apollo responds as follows:

```
P:LAXAS/213 555-0198 TERRY
  *
```

In this example, the only Y line stored in the profile is the agency phone entry. Apollo inserts the agent's name after the phone entry as instructed.

To initiate a blind move from both a MAR and BAR at the same time, enter the BAR title in place of the pseudo-city code as follows:

```
MVT/ACME‡*TERRY
```

This example moves all Y lines from the agency MAR and the BAR for the Acme company. The agent's name is added to the end of the agency phone.

CREATING AND UPDATING PROFILES

Client profiles may only be created or updated by authorized personnel, such as the agency manager or reservations supervisor. An entry-level travel or ticketing agent is primarily concerned with retrieving profiles and transferring data, but with enough experience, will eventually become responsible for creating profiles for the agency's frequent accounts.

The following entries are used to create or update client profiles:

1. Create BAR.

Format:
 BPB/<Title>

Example:

```
BPB/NUVISION
```

The BAR title must consist of at least four, and no more than 21, alphanumeric characters and may not include a slash /.

2. Build lines.

Example:
```
1N/NUVISION
2Y/P:MIAB/315 555-0012
3O/W-NUVISION☐4012 N PALM DR☐MIAMI FL Z/33316
4OF-AX6054389029887366/D0594
5N/ALWYS BK IN F CLASS
```

Copyright © 1990 by Glencoe/McGraw-Hill Educational Division. All rights reserved.

The maximum length of a single data line is 64 characters, except for a client address, which may include 128 characters. A maximum of 128 lines may be included in a single profile.

3. End.

Format:
```
BE
```

4. Change/Delete line.

Format:
```
RC:<Line><New Data>
```

Example:
```
RC: 2Y/P: LAXB/415 555-6543
```
To delete a line, leave the text portion of the entry blank.

5. Insert lines:

Format:
```
RC: /<Line to Follow>
```

Example:
```
RC: /4
```

This entry inserts a new line and renumbers all subsequent lines in the profile.

6. Create PAR:

Format:
```
BPP/<Title>-<Passenger Name>
```

Example:
```
BPP/NUVISION-PEARLE
```

Copyright © 1990 by Glencoe/McGraw-Hill Educational Division. All rights reserved.

CHECK-IN: A STUDY AID

Write the correct answer to each question.

1. What do the initials BAR stand for? _____

2. What do the initials PAR stand for? _____

3. When a client profile is displayed, what code appears next to line numbers with mandatory entries which should always be used in a PNR created for the client? _____

4. What code appears next to line numbers with optional PNR entries?

   _____

5. What code appears next to line numbers with information that is never used in a PNR? _____

6. What entry would you use to display a BAR with the title RET102?

   _____

7. What entry would you use to display a BAR with an account name of SPERRY? _____

8. What entry would move all mandatory data lines from a retrieved profile?

   _____

9. What entry would move all the mandatory data lines plus optional line 4 from a retrieved profile? _____

10. What entry would move all the mandatory data lines plus optional lines 4 through 6 from a retrieved profile? _____

11. What is the maximum length of a BAR title? _____

12. What entry will display a list of BAR titles? _____

13. What entry will display a list of PARs for the BAR titled NEWCO?

    _____

14. How would you display a PAR for passenger Clark under a BAR titled ITT?

    _____

15. Write the entry to display a BAR titled WEEKES under a PAR titled GOODYEAR. _____

Copyright © 1990 by Glencoe/McGraw-Hill Educational Division. All rights reserved.

16. Assume Apollo displays the following profile:

```
1Y/N:WEEKES/JOHN
2Y/STLB/314 555-0092
3Y/STLR/314 555-1309
40/W-GOODYEAR MFG CO□2230 S AIRWAY□ST LOUIS MO Z/63130
50/R:MS OLSON
6N/:5DELIVER TKTS AFTER 5P
```

    a. What entry would move only the name and phone items into the PNR?

        _____

    b. What entry would move the name and phone items plus the client billing address? _____

    c. What entry would move the name and phone items plus the received information. _____

    d. What entry would move all mandatory and optional lines into the PNR?

        _____

Copyright © 1990 by Glencoe/McGraw-Hill Educational Division. All rights reserved.

CHAPTER 13
APOLLO HOTELS

CHAPTER OBJECTIVES

At the end of the chapter, you should be able to perform the following tasks:

- Display the hotel index for a specific city.

- Decode room rates and bedding codes.

- Display the hotel index for a specific rate category, bedding type, or location.

- Display hotel availability.

- Display hotel availability without an air itinerary.

- Display a hotel description.

- Display hotel policies by category.

- Sell hotel space from a description.

- Interpret a hotel segment.

- Enter guarantee information with a hotel reservation.

- Modify a hotel segment.

- Record a hotel reservation booked directly with the property.

- Cancel hotel space.

Copyright © 1990 by Glencoe/McGraw-Hill Educational Division. All rights reserved.

====================

Problem

You are making travel arrangements for a client whose itinerary includes four cities. She would like to book a hotel reservation in each city near the airport. Her preference is for a major chain offering a corporate rate.

Apollo Solution

Display the hotel index in each city, check availability for your client's stay, and book reservations at properties that meet her requirements. This chapter illustrates how to utilize the Apollo hotel system.

====================

THE APOLLO HOTELS SYSTEM

Besides flight reservations and car rentals, Apollo can also book hotel reservations at participating properties in major lodging markets. Each hotel chain is identified by a two-letter code as in the following list:

Examples of Apollo Hotels

BW	Best Western	MC	Marriott
CI	Comfort Inns	QI	Quality Inns
HH	Hilton Inns	RA	Ramada Inns
HI	Holiday Inns	SI	Sheraton
HJ	Howard Johnson	TL	Travelodge
HY	Hyatt Hotels	WI	Westin Inns

A complete list of participating hotels and two-letter chain codes may be obtained by the following entry:

```
HELP HTLC
```

HOTEL INDEX

The following entry may be used to display an index of participating hotels in a particular city:

Copyright © 1990 by Glencoe/McGraw-Hill Educational Division. All rights reserved.

Format:

    HOI<City>

Example:

    HOIMIA

Response:

```
HOTELS IN MIA          RATES LOCATION-MILES FROM ARPT
HI4402 HI MIAMI DWTN   89-129C 321 PALM BLVD   -140T
SI7669 SI AIRPORT INN  88-124A 1330 OCEAN BLVD - 3CC
TL2110 TL FINANCIAL DIST 52-69 A 2112 COMMERCE - 4CC
WI0012 WI WESTIN TOWERS 89-100A MIAMI FLORIDA  - 2CC
```

Before proceeding, let us examine each line of the Apollo hotel index. Each property is identified by the chain code and property code.

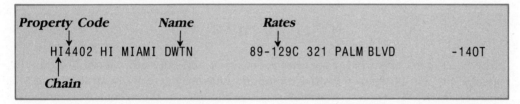

```
Property Code        Name            Rates
  HI4402 HI  MIAMI DWTN       89-129C 321 PALM BLVD        -140T
  Chain
```

The name of the property (in this case, HI MIAMI DWTN) follows the code. The rates column gives the minimum-to-maximum rate range at each hotel. In this example, the minimum room rate is $89.00 and the maximum is $129.00.

```
                                Address
  HI4402 HI  MIAMI DWTN    89-129C 321 PALM BLVD        -140T
```

The rate range is followed by a one-letter location code (C) and the abbreviated property address. In this example, the code C indicates the city center area.

```
                                          Distance
  HI4402 HI  MIAMI DWTN    89-129C 321 PALM BLVD     -140T
```

On the extreme right of each line appears the distance from the airport and type of transportation available.

```
  HI4402 HI  MIAMI DWTN    89-129C 321 PALM BLVD        -140T
```

In this example, 14 signifies that the property is 14 miles from the nearest major airport. The transportation code OT indicates that clients must arrange for their own transportation.

    The location code may be any of the following:

Copyright © 1990 by Glencoe/McGraw-Hill Educational Division. All rights reserved.

C	City center
A	Airport
R	Resort
S	Suburban

The following transportation codes may appear in the listing:

L	Limousine service
CC	Courtesy car
OT	Other transportation

Other transportation signifies that clients must arrange their own transporation, e.g., rental car, hotel van, or bus.

Modifying the Hotel Index

A location, hotel chain, or corporate rate request may be included in the entry to limit the display. The following examples illustrate this technique:

HOISFO/A	Specific location
HOISFO/HI	Specific hotel chain
HOISFO/SCR	Corporate rates

HOTEL AVAILABILITY

The hotel index tells what properties, room types, and rates are offered in a particular city, but does not tell what rooms and rates may actually be available on a particular date. To request availability with an itinerary in the agent's work area, the following format may be used:

Format:

HOA

This entry requests hotel availability in the destination city in the last segment booked. Apollo makes the following assumptions:

1. The check-in date is the same as the arrival date in the last segment.
2. The client will check out on the following day (after a one-night stay).
3. The party consists of one adult.

To indicate a different segment than the last segment booked, the following format may be used:

Format:

/<Segment to Follow>‡HOA

Example:

/2‡HOA

The example above requests hotel availability after segment 2.

The length of the stay and the number of adults may be included in the entry as follows:

Copyright © 1990 by Glencoe/McGraw-Hill Educational Division. All rights reserved.

/2‡HOA5NT2

Insert after segment:	/2
End-Item:	‡
Hotel availability:	HOA
Number of nights:	5NT
Adults:	2

The maximum number of adults per room is two. The example above requests hotel availability on the date and in the destination city shown in segment 2. A five-night stay for two adults is requested.

Example

Assume you are making travel arrangements for a client who has the following itinerary:

```
1 UA 311Y 13JAN GSOMEM HK2  840A  919A   TH
2 UA 219Y 13JAN MEMSAN HK2 1025A  223P   TH
3 UA 418Y 16JAN SANORD HK2  120P  705P   SU
4 US 624Y 16JAN ORDGSO HK2  759P 1154P   SU
```

Let's say your client inquires about hotels in San Diego, after segment 2. Two adults will be staying three nights. Based on this information, availability may be requested as follows:

/2‡HOA3NT2

When this entry is used, Apollo assumes the check-in date will be the same as the travel date in the indicated segment. The destination city (SAN) is also repeated from the air segment. Apollo responds as follows:

```
  HTL SAN              IN 13JAN-OUT 16JAN  3NT 2ADULT
 1 HI AIRPORT INN       6 SAN A 1922 ARPT BLVD      - 2NCC
  ]HOD6627   A2D-18900   A1D-149000   S1K-20000
 2 RA AIRPORT PLAZA     6 SAN A 2100 ARPT BLVD      - 4NCC
  ]HOD0615   A1D-11900   B1K-10900    B2D-9900
```

Observe that the availability display is almost the same as the hotel index, with one important difference: A second line is added to each listing, showing the various room types and rates available on the arrival date.

The new line begins with HOD, followed by the property code. This code may be used to obtain a detailed description of the hotel. The remainder of the listing is devoted to room types and rates.

Copyright © 1990 by Glencoe/McGraw-Hill Educational Division. All rights reserved.

Room Types and Rates

In general, most room rates are based on the room category and bedding. The following codes may be used to indicate various room categories:

Room Categories

A Deluxe (maximum rate)
B Superior (moderate rate)
C Standard (economy rate)
D Substandard (minimum rate)
S Suite

A bedding code is used with the room category to indicate the number and size of beds. For instance, 1K refers to a room with one king-size bed, and 2D refers to a room with two double beds. The following examples illustrate the common bedding codes found in an Apollo hotel index.

Common Bedding Codes

1K One king-size bed
1Q One queen-size bed
2K Two king-size beds
2Q Two queen-size beds
2D Two double beds
2T Two twin beds

The category and bedding code are combined to designate the room type. For example, A1K refers to a deluxe room with one king-size bed, and B2D refers to a superior room with two double beds.

Examples of Common Room Types

A1K Deluxe room/one king-size bed
A2Q Deluxe room/two queen-size beds
B1K Superior room/one king-size bed
B2Q Superior room/two queen-size beds
B2D Superior room/two double beds
C1Q Standard room/one queen-size bed
C2T Standard room/two twin beds
S2K Suite with two king-size beds
COR Corporate rate room
TUR Tour rate room

Availability with Different City

When the hotel city differs from the destination point in the preceding air segment, a slightly different format must be used:

Format:
    /<Segment to Follow>‡HOA<City><Nights>NT<Adults>

Example:

    /1‡HOASTS6NT2

Copyright © 1990 by Glencoe/McGraw-Hill Educational Division. All rights reserved.

The entry in the example above requests availability in Santa Rosa, California (STS), after segment 1.

Example

Assume a client will travel from Seattle to Los Angeles, but would like hotel accommodations in Long Beach (LGB). A five-night stay is planned, and two adults are traveling. Let's say that Los Angeles is the destination city in segment 2; the following data is required to obtain hotel availability in the requested city:

Segment to follow:	2
City:	LGB
Nights:	5NT
Adults:	2

Based on this information, the following entry may be used:

    /2‡HOALGB5NT2

Availability Without an Air Itinerary

When there is no itinerary in the agent's work area, a different format must be used to obtain hotel availability:

Format:
    HOA<In Date>–<Nights>NT<City><Adults>

Example:

    HOA10DEC-7NTNAS2

The entry in the example above requests hotel availability in Nassau, Bahamas (NAS), with check-in on the 10th of December for a seven-night stay for two adults.

Example

Assume a client inquires about hotels in Ft. Lauderdale on the 17th of January. Two travelers will be staying five nights. The following data is required to display availability:

In date:	17JAN
Nights:	5NT
City:	FLL
Adults:	2

Based on this information, the following entry may be used:

    HOA17JAN-5NTFLL2

Any entry used to display the hotel index or date availability may include optional qualifiers, as in the following example:

    HOA10MAY-2NTSFO2A

This entry requests hotel availability in the airport (A) area. Observe that the location indicator must be placed at the end of the entry, after the number of adults.

Copyright © 1990 by Glencoe/McGraw-Hill Educational Division. All rights reserved.

CHECK-IN: A STUDY AID

I. Write the correct code or description requested.

1. Give the correct meaning for each hotel location code:

C _____

R _____

S _____

A _____

2. Give the correct meaning for each transportation code:

L _____

OT _____

CC _____

3. Give the correct room code for each category:

_____ Deluxe room with two queen-size beds

_____ Standard room with one double bed

_____ Deluxe room with one king-size bed

_____ Superior room with one king-size bed

_____ Suite with two king-size beds

_____ Standard room with two queen-size beds

II. Write the correct hotel entry for each situation.

1. You are making travel arrangements for a client planning a vacation in St. Croix. What entry will display the hotel index?

_____

2. What entry will display the hotel index for Orlando, Florida?

_____

3. Write the correct entry to display the hotel index for Denver hotels near the airport. _____

4. What entry will display the hotel index for St. Louis hotels near the city center? _____

5. Write the entry to display the hotel index for Marriott properties in Chicago.

_____

6. Write the entry to display the hotel index for Hilton properties in Seattle.

_____

7. Display hotel availability after segment 1 for a three-night stay for one adult.

_____

Copyright © 1990 by Glencoe/McGraw-Hill Educational Division. All rights reserved.

8. Display hotel availability after segment 4 for a five-night stay for two adults.

_____

9. Display hotel availability in San Jose, California, after segment 2 for a two-night stay for one adult. _____

10. Display hotel availability in Tuscon without an air itinerary, checking in on the 12th of June, for a five-night stay for two adults.

_____

11. Display hotel availability for the arrival city of the last air segment booked.

_____

12. Display hotel availability after segment 4. _____

13. Display hotel availability after segment 3 for a five-night stay for two adults.

_____

14. Display hotel availability after segment 2 for a two-night stay for one adult.

_____

HOTEL DESCRIPTIONS

When the hotel index is displayed, a description may be obtained for a particular property using the following format:

Format:

    HOD<Property Code>

Example:

    HOD6039

The property code is given at the beginning of the second line of each listing in the hotel availability display.

Example

Assume you just obtained the date availability display partially shown below.

```
  HTL SFO              IN 18JUL-OUT 21JUL  3NT 1ADULT
1 HI GOLDEN GATE               SFO C 202 BAY BLVD  -18NCC
]HOD3233   A2Q-18900   A1K-189000      S2K-20000
2 HI FISHERMANS WHARF         SFO C 1432     C ST       -14NCC
]HOD5042   A1K-14900   B2K-12900      B2Q-10900
```

Let's say your client inquires about the Holiday Inn at Fisherman's Wharf (line 2), but would like to know more about the property. To display the hotel description, the following entry may be used:

Copyright © 1990 by Glencoe/McGraw-Hill Educational Division. All rights reserved.

HOD5042

A keyword may be added to the entry to display a specific subject from the hotel description. For example, assume you wish to display the guarantee policy for property 773. The following entry may be used:

HOD773/GUARANTEE

Apollo responds by displaying the desired subject as follows:

```
POLICY:
    CREDIT CARDS--AX CA CB DC
    GUARANTEE--BUSINESS NAME AND ADDRESS OR
    1 NIGHT DEPOSIT OR
    CREDIT CARD WITH EXP DATE AND CARDHOLDERS NAME AND
    ADDRESS
```

To display the available room types, the following entry may be used:

HOD773/ROOM

Response:

```
ROOM   ROLLAWAY   MAX IN
TYPE   ALLOWED    ROOM     COMMENTS:
A1K       1         3
B2T       1         3
C1Q       1         3
C2D       1         3
```

The following variation would display charges for room extras and options:

HOD773/CHARGES

Response:

```
ADDITIONAL ROOM CHARGES:
    ROLLAWAY      ADULT RA1000   CHILD RC0000   CRIB CR0000
    EXTRA PERSON        EX1000
```

Copyright © 1990 by Glencoe/McGraw-Hill Educational Division. All rights reserved.

The facilities description may be displayed by the following entry:

HOD773/FACILITIES

Response:

```
FACILITIES - 405 ROOMS MEETING FACILITIES  RESTAURANT
    COLOR TV LOUNGE COFFEE SHOP FREE PARKING
OTHER - PETS ACCEPTED ENTERTAINMENT DANCING
```

SELLING HOTEL SPACE

Hotel space may be sold from a date availability display by using of the following format:

Format:
0<Rooms><Room Type><Line>

Example:

01A1K1

Segment:	0
Number of rooms:	1
Room type:	A1K
Line:	1

The line number refers to the line in the availability display corresponding to the desired property. The entry in the example above books one room at the A1K rate at the property listed in line 1.

Example
Assume you are making travel arrangements for a client with the following itinerary:

```
1 DL 654Y 13AUG MIAIND HK1 1115A  232P   MO
2 DL 449Y 15AUG INDMIA HK1  207P  510P   WE
```

Let's say he prefers the Marriott chain. He plans a two-night stay in Indianapolis after segment 1. The following entry may be used to display availability:

/1‡HOA2NT1MC

Copyright © 1990 by Glencoe/McGraw-Hill Educational Division. All rights reserved.

Assume Apollo responds as follows:

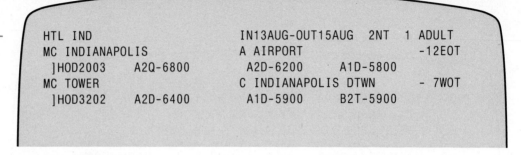

```
HTL IND                          IN13AUG-OUT15AUG  2NT  1 ADULT
MC INDIANAPOLIS                  A AIRPORT                  -12EOT
  ]HOD2003    A2Q-6800           A2D-6200      A1D-5800
MC TOWER                         C INDIANAPOLIS DTWN        - 7WOT
  ]HOD3202    A2D-6400           A1D-5900      B2T-5900
```

Let's say your client decides on the Marriott Tower (line 2). He requests a room with two double beds at the $64.00 rate. The following entry may be used to book the hotel space:

01A2D2

In this entry, the room type A2D specifies the accommodations available with two double beds.

Apollo responds by booking the hotel segment as follows:

```
2 HHL MC HK1 IND 13AUG-OUT15AUG  2NT 3202 MC TOWER
  1A2D-2/6400/AGT03543456/G-DPST/CF-83967211001
```

Before proceeding, let us examine the hotel segment in detail. Apollo labels the segment HHL to indicate a hotel reservation and gives the chain code (MC) and number of rooms confirmed, preceded by the status/action code. Following the city, the in and out dates and the number of nights are repeated.

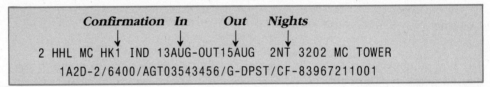

```
     Confirmation  In     Out    Nights
           ↓        ↓       ↓       ↓
2 HHL MC HK1 IND 13AUG-OUT15AUG  2NT 3202 MC TOWER
  1A2D-2/6400/AGT03543456/G-DPST/CF-83967211001
```

The property number and name are also listed in the hotel segment—followed by the room code and number of adults. Apollo automatically adds the agency's identifying ARC (or IATA) number.

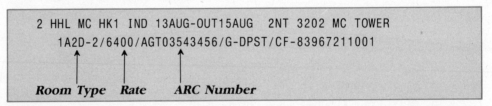

```
2 HHL MC HK1 IND 13AUG-OUT15AUG  2NT 3202 MC TOWER
  1A2D-2/6400/AGT03543456/G-DPST/CF-83967211001
  ↑        ↑        ↑
Room Type  Rate    ARC Number
```

When a confirmation number (CF) is received from the hotel, it will be added at the end of the segment.

Guarantee Information

Many hotels will only accept travel agency bookings if the reservation is accompanied by some form of guarantee. The guarantee information should be included when the space is booked. The modifier G- is used to include guarantee information when the hotel space is booked. The following entry illustrates a hotel reservation guaranteed to a credit card number:

Copyright © 1990 by Glencoe/McGraw-Hill Educational Division. All rights reserved.

The most common forms of guarantee are a valid credit card number (with account number, expiration date, and cardholder name) or the travel agency's ARC/IATA number. A cash deposit may also be required, especially when booking space at Caribbean, Hawaiian, or other overseas resorts. Some hotels (economy chains) may accept the company, client, or agency address to guarantee the reservation. In the absence of any other form of guarantee, most participating properties will assume the reservation is guaranteed by the agency's ARC/IATA number.

Room Options

Most hotels are capable of fulfilling room option requests, such as rollaway beds or infant cribs. The following codes are used to request room options:

EX	Extra adult
RA	Rollaway bed (adult)
RC	Rollaway bed (child)
CR	Crib

The following format is used to request a room option in a hotel segment:

Format:

<Basic Entry>/<Option>–<Number>

Example:

01A1K1/EX-1

Basic entry:	01A1K1
Slash:	/
Option code:	EX
Dash:	-
Number:	1

The entry in the example above stipulates an extra guest (i.e., a third adult) staying in the same room. If a rollaway bed is also required, the following entry may be used instead:

01A1K1/EX-1/RA-1

CHECK-IN: A STUDY AID

Write the correct hotel entry for each situation.

1. Display a description of the property number 943.

   _____

2. Display a description of hotel guarantee policies for property number 6723.

   _____

Copyright © 1990 by Glencoe/McGraw-Hill Educational Division. All rights reserved.

3. When hotel availability is displayed, what entry will sell one room at the B2Q rate at a property listed in line 2? _____

4. What entry will sell three standard rooms with one double bed at a hotel listed in line 5?

_____

5. What entry will sell two superior rooms with two queen-size beds at a hotel listed in line 3?

_____

6. Assume the following partial hotel index is displayed:

```
    HTL ICT              IN 12APR-OUT 15APR  3NT 1ADULT
1 HH TOWER               6 ICT S 2400 E MAIN DRAG      -18ECC
]HOD0546   A2Q-8900      A1K-8900    B2Q-7800
2 BW VILLAGE INN         6 ICT S 1430 E 14TH ST        -14ECC
]HOD0411   B2Q-7900      B1Q-7500    B2D-6900
```

a. What entry would sell one room for one adult at the $69.00 rate at the Best Western Village Inn? _____

b. What entry would sell three rooms with one king-size bed with one adult per room at the Hilton Tower? _____

c. What entry would display a description of the Hilton?

_____

7. Refer to the following hotel segment to answer the questions below:

```
3 HHL HI HK1 BOI 12JUN-OUT18JUN  6NT 0232 BOISE HI
  1C2D-2/6400/AGT03543456/G-BA483000928732110EXP794/
  CF-4F56598
```

a. To what chain does the property belong?

_____

b. On what date will the client be checking into the hotel?

_____

Copyright © 1990 by Glencoe/McGraw-Hill Educational Division. All rights reserved.

   c. How many nights will the client be staying at the hotel?

        _____

   d. What type of bedding is provided in the room?

        _____

   e. What is the room rate at which the room has been booked?

        _____

   f. What is the hotel confirmation number?

        _____

8. Assume a hotel index is displayed and you wish to book a room at the B2D rate at a property in line 2. Your client wishes to guarantee the room to his credit card number BA434659870917863; the expiration date is July 1994. Write the correct entry to book the hotel space.

_____

9. What entry will book a standard room with two double beds from a property in line 3, with an extra guest in the room?

_____

10. Assume you wish to book a superior room with one king-size bed at a property in line 2. An extra guest will be staying in the room, requiring a rollaway bed for an adult. Write the correct entry to sell the hotel space.

_____

11. Assume you wish to book a deluxe room with two queen-size beds at a property in line 3. A child's rollaway bed is requested. Write the correct entry to sell the space. _____

12. What entry would be used to request a crib, instead of a child's rollaway bed, in question 11 above? _____

MODIFYING A HOTEL SEGMENT

On occasion, a client may call to request a change in a hotel reservation that was previously booked in a PNR. A special entry may be used to make modifications without having to cancel and rebook the segment. The following entry may be used to modify room information about a hotel segment:

Format:

    HOM<Segment>R/<New Data>

Example:

    HOM2R/1B2T-1

Copyright © 1990 by Glencoe/McGraw-Hill Educational Division. All rights reserved.

Modify hotel segment:	HOM
Segment:	2
Room:	R/
New data:	1B2T-1

The example above modifies the room information to one room at the B2T rate for one adult. Observe that the new data is entered exactly as it should appear in the hotel segment.

Example

Assume you wish to change a hotel reservation in segment 4 of a travel itinerary. Your client has currently booked two rooms at the B2D rate with two adults per room. Two clients have canceled, and your client now wants two rooms at the B1D rate, with one adult per room.

The following data is required to modify the hotel segment:

Segment:	4
Room:	R/
New data:	2B1D-1

Based on this information, the following entry may be used:

    HOM4R/2B1D-1

Modifying Room Options

To modify the room options requested in a hotel segment, the following format may be used:

Format:
    HOM<Segment>O/<New Data>

Example:
    HOM2O/EX-1/RA-1

DIRECT BOOKINGS

Lodging reservations are often booked directly with the hotel (i.e., by phone) to ensure confirmation and obtain the best available rate. A direct booking should be entered in the PNR as a "passive" hotel segment, so that it will appear on the printed itinerary. To enter a direct booking, the following format may be used:

Format:
    0HTLZZBK<Rooms><City><In-Out>/W–<Property Address and Phone>

Example:
    0HTLZZBK1BOSIN20APR-OUT21APR/W-SHERATON AIRPORT INN☐BOSTON
    ☐617 555-0192

The example above records one room booked directly with the hotel. The hotel city is Boston. The client will check in on 20APR and out on 21APR. The property is the Sheraton Airport Inn. The use of the address code W– causes the hotel address and phone to be printed on the passenger itinerary/invoice that accompanies the ticket coupons. Observe that the code ZZ is always used in place of a hotel chain code.

Copyright © 1990 by Glencoe/McGraw-Hill Educational Division. All rights reserved.

If the hotel address and phone are not entered, any free-form text up to 43 characters in length may be included instead. The text may be used for the room type, rate, and confirmation number.

CANCELING HOTEL SPACE

To cancel a hotel reservation booked through Apollo, simply cancel the corresponding segment(s) in the itinerary. For example, to cancel a hotel reservation in segment 3, the following entry may be used:

    X3

If the reservation was booked directly with the hotel and afterward entered in the PNR itinerary, a CSS entry must be made to cancel the reservation. The status/action code XK is used, as in the following example:

    .2XK

This entry changes the status of segment 2 to XK, telling Apollo to remove the direct booking from the itinerary.

CHECK-IN: A STUDY AID

Write the correct hotel entry for each situation.

1. Modify a hotel reservation in segment 2, changing the room information to one deluxe room with two queen-size beds for two adults. ___HOM2R/1A2Q-2___

2. Modify segment 6 to change the room information to four standard rooms, with one double bed for one adult in each. ___HOM6R/4C1D-1___

3. Modify segment 4 to change the room information to one superior room with one king-size bed for one adult. ___HOM4R/1B1K-1___

4. Modify segment 3 to change the option information to one child's rollaway bed. ___HOM3O/RC-1___

5. Assume you previously booked a hotel reservation in segment 5. Your clients now request a crib. What entry will modify the reservation to add the option request? ___HOM5O/CR-1___

6. Assume you previously booked a hotel reservation in segment 3. Your clients request a rollaway bed for an extra guest. Write the correct entry to modify the reservation. ___HOM3O/RA-1___

7. What entry will cancel a hotel reservation in segment 2? ___X2___

Copyright © 1990 by Glencoe/McGraw-Hill Educational Division. All rights reserved.

CHAPTER 14
APOLLO CAR RENTALS

CHAPTER OBJECTIVES

At the end of the chapter, you should be able to perform the following tasks:

- Identify common car type codes.
- Display car availability by segment.
- Display car availability by pickup date, city, and rate type.
- Book a car rental from a car availability display.
- Interpret a car segment.
- Book a car rental without an air itinerary.
- Enter optional service information in a car booking.
- Modify a car segment.
- Display vendor policies and information.
- Display a car rate quote.
- Modify a car rate quote.
- Display comparative rates.
- Sell a car rental from a rate quote.

Copyright © 1990 by Glencoe/McGraw-Hill Educational Division. All rights reserved.

Problem

You are making travel arrangements for a client planning a ski trip to the Denver area. He would like to rent a car at the airport for pickup on arrival and wants to know what company offers the lowest daily rate for a station wagon with a ski rack.

Apollo Solution

Display car availability at the airport in DEN, then obtain a rate quote for a station wagon. Book the car rental, and request a ski rack. This chapter describes how to utilize the Apollo car rental program.

CAR RENTAL CHAINS

Each car rental company that participates in the Apollo computer reservation system is identified by a two-letter code. When a car reservation is requested, both the car type and the rental chain must be specified. The following are examples of car company codes for major participating chains:

Major Car Company Codes

ZE	Hertz
ZI	Avis
ZL	National
ZN	General
ZR	Dollar
ZD	Budget
TR	Tropical

CAR TYPES

Rental vehicles are divided into distinct categories, each identified by a four-letter car type code. Apollo recognizes the following car type codes:

Car Type Codes

ECMR	Economy car with manual transmission
ECAR	Economy car with automatic transmission
CCAR	Compact car

188

Copyright © 1990 by Glencoe/McGraw-Hill Educational Division. All rights reserved.

ICAR	Intermediate size car
SCAR	Standard size car
SWGN	Station wagon
LCAR	Luxury car
SPCL	Special order

CAR AVAILABILITY

When an itinerary is in the agent's work area, car availability may be displayed for any segment of the trip. The car availability entry has the following format:

Format:

/<Segment to Follow>‡CAA

Example:

/2‡CAA

The example above requests rental car availability after segment 2. This entry requests the daily rate, based on the date and arrival city that appear in the specified segment.

Example

Assume you are working with a PNR that contains the following itinerary:

```
1 TW 330Y 16DEC STLMIA HK1  515P  808P    TU
2 TW 512Y 20DEC MIASTL HK1 1030A  352P    S
```

Let's say your client inquires about rental cars at the Miami airport after the outbound trip (segment 1). The following entry may be used to display car availability:

/1‡CAA

Apollo responds by displaying a screen of car types and rental companies at the destination airport.

	A TR-TROPICAL		B ZE-HERTZ		C ZL-NATL		D ZD-BUDGET	
DAILY RATE	SPI	ON	SPI	ON	SPI	ON	SPI	ON
1. ECMR	--		--		2995		2995	
2. ECAR	2750		33/20		3300		3195	
3. CCAR	3550		35/20		3700		3500	
4. ICAR	4050		44/20		4500		2900	
5. SCAR	4550		53/20		5300		4195	
6. LCAR	6550		65/20		6700		4995	
7. SWGN	5050		53/20		4500		4195	

Each line of the car availability table is numbered. The car types are listed on the left. Each column in the table corresponds to a car company. In each column, the

Copyright © 1990 by Glencoe/McGraw-Hill Educational Division. All rights reserved.

company's daily rate is shown for each car type. Observe that the decimal point is omitted in the rate display. If a mileage charge applies, the basic rate and charge-per-mile are separated by /.

In the example above, an economy car from Tropical rents for $27.50 per day (unlimited mileage); the same car type from Hertz rents for $33.00 per day plus 20 cents per mile. (These rates are hypothetical and for illustration only. They should be not be construed as the actual rates offered by any of the car companies.)

When car availability is requested with the format above, Apollo uses the destination city and travel date shown in the specified segment. If the pickup date and point differ from the arrival information in the itinerary, or if there is no air itinerary in the agent's work area, the following format must be used instead:

Format:
    CAA<Pickup Date><Pickup City>

Example:

    CAA10MAYSFO

Car availability: CAA
Pickup date: 10MAY
City: SFO

Example
Assume you are making travel arrangements for a client who has the following itinerary:

```
1 UA 105F 18AUG SFOORD HK1   810A   224P     FR
2 UA 890Y 18AUG SFODSM HK1   653P   940P     FR
3 ARNK
4 UA 245F  4SEP ORDSFO HK1   653P   940P     MO
```

Suppose the passenger inquires about a car rental after the outbound trip (segment 2). He would like to pick up the vehicle on August 22 in Minneapolis. The following entry may be used to display car availability for this client:

    CAA22AUGMSP

Specifying a Rate Category or Vendor

The basic car availability entry assumes the daily rate is desired. A different rate category may specified as follows:

    CAA22AUGMSP-W

This entry requests the weekly W rate. The rate code may be one of the following:

Copyright © 1990 by Glencoe/McGraw-Hill Educational Division. All rights reserved.

Rate Codes

W	Weekly
E	Weekend
S	Special

Besides the rate category, a vendor may also be specified as in the following example:

CAA31JUNORD/ZD

This entry requests availability from Budget Rent-a-Car ZD. Both the rate and vendor may be specified in one entry, as follows:

CAA31JUNORD/ZD-W

This entry requests the weekly rates offered by Budget.

SELLING FROM AVAILABILITY

After car availability has been obtained, the following format may be used to book a reservation:

Format:
0<Column><Line>–<Return Date>

Example:

0A2-17MAR

Segment:	0
Column:	A
Line:	2
Return Date:	-17MAR

The column letter refers to the desired car company. The line number refers to the desired car type. Apollo assumes that one car will be rented.

Example

Assume you just obtained the car availability table partially displayed below:

DAILY RATE	A ZE-HERTZ LAX ON	B ZI-AVIS LAX ON	C ZR-DOLLAR LAX ON	D ZD-BUDGET LAX ON
1. ECAR	2995	2995	2750	3000
2. CCAR	3495	3395	3000	3295
3. ICAR	3995	3695	3600	3995
4. SCAR	4800	4400	3995	4300

Copyright © 1990 by Glencoe/McGraw-Hill Educational Division. All rights reserved.

Let's say your client would like to book a standard size car from Avis at the $44.00 daily rate. Avis ZI is the car company in column B, and SCAR is the car type in line 4. Your client plans to return the car at the airport on the 23rd of July.

Based on this information, the following entry may be used to book the reservation:

    0B4-23JUL

Apollo responds by booking the car segment as follows:

    3CAR ZI SS1 ORD21JUL-23JUL/AGT-4665545/CF-

In this example, the car reservation becomes segment 3 in the passenger itinerary. Apollo repeats the car company and shows the number of cars booked, preceded by the status/action code. Here, the code SS indicates that the reservation will be confirmed when the PNR is ended. The pickup location (the same as the arrival city in the previous air segment) is also shown. The pickup date is the same as the arrival date in the previous air segment.

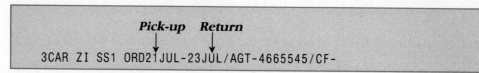

In every car segment, Apollo automatically inserts the agency's ARC/IATA number. The car company will supply a confirmation number (CF), which will be inserted at the end of the car segment.

Apollo booked one car because the number of cars was not specified. If more than one car is required, the number should be included before the column letter as follows:

    02B4-23JUL

This entry books two cars from the car rental company in column B, confirming the car type in line 4.

DIRECT-SELLING CAR RENTALS

A long or direct-sell entry may also be used to book a car rental without an availability display. With an air itinerary in the agent's work area, the following entry may be used:

Format:

    /<Segment>‡0CAR<Company>–<Return Date><Type>

Example:

    /1‡0CARZD-23AUGECAR

Insert after segment:	/1
End-Item:	‡
Car segment:	0CAR
Car company:	ZD
Return date:	23AUG
Car type:	ECAR

Copyright © 1990 by Glencoe/McGraw-Hill Educational Division. All rights reserved.

Example

Assume you are making travel arrangements for a client who has the following itinerary:

```
1 DL 575Y 11MAR DFWLAS HK2  1145A 1214A    FR
2 DL 748Y 15MAR LASDFW HK2  1120A  348P    TU
```

Let's say your client requests a car rental in Las Vegas, after segment 1. He would like a luxury car from Avis, to be returned at the airport on the 15th of March. The following information is required to book the reservation:

Segment to follow:	1
Car company:	ZI
Return date:	15MAR
Car type:	LCAR

Based on this data, the following entry may be used:

```
/1‡0CARZI-15MARLCAR
```

Technically, the return date is optional but should be included in every car rental reservation.

BOOKING CAR RENTALS WITHOUT AN AIR ITINERARY

To book a car rental without an air itinerary, the following format must be used:

Format:

0CAR<Company><City><Pickup Date>–<Return Date><Car Type>

Example:

```
0CARZIMIA7APR-12APRECAR
```

Car segment:	0CAR
Car company:	ZI
City:	MIA
Pickup date:	7APR
Return date:	-12APR
Car type:	ECAR

OPTIONAL DATA

Any entry which may be used to sell a car segment may include certain optional data. As an example, consider the following entry:

```
0C1-10MAY/PUP-DOWNTOWN/DO-LAX/ID-1233456
```

The optional data may be broken down as follows:

Different pickup location:	/PUP-DOWNTOWN
Different drop-off location:	/DO-LAX
Customer ID-number:	/ID-1233456

Copyright © 1990 by Glencoe/McGraw-Hill Educational Division. All rights reserved.

Here, the pickup (PUP) location is other than the airport, but the drop-off (DO) point is LAX. The customer's car company ID number (ID) is also included in the entry.

Other optional data codes include the following:

ARR	Arrival information
W●	Written confirmation
CD	Corporate discount number
RT	Rate input by agent (not guaranteed)
IR	Itinerary remarks
PH	Outlet phone number
SI●	Service information

CHECK-IN: A STUDY AID

NOTES TO STUDENT AFTER OPTIONAL DATA CODES BE SURE TO ADD !

I. *Write the correct code or interpretation requested.*

1. Give the correct car type code for each description:

SCAR	Standard car with automatic transmission and air
LCAR	Luxury car with automatic transmission and air
ECAR	Compact car with automatic transmission and air
ECAM	Economy car with manual transmission and air
ECAR	Economy car with automatic transmission and air
ICAR	Intermediate car with automatic transmission and air
S	Special request
SWGN	Station wagon with automatic transmission and air

2. Give the correct meaning of each rate type.

E _weekend_
W _weekly_
S _special_

3. Give the correct code for each item of optional data.

PUP -	Pick-up location (other than airport)
SI -	Service information or request
segment #	Arrival carrier, flight, and time
PH -	Outlet phone number
W -	Written confirmation

Copyright © 1990 by Glencoe/McGraw-Hill Educational Division. All rights reserved.

II. *Write the correct car entry for each situation.*

1. Assume you wish to display car availability in the arrival city of the last air segment booked. What entry would you use?

   CAA

2. How would you display car availability after segment 5?

   /5#CAA

3. What entry displays car availability from Budget after segment 2?

   /2#CAA/ZD

4. Write the entry to display car availability on April 14 in Orlando.

   CAA14APRMCO

5. Assume you would like to sell an economy car from column C, line 2 of the availability display. Your client will return it on August 26. What entry would you use? OC2-26AUG

6. How would you sell a standard car from column A, line 4 for drop-off on January 12? OA4-12JAN

7. Assume the following partial car availability table is displayed:

	A	B	C	D
DAILY	ZE-HERTZ	ZI-AVIS	ZD-BUDGET	TR-TROPICAL
RATE	FLL ON	FLL ON	FLL ON	FLL ON
1. ECMR	4995	4375	4750	4550
2. ECAR	5495	4375	4900	4700
3. CCAR	5900	5475	5200	5995
4. SCAR	6200	5950	5400	6200

   a. What is the daily rate for a standard-size automobile from Budget?

      54.00

   b. Which vendor offers an economy car with manual transmission for a daily rate of $43.75 in this hypothetical example?

      ZI -AVIS

   c. What entry would sell a compact car from Tropical for drop-off on the 23rd of April?

      OD3-23APR

Copyright © 1990 by Glencoe/McGraw-Hill Educational Division. All rights reserved.

d. What entry would sell an economy car with an automatic transmission from Hertz for drop-off on the 27th of April?

O CARZE -27APRECAR

e. What entry would sell a standard size car from Avis for drop-off on May 2? _O CARZI - 2MAYSCAR_

8. Refer to the following car segment to answer the questions below:

    3CAR ZI SS1 ORD21JUL-23JUL/AGT-4665545/CF-9Q2327861

a. What car company has confirmed the reservation?

ZI - AVIS

b. In what city will the vehicle be picked up?

CHICAGO

c. What is the drop-off date? _23 JUL_

d. What is the confirmation number provided by the car rental office?

_9Q2327861_

CARMASTER

The CarMaster Program is an enhanced version of the basic Apollo car rental program. In addition to the standard formats for availability and selling, CarMaster provides the following options to facilitate accessing and booking car rentals:

CAQ	Availability with rate quotation
CAL	Availability with low-to-high rates
CAV	Rules
CAU	Car availability update
/	Fill-in format

Qualified Car Availability

Apollo refers to a car rate quotation as a qualified availability display. The command code CAQ is used to obtain a rate quotation as follows:

Format:

    /<Segment>‡CAQ–<Return Date>

Example:

    /1‡CAQ-15MAY

A specified car type may be included in the entry:

    /2‡CAQ-21JUL.C

In this entry, C is used to request the rate for compact cars. Observe that a period . separates the return date and the car type.

Copyright © 1990 by Glencoe/McGraw-Hill Educational Division. All rights reserved.

Example

197

CarMaster

Assume you are making travel arrangements for a client whose PNR is currently in your work area. Your client would like to know the rates for intermediate size cars at the destination city in the last segment booked. He plans to return the car on the 19th of October. The following entry may be used to obtain the rate quotation:

```
CAQ-19OCT. I
```

Response:

```
SAN FRANCISCO    CA      * WEEKEND  - STAND/PROMO  * USD
  A:       HERTZ*     TERMINAL    B:      AVIS*      TERMINAL
        A R     RATE  MI   CHG        A R     RATE  MI   CHG
 1.EMAN S Q    39.99 100  .25   EMAN S G    37.00 100  .25
 2.ECAR N G    42.99 100  .25   ECAR C G    39.00 100  .25
 3.ECAR S G    49.99 150  .35   ECAR S G    44.00 100  .25
 4.ECAR S G    52.99 UNL  .00   ECAR S G    49.00 UNL  .00
```

The qualified availability display includes rate information for each car company and location. Each vendor location is identified by letter. Here, A: indicates Hertz, and B: indicates Avis, both airport terminal locations. Rate lines are numbered on the left.

```
  A:       HERTZ*     TERMINAL    B:      AVIS*      TERMINAL
        A R     RATE  MI   CHG        A R     RATE  MI   CHG
 1.EMAN S Q    39.99 100  .25   EMAN S G    37.00 100  .25
       ↗  ↑
   Status   Quoted/Guaranteed
```

To the right of the car type are two codes. The code in the column labeled A indicates the availability status: S (sell), N (need), or C (closed). The code in column labeled R indicates whether the rate is available on a guaranteed or quoted basis.

```
  A:       HERTZ*     TERMINAL    B:      AVIS*      TERMINAL
        A R     RATE  MI   CHG        A R     RATE  MI   CHG
 1.EMAN S Q    39.99 100  .25   EMAN S G    37.00 100  .25
                 ↗     ↑     ↑
              Rate  Allowance  Excess Mileage Charge
```

To the right of the rate are the mileage allowance and excess mileage charge. (UNL in the mileage column indicates unlimited mileage.) Here, Hertz allows 100 free miles at the $39.99 rate, with a .25 per mile charge for excess mileage.

Paging the Display

Because the screen size is limited, viewing all the information in a car quotation requires paging the display. The term *paging* refers to moving the display ver-

Copyright © 1990 by Glencoe/McGraw-Hill Educational Division. All rights reserved.

tically or horizontally so that more information is viewed. The following commands may be used to page the qualified availability display:

CAQ*PR	Page right
CAQ*PL	Page left
CAQ*PD	Page down
CAQ*PU	Page up
CAQ*PH	Page home

Selling from a Rate Quotation

To sell a car segment from a qualified availability display, the following format may be used:

Format:

0<Column><Line>

Example:

0A1

The column refers to the letter corresponding to the desired vendor. The line refers to the line number corresponding to the desired rate.

Example

Assume you have just obtained the following qualified availability display:

```
A:      BUDGET    TERMINAL        B:   DOLLAR    TERMINAL
        A R    RATE  MI  CHG           A R    RATE  MI  CHG
1.CCAR  N Q   26.95 100 .35      CCAR  S G   29.95 150 .30
2.CCAR  S G   34.95 100 .30      CCAR  S G   34.95 150 .30
3.CCAR  S G   39.95 100 .30      CCAR  S G   39.95 UNL .00
4.CDAR  S G   49.95 100 .35
```

Let's say your client chooses a compact car offered by Dollar at the $39.95 rate with unlimited mileage. The following entry may be used to book the car rental:

0B3

Low-to-High Availability

To display car availability with low-to-high rates, use the command code CAL as follows:

Format:

/<Segment>‡CAL–<Return Date>

Example:

/1‡CAL-15MAY

An optional car type may be specified in the entry. For example, assume you are working with the itinerary below:

Copyright © 1990 by Glencoe/McGraw-Hill Educational Division. All rights reserved.

```
1 CO 344Y 21AUG SFOIAH HK1    845A 1215P    TH
2 CO 382Y 21AUG IAHMSY HK1    122P 218P     TH
3 CO 399Y 25AUG MSYSFO HK1    100P 445P     MO
```

Let's say your client requests a car rental in New Orleans. She plans to pick up the car at the airport on arrival and return the vehicle on August 25th and she would like the lowest rates available for a compact car. The following entry may be used to display low-to-high availability:

   /2‡CAL-25AUG.C

Response:

```
NEW ORLEANS AIR LA       * WEEKLY - STAND/PROMO *   USD
A:          A R TYPE   RATE    MI  CHG  LOC ADVB  MIN  RC
1.THRIFTY N G CCAR    29.99   UNL  .00   T    7    1   ACCMP
2.NATL    S G CCAR    29.99   UNL  .00   O    3    1   SXZ
3.DOLLAR  S G CCAR    32.50   UNL  .00   O    7    3   922
4.BUDGET  S G CCAR    34.95   UNL  .00   T    7    5   COMPZD
5.AVIS    S G CCAR    37.99   UNL  .00   T    7    1   G1
```

Apollo displays the rates for compact cars available for your client's destination and travel dates, priced from lowest to highest. To the right of the excess mileage charge are several codes that do not appear in the qualified display.

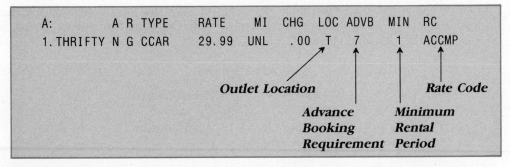

Each vendor/rate line shows the location, advance booking requirement, minimum rental period, and the car company rate code. This location is at the airport ter-

Copyright © 1990 by Glencoe/McGraw-Hill Educational Division. All rights reserved.

minal (T). The rental must be booked seven days in advance for at least a one-day period to obtain this rate.

The following location codes may appear in the low-to-high display:

Location Codes

T	Terminal
O	Off-airport
C	City
R	Resort
N	North suburban
E	East suburban
S	South suburban
W	West suburban

Specifying a Location

Unless a location is specified, Apollo will display only airport terminal and off-airport locations. To request a particular location, add the code to the end of the entry as in the following example:

```
/1‡CAL-15MAYC
```

This entry requests city locations C.

Specifying a Vendor

A vendor may be specified in any CAQ or CAL entry:

```
/1‡CAQ-15MAYT.E/ZE
```

Observe that a slash / separates the vendor code from the remainder of the entry. Here, a car type E has also been specified.

Multiple Car Types

To request rates for multiple car types, use the End-Item key ‡ to separate the car type codes as follows:

```
/1‡CAQ-15MAY.E‡C
```

The car code may consist of one to four letters, indicating the size, category, type of transmission, and air conditioning. For example, SWAR indicates a standard wagon with automatic transmission and air conditioning. The code may consist of one or more of the following elements:

Car Code Elements

	Size		Category	Transmission		A/C	
E	Economy	C	Car	M	Manual	N	No A/C
C	Compact	S	Sport	A	Automatic	R	A/C
I	Intermediate	T	Convertible				
S	Standard	W	Wagon				
L	Luxury	V	Van				
*	Any size	*	Any category				

The following examples illustrate various combinations of car code elements in a CAL entry.

Copyright © 1990 by Glencoe/McGraw-Hill Educational Division. All rights reserved.

/1‡CAL-15MAY.E	Economy size car
/1‡CAL-15MAY.IT	Intermediate size convertible
/1‡CAL-15MAY.*T	Any size convertible
/1‡CAL-15MAY.LCAR	Luxury car with automatic transmission and air conditioning

Remember not all possible combinations are available: Most vendors offer air conditioned cars and, except for economy size vehicles, offer cars with automatic transmissions. A two-letter car code is usually sufficient for most client requirements.

Rules Display

Besides availability, rates, and selling, CarMaster also permits car rules—restrictions governing rental rates—to be displayed from a rate quotation. The following format may be used to obtain a rules display:

Format:
    CAV<Column><Line>

Example:

    CAVA1

For example, assume you just obtained the following qualified availability display:

```
MIAMI       FL              * WEEKEND - STAND/PROMO * USD
A:          A R TYPE   RATE    MI  CHG  LOC ADVB  MIN  RC
1.ALAMO     S G ICAR   42.95   100 .25   0    1    1   IDY
2.BUDGET    S G ICAR   44.95   100 .25   0    2    1   2CDB
3.DOLLAR    S G ICAR   44.95   100 .25   0    1    1   765
4.GENERAL   S G ICAR   45.00   100 .30   0    1    1   G11
5.NATIONAL  S G ICAR   48.00   100 .25   0    7    3   IDAY
```

Let's say your client would like to know the restrictions for the $44.95 rate from Budget. The following entry may be used to display the rules:

    CAVA2

Response:

```
HOURS:     MON - SUN 06:00A-12:00A BUDGET ICAR
WEEKEND    STANDARD   44.95 USD      100 MI-.25MI
EXTRA DAY  44.95    100 MI-.25MI
HOURS 10.99          0 MI-.25MI MIN:
PICK UP EARLIEST: 0600A      ADBK:       1 DAY/S
PICK UP LATEST:   0100A
```

Copyright © 1990 by Glencoe/McGraw-Hill Educational Division. All rights reserved.

In the partial display at the bottom of page 201, the extra-day charge is $44.95, and a charge of $10.99 per hour is applied when a vehicle is returned late.

Car Index

To display an index of car company outlets, use the command code CAI as follows:

Format:

CAI<Pickup Date><City>/<Vendor>

Example:

CAI10MAYMIA/ZE

The example above requests outlets with cars available for pickup on 10MAY at MIA. Hertz ZE is the specified vendor.

Response:

```
MIAMI    AIR    IL       * CAR INDEX *
VENDOR COMPANY          CODE            ADDRESS
  1. ZE HERTZ           MIAT01          MIAMI AIRPORT
  2. ZE HERTZ           MIAN10          MARRIOTT
  3. ZE HERTZ           MIAW10          HOLIDAY INN
  4. ZE HERTZ           MIAS13          DOWNTOWN
  5. ZE HERTZ           MIAN18          HARBOR INN
```

VENDOR POLICY DESCRIPTION

To display a description of vendor policies, use the command code CAD as follows:

Format:

CAD<Vendor Code><City>

Example:

CADZDDEN

The example requests a description of Budget ZD rental policies in DEN.

Copyright © 1990 by Glencoe/McGraw-Hill Educational Division. All rights reserved.

Response:

```
BUDGET RENT A CAR        DEN001   DENVER              21JUL
01  AGE   AGE REQUIREMENT     02  CARS  CAR/VEHICLE TYPES
03  CDW   COLL DAMAGE WAIVER  04  DROP  DROPOFF/ONEWAY
06  GAS   REFUELING POLICY    07  HOURS HOURS-OPER/BUSNSS
08  INS   INSURANCE           09  PAI   PERSONAL ACC INSUR
11  SPEC  SPECIAL EQUIPMENT   12  TAX   TAX-STATE/LOCAL
15  COMM  COMMISSION AGENTS   16  CRED  CREDIT CARD INFO
```

When a description is requested, Apollo displays a menu of categories. Each category has a number and a keyword. For instance, category 01 pertains to age requirements of renters; the keyword is AGE.

To select a category, enter CAD/ and the corresponding code or keyword. For example, to display commission information, either of the following entries may be used:

CAD/15
CAD/COMM

Modifying Car Segments

To modify a car segment, use the command code CAM as follows:

Format:
CAM<Segment><Field>/<New Data>

Example:

CAM2D/11MAY-14MAY

The example above modifies a car rental in segment 2 to change the date information for pickup on 11MAY and return on 14MAY. Fields in a car segment are identified by the following codes:

Car Field Identifiers

D/   Rental dates
T/   Car types
O/   Optional data
X/   Cancel optional data

To modify optional data in a car segment, include the appropriate identifier as in the following example:

CAM2O/CF-5T3776762

Here, the confirmation number is being added to the car reservation in segment 2. This procedure is required when a car segment has been booked directly with the outlet, and a confirmation number is provided by phone.

Copyright © 1990 by Glencoe/McGraw-Hill Educational Division. All rights reserved.

(handwritten annotations in margins: "RETURN", "CAM2D /-18JUL", "CAM2D /18JUL", "PICK UP ONE", "/PUP", "/-RTN", "WRONG SIDE ?", "SHOULD BE ? CAM2D/18JUL")

CAM2/D-18JUL
CAM3O/SI-RQST SKI RACK
CAM4X/ID

Fill-in Formats

Any CarMaster function can be handled with a fill-in format screen instead of a direct entry. To display a fill-in format screen, add a slash / at the end of the entry:

/1‡CAQ-12MAR/

The entry above will display a fill-in screen for requesting a rate quotation. To illustrate the use of fill-in screens, note the following example.
Assume you are working with the itinerary below:

```
1 UA 181Q 18OCT SFOHNL HK2   1000A   145P    WE
2 UA 189Y 25OCT HNLSFO HK2    945A   655P    WE
```

Let's say your client requests the lowest rates at the airport in Honolulu. The following entry may be used to display the fill-in format screen for requesting low-to-high availability:

/1‡CAL/

The only difference between the fill-in entry and the standard CAL entry is the slash at the end.

Response:

```
QUALIFIED
>CAQ/*             ENTRY PARAMETERS       **DEFAULTS**
       CAR TYPES   : . . . .‡ . . . .‡ . . . .    ALL
VENDORS            : . .‡. . ‡. . ‡. .       ALL
RATE TYPE/CODE     : .  / . . . . .              DAILY/NONE
RATE CATEGORY      : .                       STANDARD/PROMO
PICKUP DATE/TIME   : . . . . ./. . . . .         AIR SEGMENT
RETURN DATE        : . . . . .               NEXT DAY
LOCATION           : . . . . . . .           AIR SEGMENT
UNL MILES ONLY     : .                       N: Y-YES
GUAR RATES ONLY    : .                       N: Y-YES
PRICE RANGE        : . . . . . . . . .           NONE
```

The fill-in screen provides blank fields (represented by dotted lines) for each possible option. To enter an option, simply type the corresponding code in the appropriate field. For instance, to specify economy cars, you would type E in the field for car types. To specify Budget, you would type ZD in the vendors field.

Copyright © 1990 by Glencoe/McGraw-Hill Educational Division. All rights reserved.

The defaults column on the right shows the options that Apollo will use by default if no specification is entered. For instance, if the car types field is blank, Apollo will display rates for all types. Likewise, if the rate type/code field is blank, Apollo will display daily rates.

A fill-in format is available for each CarMaster function, including basic availability, qualified availability, and low-to-high rates.

CHECK-IN: A STUDY AID

Write the correct CarMaster entry for each of the following situations:

1. What entry will display a rate quotation, or qualified availability display, for the destination city and date in the last air segment booked?

    _____ CAQ _____

2. Assume you wish to display a rate quotation for the destination and date in segment 3, requesting availability for all intermediate size cars. Your client plans to return the vehicle on the 21st of April. Write the correct entry.

    _____ /3 ≠ CAQ-21APR.I _____

3. What entry will display qualified availability after segment 5, requesting compact cars, for return on the 14th of January?

    _____ /5 ≠ CAQ-14JAN _____

4. What entry will display low-to-high availability for the destination and date in the last air segment booked? _____ CAL _____   *needs seq # ?*

5. Assume you wish to display comparative rates for the destination city in segment 4. Your client expresses an interest in standard size cars and prefers the Avis chain. What entry could you use to display low-to-high availability?

    /4 ≠ CAL.S/ZE _____   _____ ?

6. Assume a rate quotation (qualified availability table) is displayed. What entry will book one car from column C, line 4? _____ 0C4 _____

7. What entry will book two cars from column B, line 2, for return on the 29th of October? _____ 0B2 _____   *not applicable*

8. What character, added to the end of a CarMaster entry, will display a fill-in format? _____ / _____

Copyright © 1990 by Glencoe/McGraw-Hill Educational Division. All rights reserved.

CHAPTER 15

DIRECT LINK AND GENERAL INFORMATION

CHAPTER OBJECTIVES

At the end of the chapter, you should be able to perform the following tasks:

- Utilize the Direct Link program to access information from airline systems of participating host carriers.

- Obtain a fare quotation (tariff display) from a Direct Link carrier.

- Display a seat map from a Direct Link carrier.

- Display fare rules from a Direct Link carrier.

- Display city pair availability from a Direct Link carrier.

- Utilize the Direct Link program to access Amtrak information.

- Utilize the General Reference program to obtain weather forecasts, currency conversion rates, and other stored travel information.

- Display a Universal Profile.

- Obtain assistance from the Apollo Help program.

Copyright © 1990 by Glencoe/McGraw-Hill Educational Division. All rights reserved.

DIRECT LINK

The Apollo Direct Link program allows subscribers to obtain flight availability, tariff displays, fare rules, flight information, and seat maps from other reservation systems. (Not all Apollo agencies subscribe to the Direct Link program.)

The Apollo command code for Direct Link is L□. To access a participating carrier's reservation system, preface the desired entry (fares, availability, etc.) with L□ and the carrier code for the airline whose system you are accessing.

Format:

L □<Host>/<Entry>

Example:

```
L□AA/$DLAXMIA10MAY-EXC
```

The host refers to the airline which operates the desired computer reservation system. The entry in the example above requests excursion and children's fares from the AA computer reservation system.

Example

Assume you want to access Eastern's reservation system to display availability from Seattle to Honolulu on the 10th of May for flights departing around 8:00 A.M. The following Direct Link entry may be used:

```
L□EA/A10MAYSEAHNL8A
```

When availability is requested from a participating reservation system, seats may be sold with the normal entry. For example, to sell one seat in Y class on a flight in line 4, the following entry may be used:

```
01Y4
```

A tag is added to the end of the segment indicating the carrier whose computer system was used to book the space.

Other Direct Link Entries

L□TW/$DDENORD12JAN-NLA   Fare quotation. The display will
remain in the host system's
format, which may differ from the
Apollo fare quotation display.

208

Copyright © 1990 by Glencoe/McGraw-Hill Educational Division. All rights reserved.

| L□DL/9V/S1 | Display seat map. The seat map will be displayed in the host system's format. |
| L□EA/$V3 | Display fare rules by line number. |

AMTRAK INFORMATION

Besides other airline computer reservation systems, the Direct Link program also provides direct access to the Amtrak railway system. Basic entries for availability and tariff displays are made in standard Apollo format, as in the following examples:

L□A3/A13JULPITCHI10A	City pair availability
L□A3/A*	More availability
L□A3/A*O	Opposite (return) availability
L□A3/$DPITCHI	Tariff display (current date)

Observe that the official carrier code for Amtrak is A3.

Amtrak Cities

The following entry may be used to display cities served by Amtrak:

Format:
    L □A3–RM/*<State>/<Initial>

Example:

    L□A3-RM/*IL/S

The state must be entered using the two-letter postal code. The initial refers to the first letter of the desired city. The example above requests a list of Amtrak cities in Illinois (IL) with the initial S.

GENERAL INFORMATION

Besides air, hotel, car, and tour reservations, Apollo also stores considerable general reference information of vital and casual interest to travelers and travel agents.

General information is retrieved by keyword. In the language of computers, a **keyword** is a combination of characters or numbers used to locate data in storage. Each subject stored in the Apollo general information is identified by a keyword.

The following are a few examples of general information categories:

    WEA   Weather information
    TUR   Tourism information
    TAR   Tariff information

The command code for general information is the G key. Information is retrieved from the system by the following entry:

Format:
    G/<Category>/<Subject>

Example:

    G/TUR/MAP

Copyright © 1990 by Glencoe/McGraw-Hill Educational Division. All rights reserved.

This example requests city maps stored under the tourism category. Following are additional examples of general information entries:

G/WEA/FOR	Display weather forecasts in U.S. cities.
G/TAR/EXC	Display foreign country and currency codes for international tariffs.

UNIVERSAL PROFILES

The client profile system is also used to communicate information to Apollo subscribers. Universal Profiles, special account records containing timely information, may be displayed in the same manner as a client BAR. For example, the following entry will retrieve the Universal Profile containing information about United Airlines' in-flight services:

    S*UAL

The following are additional examples of Universal Profiles:

S*AIR	Display inter-line agreements
S*APO	Display Apollo news
S*BPR	Display boarding pass procedures
S*COM	Display Apollo commission calculations
S*CTY	Encode/decode city and airport codes
S*MPL	Display Mileage Plus policies
S*OAL	Display news from other participating airlines

THE APOLLO HELP SYSTEM

An Apollo agent may obtain instructions on the use of any command format by means of the following entry:

Format:
    HELP <Topic>

Example:
    HELP $D

The example above requests instructions on the use of the $D (tariff display) format. A keyword may be entered instead of a topic as in the following example:

    HELP SELL

A complete index of Help topics may be obtained by means of the following entry:

    HELP INDEX

Copyright © 1990 by Glencoe/McGraw-Hill Educational Division. All rights reserved.

CHECK-IN: A STUDY AID

Write the correct answer to each problem.

1. The ___DIRECT LINK___ program is used to access information stored in the computer reservation systems of other carriers.

2. What code is used to access the systems of participating carriers?
   ___L □___

3. Write the correct entry to access Eastern's system and display fares from Ft. Lauderdale to Altanta on the 23rd of December, requesting adult excursion fares. ___L □ EA / $ D FLL ATL 23DEC EXA___

4. What entry would you use to access American's system and display flights on the 15th of March from Indianapolis to Des Moines departing around 11:00 A.M.? ___L □ AA / A 15MAR IND DSM 11A___

5. Assume you have obtained a tariff display from Delta's system, and you wish to display the rules for the MRE7 fare in line 7. Write the correct entry to display the fare rules. ___L □ DL / $V7___

6. Write the correct entry to access TWA's system and display the seat map for a flight in segment 2. ___L □ TW / 9V|S2___

7. What entry will display a list of cities served by Amtrak?
   ___L □ A3 - RM / *STATE / INITIAL___

8. Write the correct entry to display Amtrak availability on the 6th of July from New York City to Boston leaving at 8:00 A.M.
   ___L □ A3 / A 6JUL NYC BOS 8A___

9. What is the entry to display train schedules for the return trip?
   ___L □ A3 / A * O___

10. What entry would you use to display Amtrak fares from Washington, D.C., to New York? ___L □ A3 / $D DCA NYC___

11. Write the correct entry to display a weather forecast in U.S. cities.
    ___G/WEA/FOR___

12. What entry would display foreign country and currency codes for international tariffs? ___G / TAR / EXC___

13. Write the correct entry to display the Universal Profile containing information on Apollo commission calculations.
    ___S * COM___

Copyright © 1990 by Glencoe/McGraw-Hill Educational Division. All rights reserved.

14. What entry would display the Universal Profile for Mileage Plus policies?

S✳ MPL

15. How would you request the Apollo Help System to display instructions regarding the T: $B (stored pricing) entry?

HELP T: $B

Copyright © 1990 by Glencoe/McGraw-Hill Educational Division. All rights reserved.

APPENDIXES

A FILL-IN FORMATS

B MAJOR AIRLINE CARRIER CODES

C PRINCIPAL CITY/AIRPORT CODES

D APOLLO QUICK REFERENCE GUIDE

Copyright © Glencoe/McGraw-Hill Educational Division. All rights reserved.

FILL-IN FORMATS

THE NEED FOR FILL-IN FORMATS

Itineraries that cannot be priced automatically by Apollo require a ticketing fill-in format. A ticket pricing record shell must be created with fare information inserted. Apollo does not automatically compute fares for the following itineraries:

- Intra-Canada itineraries
- International itineraries
- Intineraries with certain group and promotional fares
- Itineraries containing airlines that do not store fares in Apollo

The following is the basic entry to request a pricing record fill-in format:

Format:

    HHPR

Applicable modifiers including commission and form of payment should be included with the basic entry. Any applicable ticketing modifiers can be added at the time the ticket is issued.

Example:

    HHPR/Z10/FCK

Copyright © 1990 by Glencoe/McGraw-Hill Educational Division. All rights reserved.

Response:

```
] $NME  JOHNSON/DON
X CTY CR FLT/CLS DATE    TIME  ST F/B      VALUE    NVB   NVA
. ORD UA    1 Y  20NOV  1030A OK . . . .   . . . . . . . . .
O HNL AQ  364 Y  22NOV   350P OK . . . .   . . . . . . . . .
O ITO UA  118 Y  30NOV   310P OK . . . .   . . . . . . . . .
O LAX UA  104 Y  02DEC  1010A OK . . . .   . . . . . . . . .
. ORD   FARE . . .  . . . . . . . . TX . . . . . . . . .   . . TX . . . . . . . . . . . .
TTL . . .  . . . . . . . .  EQ FARE . . . . . . . . . . . .  COM 10.00/ . .  CONST..
TD 1/ . . . . . .  2/  . . . . . .   3/  . . . . . .    4/ . . . . . .             INT..
RMKS . . . . . . . . . . . . . . . . . . . . . . . . . . . . . .  PSGR 01/01
RMKS . . . . . . . . . . . . . . . . . . . . . . . . . . . . . .  BOOK 01/01
```

The response consists of a basic ticket fill-in format which represents the passenger ticket. Certain data from the itinerary has already been automatically entered into the format. Tab stops allow you to complete the format by entering the required data. There are certain guidelines that must be followed in order to complete the fill-in format correctly:

- Use the space bar or erase key to eliminate incorrect data.
- Do not erase any unused dots displayed in the fill-in format.
- Do not use the insert in line, delete in line, or the Apollo black return key.
- Type the necessary data over the dots at each tab stop. If no data are required at a certain tab stop, just tab to the next stop, leaving it blank.

Explanation of Fill-in Format Fields

$NME	Identifier for the basic ticket fill-in format. It is followed by the traveler's name as entered in the PNR Name field and will include any name remarks. This line cannot be changed.
X	Connection (X) or stopover (O) codes are placed in this column as well as a code for the origin and destination city (.). Apollo will complete as many as possible. These codes can be changed, but usually remain the same.
CTY	Airport codes for the From/To cities as entered by Apollo. These cannot be changed.
CR	Carrier code is entered by Apollo and cannot be changed.
FLT/CLS	Using the PNR itinerary, Apollo lists the flight number and class of service for each segment. Open is listed for open segments and arnk segments are left blank. The only change allowed and required is typing the correct class of service over a ‡ in the CLS column.
DATE	Using the PNR itinerary, Apollo lists the departure date for each segment, except open segments. Arnk segments are listed as void. This data cannot be changed.

Copyright © 1990 by Glencoe/McGraw-Hill Educational Division. All rights reserved.

TIME	Using the PNR itinerary, Apollo also lists the departure time of each segment except open segments and arnk segments. This data cannot be changed.
ST	Apollo also uses the PNR itinerary to indicate the status of each flight segment except open segments.
F/B	The applicable fare basis code must be entered for each segment.
VALUE	The dollar and cent amount of the base fare for each segment must be entered unless you plan to complete the linear fare construction fill-in format (*see* Linear Fare Construction).
NVB/NVA	Not valid before and not valid after dates are inserted manually or by the Apollo program.
FARE	First three dots are used for manually entering the three letter currency code of the country of origin. Apollo assumes USD unless a different code is entered. The total of the base fares listed in the Value column is manually entered over the remaining eight dots. It is possible to ask the system to calculate the fare (*see* Programmatic Calculations).
TX	Two tax boxes are provided for situations when taxes must be entered and collected for more than one country. The first tax box is for U.S. taxes and the second is for other countries' taxes. Also, when applicable, the second tax box is used for entering the "federal inspection fee." The first three dots in each tax box are used for manually entering the three letter currency code of the country where the ticket is issued. Apollo assumes USD when no code is entered. The following seven dots are for the actual numeric tax amounts to be entered manually. It is also possible to ask the system to calculate the tax (see Programmatic Calculations). The remaining two dots are used for manually entering the country's ISO country code. Apollo assumes US when left blank. When the "federal inspection fee" is listed in the second tax box, XU is to be entered in this two-dot area.
TTL	The first three dots are used for manually entering the three letter currency code. Apollo assumes USD when no code is entered. The total fare for the entire ticket is manually entered over the remaining eight dots in the currency of the country of payment. It is possible to ask the system to calculate the total fare (*see* Programmatic Calculations).
EQ FARE	If applicable, an equivalent fare paid amount is manually entered in this section. The first three dots are used for entering the three letter currency code of the country of ticket purchase. The remaining eight dots are used for entering the numeric amount.

Copyright © 1990 by Glencoe/McGraw-Hill Educational Division. All rights reserved.

COM	Commission data is manually entered unless the commission modifer is used in the initial pricing record entry. The amount may be entered as a dollars and cents amount using the $ sign and decimal, or as a percentage using the numeric amount followed by a slash. Example: $17.00 10.00/
F CONST	Apollo automatically builds fare construction when segment values are stored. In these cases, this fare construction request box may be left blank. However, the fare construction must be completed when additional information is needed such as NUCs, mileage, surcharges, differentials, etc. (*see* Linear Fare Construction). Entering a Y in this box instructs Apollo to display the fare construction fill-in format at the completion of the last book of coupons. When using this box, the segment values of the ticketing format should be left blank. A numeric in this box is applicable for PNRs containing multiple names where differing fare levels apply. For example, if the second traveler's fill-in format is being worked on and should have the same fare construction as the first passenger, enter the numeric 1.
TD	Four ticket designator boxes exist allowing separate manual inputs for each of the four ticket coupons.
INT	The international box is used for indicating an international itinerary. Apollo usually recognizes an international location in the itinerary and automatically enters an X. If an unrecognizable international city is used, an X must be manually entered.
RMKS	Two ticket remarks lines exist for manually entering any necessary ticket remarks.
PSGR 01/01 BOOK 01/01	Some PNRs have multiple passengers and/or itineraries which exceed one book (four coupons). This area automatically indicates which traveler of the total travelers is being worked on and which book of coupons of the total books of coupons is being worked on.

PRICING RECORD

All of the fields requiring money amounts should be entered in the form of dollars and cents including the decimal and excluding the $ sign. The exception is in the COM box when it is necessary to use the $ sign when dollars and cents figures are used instead of a percentage. Decimal points should be used with foreign currency entries only when that country's currency is based on a decimal system. In these cases, Apollo reads the currency code entered to check the correct placement of the decimal. If incorrect, Apollo will prompt to check the decimal placement.

In summary, the pricing record fill-in format is used for PNRs that are unable to be priced automatically by Apollo. Tab stops are reminders of actions that must be taken to manually enter the required data.

These actions include the following:

Copyright © 1990 by Glencoe/McGraw-Hill Educational Division. All rights reserved.

1. Determine and include commission and form of payment information in the initial pricing record entry.
2. Determine and enter the fare basis codes.
3. Calculate and enter the segment values.
4. Correct stopover/connection codes if necessary.
5. Compute and enter the total base fare, tax, and total fare requesting a linear fare construction fill-in format if necessary.
6. Enter any applicable equivalent fare paid amount.
7. Determine and enter any applicable data in the ticket designator and remarks boxes.

Example of completed pricing record fill-in format:

```
]$NME JOHNSON/DON
X CTY CR FLT/CLS DATE    TIME  ST F/B     VALUE   NVB   NVA
. ORD UA    1 Y  20NOV  1030A OK YEIT. . 497.00 . . . . . . .
O HNL AQ  364 Y  22NOV   350P OK YEIT. . 38.05. . . . . . . .
O ITO UA  118 Y  30NOV   310P OK YEIT. . 0. . . . . . . . . .
O LAX UA  104 Y  02DEC  1010A OK YEIT. . 497.00 . . . . . . .
. ORD    FARE ... 1032.05   TX ... 23.66. . . . TX . . . . . . . . .
TTL ... 1055.71  EQ FARE ... . . . . . . . . COM 10.00/. F CONST ..
TD 1/ . . . . . . 2/  . . . . . .  3/ . . . . . .  4/ . . . . . .        INT ..
RMKS . . . . . . . .  . . . . . . . . . . . . . . .  PSGR 01/01
RMKS . . . . . . . .  . . . . . . . . . . . . . . .  BOOK 01/01
```

Once all the mandatory and necessary data have been entered, tab to the word BOOK on the last line and enter. For itineraries that require more than one book, the next fill-in format display will appear. Once all the mandatory and necessary data has been entered in all the books, tab to the word BOOK again and enter.

Response:

       *

The asterisk response informs you that the information has been accepted. The next step is to store the pricing record with the PNR.

To store the pricing record for a single passenger record:

Format:

   HBT

If the above entry is used for the first passenger in a multi-passenger record, the response will be a display of the fill-in format for the next passenger on file in the PNR. The data previously entered in the format for the first passenger will already be included in the format for the next passenger. If the data is to remain the same, it is possible to tab to the word BOOK and make the HBT entry again. This process will repeat until formats have been displayed for all passengers in the record. This process is necessary if the fare level of any of the passengers in the record differs. In these cases, the correct information is typed over the existing data before the HBT entry is made.

Copyright © 1990 by Glencoe/McGraw-Hill Educational Division. All rights reserved.

If all the passengers in a multi-passenger record are to be fared identically, there is an easier method to store pricing records for all the passengers after the fill-in format has been completed for the first passenger.

Format:

```
HBTA
```

The result of the above entry is the storing of identical pricing records for each traveler in the PNR.

After pricing records have been stored for all travelers in the PNR, the system gives the following response.

Response:

```
PRICING RECORD ADDED
```

This results in the automatic addition of an ATFQ field to the PNR as well as a header line that informs anyone who retrieves the PNR that a pricing record exists, as illustrated in the example below:

```
T6GBYH/JJ
   PRICING RECORD EXISTS - SUBSCRIBER - $NME
1. 1JOHNSON/DON
1 UA   1Y 20NOV ORDHNL HK1   1030A   215P        SA
2 AQ 364F 20NOV HNLITO HK1    350P   431P        SA
3 UA 118Y 30NOV ITOLAX HK1    310P  1100P        TU
4 UA 104Y 01DEC LAXORD HK1   1010A   115P        TH
FONE-CHIAS/312 555-5757-JOHN
TKTG-TAU/13NOV
ATFQ-UNABLE/PZ10/FCK
FM-1032.05/23.66/1055.71 - PRICING RECORD - 12NOV
```

Since Apollo was unable to automatically price the PNR, the ATFQ field shows an unable status. However, all modifiers used with the initial pricing record entry are stored in the ATFQ field. Another addition to the PNR is the FM (fare manual) field, which was also created when the pricing record was completed and stored.

Since a ticket cannot be issued when the ATFQ field indicates unable status, it is necessary to change the unable to OK.

To change the unable status of an ATFQ field to OK:

Format:

```
T:OK
```

Response:

```
*
```

The asterisk indicates that the status of the ATFQ field has been changed to OK. To verify the change, display the ticketing field:

Copyright © 1990 by Glencoe/McGraw-Hill Educational Division. All rights reserved.

Format:

> *T

Response:

```
TKTG-TAU/13NOV
ATFQ-OK/PZ10/FCK
FM-1032.05/23.66/1055.71 - PRICING RECORD - 12NOV
```

At this point, the PNR is ready for ticket issuance and may be filed by end transaction.

DISPLAY A PRICING RECORD

At times it might be necessary to look at another display while in the process of completing a fill-in format. When this occurs, it is possible to return to the format, which will have retained all accepted data, with the following entry.

Format:

> $NME

It is also possible to display the stored pricing record in a retrieved PNR with a similar entry.

Format:

> $NME1

The above entry would result in the display of the pricing record for the first passenger in the record.

CANCEL A PRICING RECORD

Once a pricing record has been created, it is possible to cancel it with the use of the cancel key X and the pricing record code PR.

To cancel a pricing record:

Format:

> XPR

Response:

> PRICING RECORD DELETED

The result is the automatic removal of the pricing record as well as the pricing record header line, the ATFQ field, and the FM field from the PNR. However, the ATFQ and FM data will be retained the PNR's history, revealing that a pricing record has existed and what the amounts were.

Copyright © 1990 by Glencoe/McGraw-Hill Educational Division. All rights reserved.

PROGRAMMATIC CALCULATIONS

As discussed previously, it is necessary to compute base fare, tax, and total fare amounts to complete the pricing record fill-in format. The following are methods of asking Apollo to do some of the calculations.

Programmatic Calculation - A

If the entire itinerary is taxable at 8 percent and all base fare amounts have been entered in the Value column, type an A in the fare box over the first of the eight dot area.

Example:

```
. ...   FARE ... A.......  TX ... ........ ..   TX ... ........ ..
```

Response:

```
. ...   FARE USD    275.93 TX USD      22.07 US TX ... ........ ..
        TTL USD   298.00 EQ FARE ...  ........   COM  10.00/ F CONST ..
```

Apollo totals the base fares and calculates the 8 percent tax. Apollo then computes the total fare by adding together the total base fare and the tax.

Programmatic Calculation - B

If the itinerary has no applicable taxes or a specific amount of tax and all base fare amounts have been entered in the Value column, type a B in the fare box over the first dot of the eight dot area. Also insert the actual tax (if any) in the appropriate tax box.

Example:

```
. ...   FARE ... B.......  TX ... 3.00... ..   TX ... ........ ..
```

Response:

```
. ...   FARE USD    200.00 TX USD       3.00 US TX ... ........ ..
        TTL USD   203.00 EQ FARE ...  ........   COM   8.00/ F CONST ..
```

Apollo totals the base fares and calculates the total fare by adding together the base fare and the indicated tax.

SPECIAL TAX CALCULATIONS

When using the Programmatic Calculation - B method, tax may also be entered as a percentage instead of a dollars and cents amount. If a percentage is used, a slash must follow the percent amount.

Example:

```
. ...   FARE ... B.......  TX ... 9/..... ..   TX ... ........ ..
```

Response:

```
. ...   FARE USD    583.33 TX USD      46.67 US TX ... ........ ..
        TTL USD   630.00 EQ FARE ...  ........   COM  10.00/ F CONST ..
```

Apollo totals the base fares and calculates the indicated percentage of tax. Apollo then computes the total fare by adding the base fare total and the tax.

When both tax boxes are used, a dollars and cents amount may be used in one and a percent may be used in the other as long as both are entered properly. E may also be entered in the tax box when taxes are exempt.

Copyright © 1990 by Glencoe/McGraw-Hill Educational Division. All rights reserved.

UNDECODABLE CITIES

At times, an itinerary may contain a city code which Apollo does not recognize and is unable to decode. This happens when the itinerary contains little known air commuter companies and/or certain international destinations. When this occurs, Apollo will display the undecodable cities fill-in format after the HBT or HBTA entry is made.

Response:

```
$UC/UNDECODABLE CITIES
YUK . . . . . . .
```

Upon receiving this response, tab to the blank (line of dots) and type in the city name (up to 13 characters). Since the entry is free-form, Apollo will accept whatever is input and will then print it on the ticket.

LINEAR FARE CONSTRUCTION

A Linear Fare Construction is required on all tickets. Usually Apollo automatically prints the linear fare calculation; but in some cases Apollo cannot provide the proper linear codes. It is necessary to manually complete a fare construction when additional information is needed such as NUCs, mileage, surcharges, differentials, etc.

Codes Used in Linear Fare Construction

-X	No stop allowed
S	Stopover charge
Q	Surcharge
‡PAR☐	Hidden city
‡‡PAR☐☐	Point beyond
D	Class differential
/-	Arnk not included in mileage
NUC	Neutral Unit of Construction

If a Y is entered in the F CONST box of the pricing record fill-in format, a linear fill-in format will automatically be displayed after the HBT entry is made.

Example:

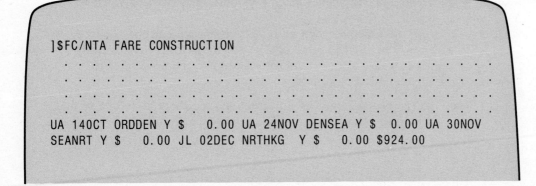

```
]$FC/NTA FARE CONSTRUCTION
    . . . . . . . . . . . . . . . . . . . . . . . . . . . . . . .
    . . . . . . . . . . . . . . . . . . . . . . . . . . . . . . .
    . . . . . . . . . . . . . . . . . . . . . . . . . . . . . . .
    UA 14OCT ORDDEN Y $   0.00 UA 24NOV DENSEA Y $  0.00 UA 30NOV
    SEANRT Y $   0.00 JL 02DEC NRTHKG  Y $   0.00 $924.00
```

Copyright © 1990 by Glencoe/McGraw-Hill Educational Division. All rights reserved.

Explanation of Format

Header line: $FC   Identifies the display as the Linear Fare Construction.

            NTA   Identifies the ticket stock as New Transitional Automated.

           FARE CONSTRUCTION   Identifies this as a Linear Fare Construction format.

Four dotted lines represent the space available for the fare construction on the actual ticket.

An abbreviated itinerary taken from the pricing record format is contained on the last two lines.

To complete the fare construction, tab to the first line of dots and type in the necessary fare information.

Example:

```
]$FC/NTA FARE CONSTRUCTION
 14OCT CHI UA DEN UA SEA UA TYO JL HKG M924.00 USD924.00. . . .
 . . . . . . . . . . . . . . . . . . . . . . . . . . . . . . .
 . . . . . . . . . . . . . . . . . . . . . . . . . . . . . . .
 . . . . . . . . . . . . . . . . . . . . . . . . . . . . . . .
 UA 14OCT ORDDEN Y $   0.00 UA 24NOV  DENSEA Y $  0.00 UA 30NOV
 SEANRT Y $   0.00 JL 02DEC NRTHKG  Y $   0.00 $924.00
```

Explanation of Data Required

1. Type the originating date of travel in the basic date format which consists of a one- or two-digit day followed by the three-letter code for the month.
2. Indicate the routing of the itinerary using the three-letter city codes and carrier codes in alternating order.
3. Insert the fare in the routing sequence after the city code which indicates the construction point. All fare entries must be in the same currency. The codes listed previously may be used when applicable.
4. Indicate the total preceded with the appropriate currency code. A $ sign may be used in place of USD when the itinerary is entirely domestic. When NUCs are used to determine the fare, precede the total with the NUC code.

Note: NUCs (Neutral Units of Construction) represent a method of determining a fare when multiple currencies are involved.

Copyright © 1990 by Glencoe/McGraw-Hill Educational Division. All rights reserved.

Example:

```
]$FC/NTA FARE CONSTRUCTION
 14OCT DEN UA -XMIA PA CCS Q15.00 M450.50 PA NYC S30.00 UA  . .
 DEN M450.50 USD946.00. . . . . . . . . . . . . . . . . . . . .
  . . . . . . . . . . . . . . . . . . . . . . . . . . . . . .
  . . . . . . . . . . . . . . . . . . . . . . . . . . . . . .
```

The -XMIA entry indicates there is no stopover in Miami.
The Q15.00 entry indicates the weekend surcharge (after the overwater routing).
The S30.00 entry indicates the stopover charge (after the point of stopover).

Notes: Always use city codes, not airport codes.
Always use base fares or NUC amounts excluding taxes.
Use the tab key to move from one line to another when necessary.
Always type within the parameters of the dots.
Do not use the delete-in-line, insert-in-line, or Apollo's black return key.

Copyright © 1990 by Glencoe/McGraw-Hill Educational Division. All rights reserved.

MAJOR AIRLINE CARRIER CODES

Code	Airline	Code	Airline
AA	American	LH	Lufthansa (Germany)
AC	Air Canada	LY	El Al Israel Airlines
AF	Air France	ML	Midway
AI	Air India	MX	Mexicana Airlines
AS	Alaska Air	NW	Northwest
AM	Aeromexico	OS	Austrian Airlines
AR	Aerolineas Argentinas	PA	Pan American
AV	Avianca	PR	Philippine Airlines
AY	Finnair	QF	Qantas (Australia)
AZ	Alitalia	RK	Air Afrique
BA	British Airways	SA	South African Airlines
CO	Continental Airlines	SK	Scandinavian Airlines
CP	Canadian Airlines	SH	SAHSA (South America)
DL	Delta	SR	Swiss Air
EA	Eastern	TE	Air New Zealand
EI	Aer Lingus (Ireland)	TM	Mozambique Airlines
FI	Icelandair	TW	TWA
HP	America West	UA	United
JL	Japan Airlines	US	USAir (previously AL)
JU	JAT (Yugoslavia)	UT	UTA French Airlines
KL	KLM (Netherlands)	WT	Nigeria Airways
LA	LAN (Chile)		

Copyright © 1990 by Glencoe/McGraw-Hill Educational Division. All rights reserved.

PRINCIPAL CITY/AIRPORT CODES

The following list is arranged alphabetically by **code.**

North American

Code	City	Code	City
ABE	Allentown, Pennsylvania	BDR	Bridgeport, Connecticut
ABI	Abilene, Texas	BGI	Barbados
ABQ	Albuquerque, New Mexico	BGR	Bangor, Maine
ABY	Albany, Georgia	BHB	Bar Harbor, Maine
ACA	Acapulco, Mexico	BHM	Birmingham, Alabama
ACT	Waco, Texas	BIL	Billings, Montana
ACV	Eureka/Arcata, California	BMG	Bloomington, Indiana
ACY	Atlantic City, New Jersey	BMI	Bloomington, Illinois
AGS	Augusta, Georgia	BNA	Nashville, Tennessee
AHN	Athens, Georgia	BOI	Boise, Idaho
ALB	Albany, New York	BON	Bonaire, Netherlands Antilles
ALO	Waterloo, Iowa	BOS	Boston, Massachusetts
ALW	Wallawalla, Washington	BRO	Brownsville, Texas
ANC	Anchorage, Alaska	BPT	Beaumont/Port Arthur, Texas
ASE	Aspen, Colorado	BTM	Butte, Montana
ASO	Andros Island, Bahamas	BTR	Baton Rouge, Louisiana
AUA	Aruba, Netherlands Antilles	BTV	Burlington, Vermont
AUG	Augusta, Maine	BUF	Buffalo, New York
AZO	Kalamazoo, Michigan	BUR	Burbank, California
BBR	Basse-Terre, Guadeloupe	BWI	Baltimore, Maryland
BDA	Bermuda	BZE	Belize City
BDL	Hartford, Connecticut	CAE	Columbia, South Carolina

Copyright © Glencoe/McGraw-Hill Educational Division. All rights reserved.

CAK	Akron/Canton, Ohio	GAD	Gadsden, Alabama
CCE	St. Maarten, Netherlands Antilles	GCM	Grand Cayman, Cayman Islands
CEC	Crescent City, California	GCN	Grand Canyon, Arizona
CHI	Chicago metropolitan area	GEG	Spokane, Washington
CHO	Charlottesville, Virginia	GGT	Georgetown, Bahamas
CHS	Charleston, South Carolina	GJT	Grand Junction, Colorado
CIC	Chico, California	GNV	Gainesville, Florida
CID	Cedar Rapids, Iowa	GRB	Green Bay, Wisconsin
CKB	Clarksburg, West Virginia	GRR	Grand Rapids, Michigan
CKV	Clarksville, Tennessee	GSO	Greensboro, North Carolina
CLE	Cleveland, Ohio	HAR	Harrisburg, Pennsylvania
CLM	Port Angeles, Washington	HAV	Havana, Cuba
CLT	Charlotte, North Carolina	HGR	Hagerstown, Maryland
CMH	Columbus, Ohio	HHH	Hilton Head, South Carolina
CMI	Champaign, Illinois	HNL	Honolulu, Oahu, Hawaii
CNM	Carlsbad, New Mexico	HOU	Houston, Texas (Hobby airport)
COU	Columbia, Missouri		
CPR	Casper, Wyoming	HSI	Hastings, Nebraska
CRP	Corpus Christi, Texas	HSV	Huntsville, Alabama
CUN	Cancun, Mexico	HUF	Terre Haute, Indiana
CVG	Cincinnati, Ohio	HUT	Hutchinson, Kansas
CYB	Cayman Brac, Cayman Islands	HVN	New Haven, Connecticut
CYS	Cheyenne, Wyoming	HYA	Hyannis, Massachusetts
CZM	Cozumel, Mexico	IAD	Washington–Dulles airport
DAB	Daytona Beach, Florida	IAH	Houston Intercontinental airport
DAY	Dayton, Ohio		
DCA	Washington, D.C. (National airport)	ICT	Wichita, Kansas
		IDA	Idaho Falls, Idaho
DEN	Denver, Colorado	ILG	Wilmington, Delaware
DEC	Decatur, Illinois	IND	Indianapolis, Indiana
DFW	Dallas–Ft. Worth, Texas	IPT	Williamsport, Pennsylvania
DLH	Duluth, Minnesota	ISO	Kinston, North Carolina
DOM	Dominica, West Indies	ISP	Long Island, New York
DSM	Des Moines, Iowa	ITH	Ithaca, New York
DTT	Detroit, Michigan (city)	ITO	Hilo, Hawaii
DTW	Detroit, Michigan (airport)	JAC	Jackson, Wyoming
EAU	Eau Claire, Wisconsin	JAN	Jackson, Mississippi
ELH	North Eleuthera, Bahamas	JAX	Jacksonville, Florida
ELM	Elmira, New York	JFK	New York–Kennedy airport
ELP	El Paso, Texas	JHW	Jamestown, New York
ERI	Erie, Pennsylvania	JNU	Juneau, Alaska
EUG	Eugene, Oregon	KIN	Kingston, Jamaica
EVV	Evansville, Indiana	KOA	Kona, Hawaii
EWR	Newark, New Jersey	KTN	Ketchikan, Alaska
FAI	Fairbanks, Alaska	LAF	Lafayette, Indiana
FAR	Fargo, North Dakota	LAM	Los Alamos, New Mexico
FAT	Fresno, California	LAX	Los Angeles, California
FAY	Fayetteville, North Carolina	LBB	Lubbock, Texas
FDF	Fort de France, Martinique	LBF	North Platte, Nebraska
FLG	Flagstaff, Arizona	LCH	Lake Charles, Louisiana
FLL	Ft. Lauderdale, Florida	LEW	Lewiston, Maine
FPO	Freeport, Bahamas	LEX	Lexington, Kentucky
FWA	Ft. Wayne, Indiana	LGA	New York–LaGuardia airport
FYU	Ft. Yukon, Alaska	LGB	Long Beach, California

Copyright © 1990 by Glencoe/McGraw-Hill Educational Division. All rights reserved.

LHU	Lake Havasu City, Arizona	PMD	Palmdale, California
LIH	Lihue, Kauai, Hawaii	POU	Poughkeepsie, New York
LIJ	Long Island, New York	PUB	Pueblo, Colorado
LIT	Little Rock, Arkansas	PUW	Pullman, Washington
LNK	Lincoln, Nebraska	PVD	Providence, Rhode Island
LNS	Lancaster, Pennsylvania	PVR	Puerto Vallarta, Mexico
LUP	Malaupapa, Molokai, Hawaii	QCE	Copper Mountain, Colorado
LWS	Lewiston, Idaho		
MBJ	Montego Bay, Jamaica	RAP	Rapid City, South Dakota
MBS	Saginaw, Michigan	RDG	Reading, Pennsylvania
MCI	Kansas City, Missouri (airport)	RDU	Raleigh-Durham, North Carolina
MCO	Orlando, Florida		
MDH	Carbondale, Illinois	RIC	Richmond, Virginia
MEM	Memphis, Tennessee	RNO	Reno, Nevada
MEX	Mexico City, Mexico	ROA	Roanoke, Virginia
MFR	Medford, Oregon	ROC	Rochester, New York
MGM	Montgomery, Alabama	ROW	Roswell, New Mexico
MHK	Manhattan, Kansas	SAB	Saba, Netherlands Antilles
MHT	Manchester, New Hampshire	SAN	San Diego, California
		SAT	San Antonio, Texas
MIA	Miami, Florida	SBA	Santa Barbara, California
MIE	Muncie, Indiana	SBN	South Bend, Indiana
MKC	Kansas City, Missouri (city)	SBP	San Luis Obispo, California
MKE	Milwaukee	SCF	Scottsdale, Arizona
MLI	Moline, Illinois	SDF	Louisville, Kentucky
MLU	Monroe, Louisiana	SEA	Seattle, Washington
MOB	Mobile, Alabama	SFO	San Francisco, California
MRY	Monterey, California	SHV	Shreveport, Louisiana
MSO	Missoula, Montana	SJC	San Jose, California
MSP	Minneapolis, Minnesota	SJD	Los Cabos, Mexico
MSY	New Orleans, Louisiana	SJU	San Juan, Puerto Rico
MVY	Martha's Vineyard, Massachusetts	SLC	Salt Lake City, Utah
		SLU	St. Lucia, West Indies
MYR	Myrtle Beach, South Carolina	SNA	Orange County, California
		STL	St. Louis, Missouri
NAS	Nassau, Bahamas	STS	Santa Rosa, California
NPT	Newport, Rhode Island	STT	St. Thomas, Virgin Islands
NYC	New York metropolitan area	STX	St. Croix, Virgin Islands
OAK	Oakland, California	SUX	Sioux City, Iowa
OKC	Oklahoma City, Oklahoma	TAB	Tobago, Trinidad/Tobago
OKK	Kokomo, Indiana	TCL	Tuscaloosa, Alabama
OLU	Columbus, Nebraska	TEX	Telluride, Colorado
OMA	Omaha, Nebraska	TLH	Tallahassee, Florida
OME	Nome, Alaska	TOL	Toledo, Ohio
ORD	Chicago—O'Hare airport	TOP	Topeka, Kansas
ORF	Norfolk, Virginia	TUL	Tulsa, Oklahoma
OSH	Oshkosh, Wisconsin	TUS	Tucson, Arizona
PCT	Princeton, New Jersey	UCA	Utica, New York
PDX	Portland, Oregon	VDZ	Valdez, Alaska
PHF	Newport News, Virginia	VIJ	Virgin Gorda, British Virgin Islands
PHL	Philadelphia, Pennsylvania		
PHX	Phoenix, Arizona	WAS	Washington, D.C. metropolitan area
PIA	Peoria, Illinois		
PIR	Pierre, South Dakota	WZY	Nassau—Paradise Island, Bahamas
PIT	Pittsburgh, Pennsylvania		

Copyright © 1990 by Glencoe/McGraw-Hill Educational Division. All rights reserved.

YEG	Edmonton, Alberta
YMX	Montreal, Quebec
YVR	Vancouver, British Columbia
YYC	Calgary, Alberta
YYZ	Toronto, Ontario
YXU	London, Ontario
ZBS	Mesa, Arizona

International

AKL	Auckland
AMS	Amsterdam
BEG	Belgrade
BEY	Beirut
BNE	Brisbane
BOB	Bora Bora
BOG	Bogota
BOM	Bombay
BUD	Budapest
CAI	Cairo
CAS	Casablanca
CCS	Caracas
CCU	Calcutta
CDG	Paris (Charles de Gaulle airport)
CPH	Copenhagen
DBV	Dubrovnik
DEL	Delhi
DUB	Dublin
DUS	Dusseldorf
FCO	Rome (Leonardo Da Vinci airport)
FRA	Frankfurt

GIG	Rio de Janeiro (airport)
GUA	Guatemala City
GVA	Geneva
HEL	Helsinki
HKG	Hong Kong
IST	Istanbul
JKT	Jakarta
JNB	Johannesburg
KWI	Kuwait
LGW	London (Gatwick airport)
LHR	London (Heathrow airport)
LIM	Lima
LON	London (city)
LUX	Luxembourg
MAA	Madras
MAD	Madrid
MOW	Moscow
MOZ	Moorea
ORY	Paris (Orly airport)
OSL	Oslo
PEK	Beijing
PPG	Pago Pago
PPT	Papeete (Tahiti)
PTY	Panama City
RIO	Rio de Janeiro
ROM	Rome
SAO	São Paulo
SEL	Seoul
SHA	Shanghai
SIN	Singapore
STO	Stockholm
SYD	Sydney
TLV	Tel Aviv
TPE	Taipei
TYO	Tokyo
WAW	Warsaw
ZHR	Zurich

Copyright © 1990 by Glencoe/McGraw-Hill Educational Division. All rights reserved.

APOLLO QUICK REFERENCE GUIDE

SIGN ON/OFF

Sign On	SON/12T
Sign Off	SOF

AVAILABILITY

By departure time	A10MAYSFOMIA8A
By arrival time	A10MAYSFOMIAA5P
Opposite availability	A*O10MAY/5P
Additional availability	A*
Change date	A17MAY
Change departure time	A*3P
Change departure city	AOAK
Original availability	A*R
Specified connecting city	A10MAYSFOMIA8ADEN
Specified class	A/Q/10MAYSFOMIA
Specified carrier	A10MAYSFOMIA‡UA
Direct flights only	A10MAYSFOMIA8A/D

SELL

From availability	01Y1
Connection	01Y1Y2
Direct-sell flight	0AA334Y22OCTLAXORDNN2
Direct-sell UA flight	0440Y12FEBSFOHNLNN2
Waitlist	0DL1442Y12OCTATLLGALL2
UA priority waitlist	0910M24JANORDLGAPB1

Copyright © 1990 by Glencoe/McGraw-Hill Educational Division. All rights reserved.

Within 24 hours	0910M24JANORDLGAPC1
Open segment	ODLOPENYPITSFONO1
Direct book	ODL584F22SEPDFWATLBK2
Arnk (surface segment)	Y

PASSENGER DATA

Name	N: LINDBERG/C
Multiple passengers	N: 2GREENBERG/L MR/R MRS
Multiple last names	N: FORREST/T MR‡N: TREE/A MRS
With ID number	N: WIGGONS/C MR*B65432
Unaccompanied minor	N: WILEY/DORIS MISS*UM08
Phone	P: SFOAS/415 555-0198-JANET
Ticketing	T: TAU/10MAY
Received	R: P
End transaction	E
Ignore transaction	I

SUPPLEMENTARY DATA

Client address	W-ABC CO☐123 MAIN☐TUCSON AZ/Z83210
Remarks	☐5: QTD 139.00 FARE/12JUL
OSI	☐: 3OSIYY VIP PRES ABM CORP
SSR	☐: 3SSR VGML AA NN1 AA181Y2MAYLAXDFW

DISPLAY

Retrieve PNR by name	**-FROST
From similar name list	*3
By departure date/name	**26MAR-SMITH
By flight/origin/name	*AA374/10AUGDFW-MICHAELS
By record locator	*Z4QX2V
Redisplay record	*R
Display itinerary	*I
Name items only	*N
Passenger data	*P
OSI information	*PO
SSR information	*PS
Phone items only	*PP

Copyright © 1990 by Glencoe/McGraw-Hill Educational Division. All rights reserved.

Cancel segment	X2
Cancel and rebook	X2/0126Q10JULSEALAXNN2
From availability	X2/01Q3
Cancel range	X2-5
Multiple segments	X1‡3
Cancel itinerary	XI
Cancel air only	XA
Insert after segment	/1
Insert and book	/3‡0CO252Y23OCTSFODENNN2
From availability	/3‡02Y3
Insert arnk segment	/4‡Y
Change segment status	.1HK
Add flight times	.3T/1010A245P

PNR EDITS

Change name item	C:2N:JOHNSON/HOWARD
Delete name item	C:2N:
Change phone item	C:3P:SFOR/415 555-0112
Delete phone item	C:4P:
Change remark	C:2□:5QTD 89.00 FARE/8FEB
Delete remark	C:3□:5
Change ticketing item	C:T:TAU/28JUL
Reduce number in the party	C:-1
Divide PNR	DN2
Divide by name reference	DN1-3
Multiple name reference	DN1-2‡1-3

FARES

Fare quotation	$DSFOMIA10MAY
Specified fare basis	$DSFOMIA9APR□QVAP7
Specified fare category	$DSFOMIA9APR-NLA
Specified carrier	$DSFOMIA9APR*CO
Fare category and carrier	$DSFOMIA9APR-M*DL
Joint fares	$DLAXMIA13FEBATL
Display connecting points	$DLAXMIAC
Rules display from tariff	$V5
From rules menu	$V/10
Specified carrier	$V5*CO
Without a tariff display	$VSFO/MIA/10MAY/□QHHE70

Copyright © 1990 by Glencoe/McGraw-Hill Educational Division. All rights reserved.

ITINERARY PRICING

Full-price adult	$B
By passenger type	$B*C10
Multiple passenger types	$BN1‡2*C8
Segment selection	$BS‡/2
Name selection	$BN1-2
Forced connection	$BX2
Different class	$BS1☐Q
Multiple segments/class	$BS1☐Y‡2*4
Specified fare basis	$B☐ME70
Lowest fare available	$BB
Multiple types/lowest fare	$BBN1-1‡1-2*C8
Store pricing instructions	T:$B
Form of payment	F-CK
Print itinerary/invoice	T:$BDID
Print ticket only	T:$BDTD
Free ticket	T:$BGF/FS
Omit amount on itinerary	T:$BGIN
Separate itinerary/invoice	T:$BGIS

TICKETING/INVOICING

Issue ticket	HB:
With form of payment	HB:FCK
With name selection	HBN1-2‡1-3
With segment selection	HBS1‡3
Separate invoices	T-SD
Separate invoices by product	T-SA
Single invoice by date	T-CD
Single invoice by product	T-CA
Print message on itinerary	T-IR
Itinerary without amount	T-ID

CLIENT PROFILES

Display BAR	S*ABM
Display PAR	S*ABM-THOMPSON
Display BAR titles	SLB
Display PAR names	SLP/ABM
Move mandatory Y lines	MV/
Move Y lines plus 0 line	MV/5
Multiple 0 lines	MV/7-9
Move from BAR	MVB/

Copyright © 1990 by Glencoe/McGraw-Hill Educational Division. All rights reserved.

Blind move from MAR	MVT/Q0X‡*JANET
Create/update BAR	BPB/ACME
Add data line	1Y/P:SFOB/415 555-0987
Change data line	RC:3P:SFOB/415 555-6543
End and save	BE

SEAT ASSIGNMENTS

No-smoking window	9S
No-smoking aisle	9S/A
No-smoking aisle across	9S/AA
Smoking window	9S/X
Smoking aisle	9S/XA
Assign specific seat	9S/14C
Multiple seat assignments	9S/14ABC
Display seat map	9V/S1
Without itinerary	9V/189Y10MAYSFO
Display seat information	9D
Cancel seat assignments	9X
Mileage Plus number	MP*838261/N1-1

QUEUES

Queue count	QC/18
Access queue	Q/18
Remove PNR from queue	QR
Exit and end transaction	QX‡E
Exit and ignore	QX‡I
Queue placement	QEP/44
Continuous queue ticketing	HB:Q
Ticket queue 10	HB:Q/10
Record count for ticketing	ORC/TAU/17SEP
Move TAU records to queue	ORB/TAU/17SEP-Q36
Remove all records	QFREE/43

HOTELS

Hotel vendor codes	HELP HTLC
Hotel index by city	HOISFO
Specific location	HOISFO/A
Specific chain	HOISFO/HI
With rate modifier	HOISFO/SCR
Availability from index	HOA
From itinerary	/1‡HOA5NT2

Copyright © 1990 by Glencoe/McGraw-Hill Educational Division. All rights reserved.

With different city	/1‡HOASTS6NT2
Without air	HOA10DEC-7NTNAS2
Hotel description	HOD773
Policy description	HOD773/ROOM
Description by property code	HOD2303
Sell from description	01A1K1
With form of guarantee	01A1K1/G. . .
With room options	01A1K/EX-1/RA-1
Modify hotel segment	HOM2R/1B2T-1
Direct booking	OHTLZZBK1BOS. . .
Cancel hotel segment	X3
Cancel direct booking	.2XK

CAR RENTALS

Availability after segment	/2‡CAA
With pickup date and city	CAA10MAYSFO
Date/city/rate type	CAA22AUGMSP-W
Date/city/rate/vendor	CAA22AUGMSP/ZD-W
Sell from availability	0A2-21AUG
Rate quotation	/2‡CAQ
With date and car type	/2‡CAQ-10MAY.SC
Low-to-high rates	/2‡CAL
Sell from rate quotation	0A3-17MAY
Vendor index	CAIZDLAX
Policy description	CADZLLAX
Modify car segment	CM3/CF-7670928

DIRECT LINK

Tariff display	L☐AA/$DLAXMIA10MAY-EXC
Availability	L☐DL/A10MAYSEAHNL8A
Seat map	L☐DL/9V/S1
Fare rules	L☐CO/SV3
Amtrak availability	L☐A3/A13JULPITCHI10A
More Amtrak availability	L☐A3/A*
Opposite Amtrak availability	L☐A3/A*O
Amtrak tariff display	L☐A3/$DPITCHI
Amtrak city codes	L☐A3-RM/*IL/S

Copyright © 1990 by Glencoe/McGraw-Hill Educational Division. All rights reserved.

Index

Copyright © 1990 by Glencoe/McGraw-Hill Educational Division. All rights reserved.

Copyright © 1990 by Glencoe/McGraw-Hill Educational Division. All rights reserved.

Copyright © 1990 by Glencoe/McGraw-Hill Educational Division. All rights reserved.